Negotiating Control

STUDIES IN MOBILE COMMUNICATION

Studies in Mobile Communication focuses on the social consequences of mobile communication in society.

Series Editors
Rich Ling, *Nanyang Technological University, Singapore*
Gerard Goggin, *University of Sydney, Australia*
Leopoldina Fortunati, *Università di Udine, Italy*

Haunting Hands: Mobile Media Practices and Loss
Kathleen M. Cumiskey and Larissa Hjorth

A Village Goes Mobile: Telephony, Mediation, and Social Change in Rural India
Sirpa Tenhunen

Negotiating Control: Organizations and Mobile Communication
Keri K. Stephens

NEGOTIATING CONTROL

Organizations and Mobile Communication

Keri K. Stephens

OXFORD
UNIVERSITY PRESS

OXFORD

UNIVERSITY PRESS

Oxford University Press is a department of the University of Oxford. It furthers
the University's objective of excellence in research, scholarship, and education
by publishing worldwide. Oxford is a registered trade mark of Oxford University
Press in the UK and certain other countries.

Published in the United States of America by Oxford University Press
198 Madison Avenue, New York, NY 10016, United States of America.

© Oxford University Press 2018

Library of Congress Cataloging-in-Publication Data
Names: Stephens, Keri K., author.
Title: Negotiating control : organizations and mobile communication / Keri K. Stephens.
Description: New York, NY : Oxford University Press, [2018]
Identifiers: LCCN 2017057403 (print) | LCCN 2017059399 (ebook) |
ISBN 9780190625528 (updf) | ISBN 9780190625535 (epub) |
ISBN 9780190882327 (online resource) | ISBN 9780190625511 (pbk. : alk. paper) |
ISBN 9780190625504 (cloth : alk. paper)
Subjects: LCSH: Information technology—Management. | Mobile communication systems. |
Communication in management. | Knowledge workers.
Classification: LCC HD30.2 (ebook) | LCC HD30.2 .S78325 2018 (print) |
DDC 658/.054167—dc23
LC record available at https://lccn.loc.gov/2017057403

9 8 7 6 5 4 3 2 1

Paperback printed by Webcom, Inc., Canada
Hardback printed by Bridgeport National Bindery, Inc., United States of America

Dedicated to Tab, he's been with me since my
mobile story began, Sarah Kay, and Kyle

CONTENTS

Negotiating Control

Introduction

Managers, employees, and organizations constantly experiment with new ways to communicate more effectively when working. Typically, these are respectful negotiations. But Delilah, for one, was not so blessed.

A 30-year-old mother of three, Delilah (a pseudonym) worked in the dispatch bullpen at a metropolitan police department. She was responsible for taking inbound calls, locating the appropriate officers in the field, and then forwarding the calls to them. Doing that kept her plenty busy most days. Like her colleagues in dispatch, she normally communicated by phone, whereas for most of her non-urgent internal communication, such as with her co-workers and manager, she used email. The police department provided each dispatcher with his or her own computer, software, landline phone, and headset—but no cell phone.

In 2009, Delilah's team got a new manager who didn't like email. He much preferred texting. One day he sat the team down and explained how wonderful it would be if they could all switch from sending so many emails and, instead, simply text him directly or create a group text. After all, he said, there was a lot of talk about email causing people to feel overloaded.

Everyone courteously nodded their assent, and the group dispersed.

A week later the manager sat the team back down and expressed his frustration that *certain* members of the team weren't participating in the group texts. He chastised the group and called those unresponsive members "poor team players." Delilah, who was one of the guilty parties, came forward to politely explain herself. "My personal cell phone is an emergency phone," she said, "and I have to pay for every text message and phone call I make. I'm not in a position to use my minutes for work text messages. I am in the dispatch office every day that I'm at work, so people can come find me with requests or send me an email. Those ways of reaching me don't cost me out of pocket."

Delilah paused at this point in telling her story. We were in a small focus group with three other police department employees who worked in positions other than dispatch. Delilah described her manager's response: "He flicked a nickel across the table and said sarcastically, 'Really? There, I'll pay for your damn text message this time. Find a way to be a team player.'"

Suddenly scared for her job, she wasn't about to challenge the man. She felt she had no choice but to find a way to pay for those extra text messages.

POWER AND CONTROL IN ORGANIZATIONAL MOBILE USE

Delilah's story has bothered me ever since she shared it back in 2009. I call it the "Flicked Her a Nickel" story because her situation captured a prominent downside of mobile phone use in the U.S. at that time. People had to pay for the number of minutes they used, and both plans and devices were expensive, at least in this country. Most Americans simply couldn't afford a personal mobile device. While companies often provided one—typically a BlackBerry—for their higher-level and mobile employees, most workers had to fend for themselves.

As an organizational scholar, I run across unequal power relations like this in most of the cases I study. Delilah's experience illustrates the complexity involved in negotiating workplace device use in virtually any hierarchical power structure. Delilah liked her job, despite making only slightly over minimum wage. She saw herself playing an important role in society by being the connector between citizens in need and their police department. Her manager, meanwhile, with his much larger paycheck, had no problem purchasing a mobile plan with unlimited minutes of text and talk. He never stopped to think that worker bees like Delilah weren't nearly so lucky.

I never got to interview that particular manager, so I never learned if he was even aware of the burden his texting preference placed on his subordinates; but I suspect that this story is hardly unique. Perhaps his arrogance wasn't either. Managers often push their communication preferences on subordinates either consciously or unconsciously.

In writing this book, I find myself in a unique position to understand the shifting control issues around organizational mobile use. I was a mobile knowledge worker—a field engineer working for Hewlett-Packard—in the 1990s who used various types of cellular and mobile devices. I was often in a car, stuck in traffic, trying to reach my Southern Californian customers in the biopharmaceutical, environmental, and industrial chemical industries. Then, in the late 1990s I returned to academia to become a social scientist studying information and communication technologies (ICTs).

My winding early career path means that I have data spanning from 1990 until 2016. It's my hope that capturing a historical perspective on mobile communication can help readers understand the contemporary tensions that exist between companies, mobile-use policies, and employees. This perspective also invites readers to consider multiple perspectives, such as how traditional organizational power structures seem to be observed in mobile communication practices.

Let me begin by defining some key concepts used throughout the book.

MOBILES AS COMBINATORIAL ICTs

What are mobiles, mobile devices, and mobile technologies? To answer this question, this book takes a multifaceted approach. In 1992, Roger Silverstone and his colleagues,[54] who were studying media technologies in the household, found that these technologies weren't just functional tools designed for a specific purpose. But rather, when people used media, their decisions and practices surrounding this use conveyed additional symbolic, as opposed to content, messages. Silverstone's team termed this "double articulation" (p. 21), meaning that media can both be a material object and play an integral role in creating meaning. Rich Ling[32] built on the early work of Silverstone and Haddon[15] to focus specifically on cell phones and their impact on society in the early 2000s. Most of the scholarly research on mobiles stresses the importance of doubly articulating mobiles.

The notion of double articulation is central to much of the current research in organizations and technology. Today's scholars stress the importance of looking beyond the technological devices themselves, such as a cell phone, an iPad, or a laptop, to consider how meaning—also called "social" or "symbolic"—is entwined with them.[44,45] So while I might refer to a specific device, or more broadly call a device a mobile, I'm also considering how people interact and interpret those devices as part of their communication practices. This book builds on that expanded idea of technology but concentrates on studying mobiles in organizational life. Yet, instead of focusing purely on how communication occurs through mobiles, I emphasize the communication occurring *around* mobiles.[52] This allows me to discuss important organizational communication topics like *power, norms, policies,* and ultimately what I call the *negotiation for control.*

Besides taking this more comprehensive view of mobiles, this book situates each mobile device as a type of ICT. Ron Rice and Paul Leonardi define ICTs as "devices, applications, media, and associated hardware and software that receive and distribute, process and store, and retrieve and analyze digital information between people and machines (as information) or among people (as communication)"[52] (p. 426). While this definition is broad, it accurately captures the diverse ways that ICTs can be used. It also highlights the integrated nature of information and communication, something we clearly see with contemporary mobile devices. They are used for both communication and more information-focused activities.

Contemporary mobile devices, such as smart phones, iPads, and laptops, exemplify what scholars have called "combinatorial ICT use," "multiple media use," "media mixes," "intermediality," and "multiple ICT use."[17,19,20,30,46,51,57,65,73] Over time, mobile devices have become increasingly combinatorial, reflecting the proliferation of ingenious new features available for users. For example, Chapter 1 discusses the car phone, originally a fairly limited mobile device used to make phone calls to others. Yet by Chapter 4, the BlackBerry has expanded mobile capabilities to the point where it becomes more of a combinatorial ICT than just a single-function communication device. This is why it's important to define a mobile device as a combinatorial ICT. Today, people can use the same device to make phone calls, send text messages, check email, access the cloud for a variety of information, and post or read social media.

AFFORDANCES

Besides physical devices, this book also considers what are called "affordances" of technologies. These are the material features that don't define how individuals use ICTs but instead provide possibilities for use depending on how people interact and relate while communicating with others.[12] An affordance approach was originally described by James Gibson, an American psychologist.[12] His work was not technology- or organization-specific, but communication scholars have used his brainchild to provide framing that helps move conceptual thinking beyond deterministic assumptions of technology use.[10,11,26,27,28,37,47,50,53,66]

This notion has prompted media scholar Andrew Schrock to look specifically at the affordances of mobile devices,[53] while scholars like Ron Rice and his team are looking at how to combine media and create broader understandings that they call "organizational media affordances."[50] Multifaceted thoughts about affordances and multiple ICTs are important because one thing's for certain with mobile communication: the devices will change! From mobile phones to mobile watches, these devices invite continued study. Furthermore, as the affordances of individual media begin to overlap, they likely will change the perceived usefulness of mobile devices[17]—and possibly their fundamental functions, too. I elaborate on these issues in Chapter 11.

THE ORGANIZATION OF THIS BOOK

I've organized and written this book with the hope that people from different backgrounds—scholars, human resource (HR) managers, information systems (IS) professionals, and students—can all understand and learn from the stories and data analyzed here. In keeping with these goals, theory concepts and research literature appear throughout the book, often as stand-alone chapters or as the framing for the narratives shared. Altogether, there are stories of over 55 different workers and managers, out of a combined data set representing over 500 individuals whose data I've collected over two decades.

Chapters 1 and 2 provide a historical perspective on cell phones as business tools. In the 1990s and early 2000s, organizations supplied their highly mobile workers with these communication opportunity–expanding devices, but, as you'll see, some of these employees started bringing their personal devices to work. During these early years, employees and managers began jockeying for control over these mobile resources, so in Chapter 3, I develop the theoretical background on organizational control. That chapter provides the grounding to make sense of what happened in the early years and sets the stage for what's to come as the BlackBerry, and eventually the iPhone, surge into organizations from almost all hierarchical directions.

The next section presents a mix of workers and focuses on how they cope with informal and formal rules, policies, and resources that are often under managerial control. Chapter 4 presents the stories of "knowledge workers"—a term coined by Peter Drucker to describe autonomous employees whose jobs involve generating knowledge—trying to navigate how to use their mobile devices in meetings. Then, in Chapter 5, I share an opposite story: how one organization banned its janitorial staff from even bringing a mobile device to work. Chapter 6 elaborates on a specific type of formal organizational policy called bring your own device to work, or BYOD, a topic often discussed in the management information systems (MIS) literature. Then, in Chapter 7, I present data from college interns and raise concerns about whether new employees are always ready to be productive when they are required to provide their own tools—mobile devices.

The next two chapters focus on customer-facing work in a variety of occupations and jobs. Chapter 8 provides a detailed analysis of a hospital trying to implement its permissive BYOD policy by using employees' own mobile devices to help coordinate patient care. Chapter 9 focuses on customer-facing employees and how they, their managers, and their friends and family use mobiles to stay connected before, during, and after work.

The final three chapters synthesize the data as a whole, compare mobile use across types of workers, and develop the theoretical and practical understanding of how control around mobile communication is negotiated. Specifically, Chapter 10 provides a comparison of the diverse people whose stories are shared in the book. My analysis identifies four key characteristics of jobs that enable and constrain workers' control over their own mobile communication: degree of autonomy, mobility, task variability, and communication focus. Chapter 11 develops the four theoretical contributions: (1) the longitudinal perspective linking personal device diffusion, societal norms of connectedness, and control negotiations; (2) an elaboration of the temporal affordance of reachability; (3) the role of power and people's subjective perceptions in mobile-use acceptability; and (4) a multilevel model of negotiating control over mobile communication. Finally, Chapter 12 is a brief, practical chapter that helps you grasp the vast differences in perceptions of organizational mobile communication and proposes several steps for future research.

You'll probably notice I've included only limited data on knowledge workers and their love–hate relationships with work–life intrusion because these topics have been heavily emphasized in organizational technology research.[13,14,18,39,40,41,43,48,64] In this book, by including many types of workers, I unearth several surprises, like the intruding role that friends and family play when they try to reach their loved ones during their work hours. In general, the findings suggest workers can't erect boundaries very well, and most people do an unbelievably poor job negotiating control over their own time.

If you're curious about the data sets used for each chapter, the analyses, and my research questions, I've shared some information in each chapter, but you'll find the details in Appendix A. There is also a dedicated Appendix B that carefully thanks the host of people who've contributed insight, data, opinions, and support for this book. I'm very fortunate to have such helpful friends, family, colleagues, and students because many ideas need to be shared before they can be further developed.

Because this is a scholarly book, I'll close with a brief summary of the key contributions.

CONTRIBUTIONS TO MOBILE, ORGANIZATIONAL, AND MIS SCHOLARSHIP

Mobile communication scholars have spent the past decade articulating the nuanced role that mobile devices play in facilitating societal norms of connectedness.[1,6,8,21,22,31,32,33,34,35,36,42,53,55,61] This vast, interdisciplinary, international research has examined several work-related issues ranging from the paradoxes created when people feel both liberated and enslaved by having a mobile device 24/7[2,18,64,70,71,72] and the use of mobiles by isolated workers.[7,65,74,76] Organizational scholars also have studied work–life issues[13,14,39,40,41,43,47,48,64] as well as conducted considerable research on knowledge workers' use of ICTs,[3,4,5,50,62,63,66,67,73] and using mobiles in meetings.[49,58,59,60,68,69] Finally, MIS scholars have provided an additional area of effort around organizational policies and mobile devices.[16,23,24,25,38,56,75]

This book is motivated by my own training in organizational communication and technology and it combines these three disciplines to zeroe in on things we're missing in these bodies of research. One advantage of having data spanning two and half decades is that it provides a longitudinal perspective on the dynamics involved in organizational mobile-device use. Mobile scholars will see how societal norms of connectedness function to enable and constrain the control that organizations, and their diverse workers, each have in how the workers use mobile devices. But this control is not one-directional; individuals push back and find creative ways to hide their use, and many organizations actually *need* their employees to bring their devices to work. Furthermore, the diverse data helps me elaborate and develop the temporal affordance of reachability. It might look a bit different depending on job role and industry, but it's a surprisingly pivotal issue that people struggle to understand because they tend to think that everyone is reachable upon demand. Organizational researchers will find that this book closes a gap in understanding how "technologies produce, maintain, and change knowledge"[52] (p. 442). Specifically, the data shows that workers in all types of jobs, with all levels of education and responsibility, produce knowledge and need access to information. This book also responds to a complaint made by organizational-technology scholars, namely, that the field has overlooked the role of power in technology change.[29] Power and control are the threads in all the data.

Finally, I've reached into the information-science and MIS literature to bring a theory-driven human communication perspective to the growing work in policies that guide mobile-device use at work. These sanctioned rules are ever-changing, and by examining such a broad data set, this book proposes that they be expanded to include all types of workers. But I also raise some concerns that if everyone is expected to bring a device, there likely will be some new training needs to ensure that what looks like an inclusive policy doesn't actually create new divides that could harm individuals and their organizations.

CHAPTER 1
Early Mobile Use

Walking down the aisle on United Flight 579 to Denver on a Thursday morning in 2016, I started counting: iPad, iPhone, laptop, Kindle, other mobile phone, newspaper, paper notepad. . . . This flight is filled with business travelers, suited and casual, carrying their briefcases, unpacking their multiple devices for the flight. One man has a newspaper open, his iPad in his lap, and is composing a text message on his phone. He will probably use the plane's Wi-Fi to send that message. This is common in 2016. Even in the confined seating on an airplane, people use their mobiles for work and play.

The introduction of personal mobile devices and smartphones in the U.S. between 2000 and 2010 created an explosion of mobile users. This relatively recent phenomenon still sets many information-technology (IT) and human-resources executives to worried wondering. Is our company data safe? Are our employees using mobile tools to enhance their productivity or too often for purely personal reasons? Should we pay for these mobile tools? These are just a few of the questions organizations are raising, now that many workers bring their own mobile devices into the workplace. I see no easy answers, and the answers will likely change over time.

To gain some perspective on why these workplace mobile-device conversations exist today, let's step back in time to when organizations virtually monopolized mobile communication. The chief question addressed here is: *How did early mobile-device use at work set the stage for the resulting negotiation for control over mobile communication?* First, I'll share my story of working in industry in the early 1990s with my car phone. Car phones were business tools then, paid for by the few companies willing to cover their expense. This conversation includes my mentor, who worked with me at the time, to verify and add to my story since this isn't data that was collected as part of a research study. Next, I'll share a series of narratives from data collected over the past 15 years that illustrates how employees in the later 1990s and early 2000s were bringing their own devices to work, long before we had a term to describe this practice. The chapter ends by examining literature that explains these early behaviors.

CAR PHONES AS BUSINESS TOOLS

It is 1990. Car phones have only recently hit the American market, and they're expensive, so few business people are using them. Besides, they're bulky and generally remain permanently mounted in cars, thus limiting their usefulness (see Figure 1.1). Fax machines, though, are now common and considered indispensable for transmitting documents. Email, while growing in popularity, remains limited to those desktop and laptop computers blessed with a wired connection into a special system, hence only used by the more technologically savvy companies. Wi-Fi and mobile apps, meanwhile, are still to come, so people still send holiday cards— handwritten or typed on a computer—via snail mail.

In 1990 I was a young college graduate plying my first job as a sales rep in the high-tech industry in Los Angeles. My employer, Hewlett-Packard (H-P), then renowned as a provider of sophisticated scientific instruments, provided me, and indeed the entire field organization (sales, service, and managers), with tools to maximize our productivity. These included a

Figure 1.1. An image of a bulky car phone

laptop, a Ford Taurus, and a car phone, the latter permanently mounted on the front floorboard with its antenna attached to the outside of the trunk, like with police cruisers. Very cool.

I had never heard of a car phone before taking that job. And though the device struck me as altogether glamorous, it wasn't described as a benefit of employment. H-P considered it an integral part of my job. After all, our sales and service goals required us to maximize our face time with customers, not hole up in the office. The car phones greatly improved our ability to accomplish that goal.

In the course of my workday, I was frequently stuck in traffic. Not normal traffic, but LA traffic, the kind where people could lose 2–4 hours of their lives just sitting with their cars on some freeway. Having a car phone meant I could get a jump on the day. I could leave home at 6 a.m. before traffic picked up and then, while driving, make calls to various people at the manufacturing facilities that H-P owned on the East Coast. Living in California was an advantage because I could reach those folks early in their workday. I often even had time to stop at a coffee shop, finish up my previous day's paperwork, and still make my first appointment at 8 a.m. By the way, there was no digital help finding customers' addresses. My only navigation help consisted of four different Thomas Guides, iconic mapbooks covering the various counties in Los Angeles.

After my first appointment, the car phone became an integral part of my workday. Instead of having to stop periodically at pay phones, then still a fixture at many street corners in Los Angeles, I could sit comfortably in my car and contact colleagues in the main office, for I'd often need to check on the availability of equipment, request that a quote be generated, or check on the latest financing options for my customers. I had email then; but as this was 1990, there was still no Wi-Fi, and response expectations were days, not hours. Having a car phone allowed me to be ultra-responsive to my customers' requests, and they noticed. I could call in a quote and—eureka!—it would be faxed to the customer the same day! Then, in between other sales calls, I could contact the customer and discuss the quote. My car phone was a godsend. It sped up the sales process, made me more efficient, and helped me stay in close contact with my office and my customers.

Many of my calls were to H-P colleagues. We were a team that lived and worked out of our cars. The service engineers had my back, and they knew I wouldn't call unless I really needed their help. It was important that this field team be connected because when a problem arose, we needed to move fast, and borrowing a customer's landline phone was thought tacky.

In addition to being more responsive and efficient, I felt that my car phone kept me safe. My sales territory included some industrial-chemical facilities in Central and East Los Angeles, and on one occasion I was stopped by police and told that a young businesswoman should not be driving in that part of town. In 1991, shortly after the Rodney King verdict was announced, I was in Central LA helping a customer board up his windows before the rioting reached his business. As I was leaving, that customer, in gratitude, gave me a purchase order, and it helped me make my month's quota. Driving homeward from his office, I could see the fires in my rear-view mirror.

My customers often had secured parking located behind a locked gate. After I established a relationship with them, they would ask me to drive up, give them a quick call, and then they'd buzz me in to park in their secured lot. But without my car phone, I would have had to park on the street and walk sometimes several long blocks.

H-P had a policy that the car phones were for company use only. However, my sympathetic manager okayed my calling home to say I was running late or to ask if I could pick something up for dinner. Since my husband and other family members didn't have car phones, the policy was not a burden. I could only reach my friends and family members at work or after they came home for the evening. The average car phone bill in my office ran around $850/month. I remember a colleague once turning in his for $1,300. My boss asked him if he was using the phone for personal use. My colleague paused and simply said, "I'm a busy guy." For the next few months, the company monitored all our phones and insisted we keep our bills under $800/month. While similar grillings came up a couple of times a year, I don't remember anyone ever getting penalized for extravagance. Basically, its formal policy notwithstanding, H-P seemed to feel that as long as we were out paying calls on our customers, it was OK if we made some personal calls in between. H-P got a lot more hours of work from our sales and service team by looking the other way.

After I had worked for the company for about a year, H-P upgraded me to something called a "bag phone." This one was more portable because the entire device fit in a rectangular bag roughly 10″ by 16″. I could still mount it on the floorboard for when I was driving, but I could also unplug it and take it with me into my house at night. It proved really convenient if others wanted to reach me when I was working from home, but it was too expensive for me to make many outgoing calls with it there and quite unnecessary, since I had my landline phone right at hand.

I rarely received calls on my bag phone after work hours—in fact, so infrequently that I still remember how odd it was when one of my customers called me on it one evening when I was at home. I had been trying to help him get financing so that he could purchase around $100,000 worth of our equipment, so I assumed he was calling for a quick update. But no, that wasn't the reason. Slurring his words, and with loud music playing in the background, he wanted to invite me to come to his house for a party. Dumbfounded, I quickly told him I was busy and hung up—then spent the next hours, and days, worrying that he'd cancel his big order. But a week later, to my vast relief, the order came through. I made a point, though, of never calling on that customer alone again. I always took a colleague with me.

SMALLER EAST COAST–BASED COMPANY

After my stint at H-P, I went to work for a smaller company that had a more restrictive car-phone policy. This company still paid for the phone, but each month I had to highlight all personal calls on my bill, none of which could be turned in on my expense account. I remember resenting having to spend a good half-hour scrutinizing 15–20 pages of an itemized bill simply to deduct some $30 worth of personal calls.

One month, management decided that the field staffers' car-phone bills were excessive, so it decreed that the company would only pay for the first $400 of our bills, the rest being our responsibility. This smaller company was based on the East Coast, and it had a field sales-and-service team spanning the entire U.S. Some of the field personnel, especially those close to the home office, were blessed with very small territories. In addition, they often had temporary offices located inside their major accounts there, so they had near-constant access to a private landline phone. In my own case, however, I had to cover six states in the western U.S., and my territory included traffic-heavy Southern California. Making matters worse, it also included desolate drives through Death Valley into Arizona and New Mexico. A few of my colleagues were similarly disadvantaged. So together we appealed to our manager, explaining that we needed a larger allocation of the car-phone budget because we were often in traffic and covered huge territories. Fortunately, he was willing to negotiate for us and got our stipend raised from $400 to $500 a month.

In the early 1990s that still wasn't enough to cover basic business calls, so I had to cut corners. For example, I began limiting my phone conversations with the home office so that I'd have more minutes left to converse with customers, service engineers, and co-workers, especially on time-sensitive matters. But that decision jeopardized my relationships with people at the main office. When I realized that, I planned a week-long trip to headquarters and had one-on-one visits with my colleagues. Fortunately, travel expenses came out of a separate budget.

While my car phone was certainly a business tool, I do remember feeling "cool" because I had a car phone when practically no one else did. I could fantasize myself chillin' in my Infinity G20, pretending to talk on the phone and sticking my head out the sunroof for all the world to see. I was 22, had a cool job, a company car, and a gadget no one else had. As I reflect on this feeling, I'm not sure how much of the "cool" factor can be attributed to having the latest technology and how much of it to my being in my early 20s and having a great job that provided me the latest technology. After all, while I was technically an early adopter of car phones, so was everyone in my job role at the companies where I worked. In truth, I wasn't really a technology early adopter then, nor am I now. Some people might even call me a late adopter. I'm not the type of person who rushes out to purchase the latest technology, for I'm simply not a gadget person. I wait until new technology works well enough for me to use it to accomplish my goals.

MY STORY AS THE STARTING POINT

These recounted experiences are among the few pieces of data in this book that I didn't directly collect through a formal research study process. But I wasn't an academic in the early 1990s. I worked in industry then. And it wasn't until I began developing ideas for this book that conversations with others helped me see the value of using my lived experiences as an anchoring point for understanding, more generally, how mobile use in organizations has evolved.

BRINGING THEIR DEVICES TO WORK BEFORE ANYONE KNEW THIS WAS A THING

By the late 1990s, organizations were seeing more personal mobile devices being brought into the workplace by their employees. While these portable devices (e.g., tablets, personal digital assistants) were still rather expensive in the U.S., early adopters bought them initially for personal use and then gradually began also leaning on them at work. There were likely many reasons for their doing so, so next I will share a set of examples illustrating the breadth of this early trend. These examples stand in stark contrast to the earlier, pervasive *organizational control* of mobile communication practices that I documented in my story of the car phone in the 1990s.

The data constituting the first story of Bill, a semiconductor engineer, was collected at two points in time. I first interviewed him in 2001 as part of my dissertation data collection on how people used multiple technologies to communicate at work. I reinterviewed him in 2016 to get a fresh perspective on how his mobile use had changed. During our first interview, I was intrigued by his creative use of multiple technologies that he had researched, brought to work, and paid for by himself. This was uncommon in the late 1990s because traditional knowledge workers, like Bill, received company-provided computers and laptops. I contacted him again in 2016, reminded him of what we had discussed in 2001, and asked him to reflect on his past and present experiences using mobile devices. Bill's narrative data that I share here is a combination of those two interviews.

After exploring how and why Bill brought his devices to work, the next set of narratives reflect personal digital-assistant use between 2000 and 2002. This data was collected as part of my dissertation project on how people used multiple technologies to communicate at work. It illustrates the growing dynamics involved in struggles for control over personal time—a struggle with self-discipline—and control over data. Organizations and work situations constituted the context for this new type of mobile use, but at this time in workplace mobile-use history, the negotiation for control was more intrapersonal, not between organizations and individuals.

MOBILE TABLETS AND TWO-WAY PAGERS IN THE SEMICONDUCTOR INDUSTRY

Bill was working as a semiconductor engineer in the late 1990s, spending most of his days in a so-called clean room—a low-particle environment where semiconductors could be antiseptically researched and manufactured. Barely 30 years old, Bill was a fast-talking Texan with a reasonably thick drawl. A genuinely nice guy, nerdy like many people in his industry, he had the rare combination of intelligence with a humble demeanor. Before entering the clean room, Bill and his co-engineers had to don oversized, paper-like "bunny suits" that covered all their clothing, hair, and shoes and then—the finishing touch—don a surgeon's face mask. Thus garbed, they looked like space age clones. Meanwhile, whatever they proposed to carry in—normally clean-room notebooks—also had to be wiped down to remove any dust. As a last precaution, they had to pass through an air shower that blew air over them, eliminating any remaining air contaminants they might still be carrying.

"Efficient," "master documenter," "early adopter"—that's how Bill's admiring colleagues liked to describe him. Take, for example, how he modified the standard pen-and-paper method everybody used to document their work in the clean room. That old-school method—quaint to Bill—badly cramped his work style. True, some work computers were available there, but not enough of them, or not always close enough by; and he often needed to be right next to his experiment to document his research. "At that time," he recalls, "my company was basically happy with the non–clean room laptops they provided [us], so they weren't interested in looking at new mobile tools. I am willing to provide my own money—that they pay me—to keep my technology tools functioning at a higher level." His colleagues respected that perfectionism. And "everybody knew I was an early adopter of new technology." So when he arrived in the clean room one day with his own new tablet computer, it got their attention. He even lent it out to them in hopes of generating support for the device. But, he says, "management never saw the need" for tablets, despite their being portable and easily cleaned.

Bill's first tablet was small enough to put in a clean room–approved, 10″ by 12″ clear plastic case that he could then wipe dust-free. He loaded all the same data-security software on that tablet that was on his company-provided laptop, and this became his clean-room documenting tool. His goal wasn't to work around IT policies; it was simply to have the latest technology to make him more efficient. Tablets of the 1990s and early 2000s could be configured to have as much storage as laptop computers. The storage capacity of these early tablets made them more like minicomputers than contemporary tablets like iPads. He explains, "My ability to store data and capture information about me and my environment was focused on this tablet." It eventually replaced his laptop altogether. Keep in mind that laptop computers in the early 2000s were big, bulky, and heavy. Bill's handy tablet was his portable computer.

TWO-WAY PAGERS AND BARBIE LAPTOPS

In the late 1990s and early 2000s, Bill's company didn't provide him a cell phone, but it did provide him a pager. Today pagers aren't particularly common mobile tools (though hospitals still use them in the mid-2010s), but most pagers of that earlier era were 3-by-4″ devices that had a display that could show a phone number (see Figure 1.2). They'd beep or vibrate when you received a page, which was simply a request to call the person. Their number in hand, you'd then have to find a phone to do that. Some

Figure 1.2. An image of a two-way pager

brands also offered more upscale models, slightly larger, that included tiny keyboards. Those were "two-way pagers" because not only could they receive requests for a return call but people could use them to input a request for a call back. Pagers worked on a different type of data network than cell phones.

Even though Bill was an early adopter of most technologies, he "was a very, very late adopter on cell phones," he confesses. "It took me a long time to convince my wife that I needed a cell phone because my company [had] provided me a two-way pager. I remember having to stop and find a pay phone in the early 2000s because I had to call my wife back when she sent me a page." But Bill elaborated that he didn't use his mobile tablet like he would use a cell phone today: "For the amount of notes that I take, the cell phone would have been too small [to be useful at work]."

When I reinterviewed Bill in 2016, he provided some insights into how the notion of a pager has changed over time:

> If I say to my daughter now [the word] "paging," in my mind I remember two-way pagers. It was texting. We had texting before texting was common. It was two-way with a tiny screen and tiny little keyboards where we could exchange messages with other people who had the same devices. When I think of the word "pager," I think of texting. These were great because they were asynchronous.

Bill recalls sitting in a conference one day in 1999 when he noticed that a vendor was showing slides that contained some of the data he had collected in his company's clean room. Concerned, Bill promptly sent a two-way page to his boss asking if the vendor had permission to show what seemed proprietary data. Within 3 minutes he and his boss had exchanged messages, determined that the data was indeed proprietary, and decided upon a course of action. When the presentation was over, Bill approached the vendor, knowing that his actions were sanctioned by his manager, and told the man that he could not continue sharing the proprietary data. Bill elaborated on this situation during his reinterview, saying, "You would not think twice about this kind of situation today, but at that time, it was novel." Very few people had two-way pagers then, and the unobtrusive nature of "texting before texting was common" allowed Bill to access people remotely and make fast decisions.

Many engineers at Bill's company were provided these two-way pagers, but the managers had a higher-end version affectionately called a "Barbie laptop." Bill laughed upon recalling how "there were 250-pound men running around texting on what they called their Barbie laptops. They looked like toys—something Barbie might use!" These devices were slightly larger, and they even had functions that resembled modern-day apps. The companies had to pay considerably more for these large, portable pager/mini-laptop devices, but the added functionality is something that managers argued they needed because of their highly mobile jobs.

CONTROL OVER DATA AND WORK

Bill cheerfully fits the species known as the "electronic data hoarder," but that zeal for organizing and stockpiling all his data has made him an asset in every job he's had since his early semiconductor days. His willingness to go out of his way to provide his own mobile tools has also helped establish him as a documentation and historical-information expert. By providing his own tools, he has control over how he stores the data; and over time, he has learned to retrieve that data very quickly. He centralizes it on a single computer that's fully encrypted and that has multiple backups. This means he enjoys a unique advantage when interacting with colleagues and clients. He offers a couple of examples:

> If I go into a meeting in Shanghai and our customer asks me, "How much did you pay for pig feed in 1978?"—I'm not sure that question would come up, but if it did—I can actually provide them a receipt on the spot. Another example is that I got a call from a colleague asking details about an engineering project I worked on 13 years ago. In 5 minutes, I found the data and provided it to the person. This had literally been sitting on my machine, unused, for at least 11 years, and the only reason it took me 5 minutes to find it is that I had to look for the specific details that my colleague wanted.

In the early 2000s, Bill's company realized that with cable modems and Internet connections going to their workers' homes, their employees could log into company servers after work hours. So, to encourage this behavior, they opted to pay for Bill's Internet access. That company benefit alone saved him about $50/month. He told me then:

> I was an engineer working on special projects in a manufacturing facility that ran 24/7. Fairly often the technicians would reach a point in the manufacturing process where things would stop—we called this "going on hold." Looking back on that, there was a psychology involved where if someone else [my company] was paying for my Internet access, I felt obliged, anytime I thought about it, to go check and see the status of the project. They were paying for some of my fun Internet access, too, so at 11 o'clock at night, I'd also go into the system to be sure things were running smoothly instead of waiting until I got to work the next morning.

But then, around 2008, that nice benefit went away, with no explanation, and he had to pay for his own Internet access. Unsurprisingly, it immediately changed how he worked:

> When they stopped paying for my cable access, I didn't feel obliged to them to go, not only out of my way, but well out of my way, to check on anything. There were probably lots of reasons the company decided to stop paying. Maybe they didn't want to pay for people doing naughty things on the Internet, and I understand that. But if it was just a cost-savings measure, they probably didn't realize the productivity they were losing because people were not doing extra work.

PRIVATE IPHONE USE IN POLICING

It's 2008 and Ted, a police officer, has just attended a focus group I ran on using technology at work. Ted approaches me and pulls out his iPhone; still shiny and unscratched. He explains that police radios are important, but it's his mobile device that is truly his hidden partner when he's on duty. He shows me a website where he can look at pictures of the latest drugs of abuse and compare those to substances—often pills—found in a suspect's car. Within minutes he has what he needs to make an arrest and confiscate the tentatively identified substance. Ted continues sharing and explains that since he owns his iPhone and many of his fellow officers also have personal mobile devices, they regularly use them to swap stories and jokes that are against policy when shared on a police radio. Ted loves being an innovative officer, and having mobile access helps him do a great job.

But at this time in 2008, his supervisor and the entire policing organization were still relying on landline phones and police radios, assuming this was how their police force communicated. The organization couldn't keep up with the tools that their employees brought to work. Mobile devices were expensive and frequently only provided for people in upper management roles. At that time, this organization didn't have policies guiding the use of mobile devices, so these officers weren't necessarily breaking the rules. This example is almost a decade old, and we still hear these same stories today. People in an organization and the organization itself aren't always aligned in how they use and regulate mobile-device use. Alignment issues raise many questions concerning how organizations (employing and more voluntary) can and should address the fact that most people around the globe have a mobile device in their pocket. This book explores mobile-device use by focusing on the challenges and opportunities that organizations face now that mobiles are so diffused.

CONTROL AS A FORM OF INDIVIDUAL AGENCY

These examples reveal the growing power that individuals and organizations were experimenting with in the early days of mobile devices. While organizations began realizing that they had the power to provide resources, like home-based Internet services, and were also providing more portable computing solutions, there were few formal policies regulating how people brought these personal devices to work. On the surface, Bill's behaviors might seem contradictory: he buys his own mobile tablet and creates innovative data-storage practices but is annoyed when his company stops paying for his Internet access. But these stories are finally not about money and who pays for technology and access. These stories are more psychological; they're about *control*. Bill enjoyed control over his data and portable devices—and being at no risk of violating any company policies. Actually, if his company was like many of the other companies I've studied, they were probably only beginning to formulate policies around personal mobile tools in the early 2000s.

PALM PILOTS AND PERSONAL DIGITAL ASSISTANTS: PORTABLE AND INFORMATION STORAGE

Bill introduced us to early mobile devices like tablets and two-way pagers, but there was another mobile tool emerging in organizations around the late 1990s: the artfully named Palm Pilot. Perusing the data I collected with

Figure 1.3. A photo of a personal digital assistant (PDA)

a team of researchers[4] in the early 2000s, I was struck by how many of our U.S. interviewees mentioned a Palm Pilot or a personal digital assistant (PDA). These devices, at 8 by 6″, were the size of a small paper day planner, didn't quite fit into a pocket, and functioned as both calendar and self-contained document-storage device (see Figure 1.3).

Before I share my examples, let me describe how this data was collected.

I began collecting data on the workplace use of information and communication technology (ICT) in the late 1990s, back when I'd returned to graduate school after having worked in industry for the first decade of my career. For my dissertation, I worked with a team to collect over 72 interviews in the U.S. and Norway that revealed how knowledge workers used multiple ICTs to accomplish their work. Mobile devices played an important role in these interviews, even though at the time I didn't realize what I was seeing in the data.

I approached the data collection for that large project with an overarching question: *How do people combine ICTs and use them in sequences?* I used the data from 66 of the interviews to develop ICT succession theory,[17] where I articulated propositions predicting when people will combine ICTs. Our team also published an empirical paper focused on the reasons knowledge workers use sequences of ICTs in organizations[18] In that article we content-analyzed the interviews and coded for the use of discrete and combinations of ICT use. We found that when people hope to persuade others, they are more likely to use sequences of ICTs instead of a discrete ICT. When these people sent an email and had not heard a response in a couple of days, they picked up the phone and called the person they were trying to reach. Simply sending an email was often not enough to entice a response. People needed multiple reminders through different ICTs.

We also drilled down into why people use certain ICTs to follow up from an initial communication attempt. We classified follow-up ICTs into two dimensions: degree of connection with others and availability of auditory information. The phone and face-to-face communication had availability of auditory information and allowed communicators to connect directly with others. Email, on the other hand, did not have any auditory capability at the time we conducted that study. We also conducted an analysis comparing national cultural dimensions of technology use in Norway and the United States.[16] Finally, our team used 16 interviews from the data set to write narratives that situated ICT use broadly[4] in the early 2000s. These narratives illustrated diverse workers' use of multiple ICTs.

Looking back on the interviews my team collected provides me a window now into how work practices have changed in the past two decades. This early data on mobiles also illustrates how a key mobile device affordance—connectivity—that happened around 2005–2010 both answered a call from our interviewees in the early 2000s and provided these workers with opportunities to change their work practices. Affordances can be considered features that people have the capacity to use, if they choose that path. At that time, connectivity was more of an individual-level affordance that provided *individuals* with opportunities to connect with data, not necessarily other people, especially not with people outside their work context.

As I share some examples from that data set, it's important to realize that our team decided, before we began collecting data, that we wanted a mix of workers whom we identified as either internally or externally focused—that is, either (a) those whose communication practices were primarily aimed inside their organization or (b) those who were mobile and often communicated with others who were not officially affiliated with their organization. At the time we collected this data, our team did not clearly identify mobility and mobile tools as being unique.[4] But almost every interviewee who identified as what we would call today a "mobile worker" mentioned that laptops were essential for their work and that the biggest need was to expand wireless access. As I reflect on this data, I realize that our team knew there were differences between these internal and external workers, but it was only after mobile devices allowed workers access to the Internet that those differences became clear.

To provide some perspective on this early mobile use, I'll begin by sharing data on PDA use from people in IT-related industries who told their ICT-use stories in 2000 and 2001 as part of this larger data set. These devices were called personal digital assistants (PDAs), and the most common brand was called a Palm Pilot. These devices resembled small tablets or larger mobile phones, but they had limited connectivity to the Internet because

Wi-Fi was not readily available. They also had limited storage ability, and most people used them to manage their calendars. I had some personal experiences myself with a Palm Pilot, which I used in the late 1990s. My most vivid memory of using it was when I attended networking events in Austin, Texas. I remember being at Chez Zee, a popular restaurant there, and having a conversation with three people concerning when we would meet again. Every one of us stopped talking, pulled out our Palms, and flamboyantly started using our stylus to click around on our calendars. I still remember one person saying, "Well, my Palm says that I'm available Thursday at 4. Are you?"

Our PDAs were useful as a portable day planner, but they were also a badge of our being tech-savvy and an early adopter, things highly valued in Austin's entrepreneurial community at that time. By the way, I stopped using my Palm Pilot when I returned to graduate school in 1999 because I didn't see that it actually added enough value to my work; also, none of my peers used one, which confirmed that impression.

Let's now examine three stories of PDA use from the data.

PDAs DURING TRAVEL AND AS PORTABLE STORAGE

Samantha was a new college graduate working, in the early 2000s, for a digital-learning start-up headquartered in a major city in the southern U.S. As many employees in start-ups often do, Samantha wore several hats. Her primary one was sales and customer service, so she was constantly monitoring industry and national news to keep on top of emerging trends. She also occasionally traveled to meet with her clients. But she didn't worry about missing news on those trips because it was readily available. "I normally put on the news channel when I'm in the hotel," Samantha explained. "And airports normally have CNN, so I can get some news there. I'll read the headlines in newspapers. But if I see a computer and no one is on it, I will certainly hop on and jump to CNN."

In 2001 in the U.S., people got news from either the TV or a computer with an Internet connection because most cellular phones and PDAs lacked that capability. But even then, many of our interviewees could envision that mobile Internet access was on the horizon. Samantha explained that if her PDA were Internet-enabled, she would check the Internet for news. She also had a vision of the type of connectivity she needed. "If only my hand-held were Internet-enabled," she said. "I'm sure I will [be able to use my devices to check the Internet] eventually. I think all salespeople are going to get these little guys [pointing to her PDA] because we do demos and things like that. I would also use a cell phone if I could afford the $500/month gadget." Even in the early 2000s, cell phones were still pricey in the U.S. after you figured in both the device itself and some providers' byzantine usage plans.

Yet this example of PDA use shows how these mobile devices were starting to have some meaningful mobile capabilities. Samantha had purchased her PDA only a month before our interview, but, she said, "I use it ten times more than I thought I would." Now becoming more comfortable with it, she found she could download helpful information, and she was learning to use Expedia for travel and maps. Though accounting herself no techie, she was finding her PDA easy to use and genuinely helpful on her travels.

GABRIELLE, THE RURAL BANKER

Samantha's growing interest in using her PDA as a portable storage device was similar to that of another of our interviewees, Gabrielle, a middle-aged banker from a tech-savvy rural community also located in the southern U.S. Gabrielle's ICT-use story has been shared before,[4] but her PDA use is particularly helpful in understanding early mobile use. Gabrielle prized both efficiency and information currency. She had her team conducting business online before 2000, and they used banking rate consolidators before many other metropolitan banks. She realized that, hers being a rural bank in a wealthy community, she had to find ways to be competitive, or her clients would shift to a large bank in a bigger city. Having the latest information helped Gabrielle stay on the cutting edge, and her PDA became a convenient way for her to take information with her and fill her downtime by reading. Browning and colleagues shared this remark from Gabrielle:

> "I use it [Palm Pilot] when I go to doctor's appointments and have time waiting in their lobby. Before I go, I'll download a couple of magazines just for our [the Bank's] sake, and some for personal use, including *Rolling Stone Magazine*. I'll also download parts of the *Wall Street Journal*—and even entire books."

By today's lights, her practices may seem a little ho-hum since our own mobile devices don't even need to download this type of information, thanks to streaming and mobile apps. But remember, this was 2001; mobile devices were used more for *portable storage*, not as tools that allowed for real-time connections and access to information.

EVAN, THE WEB-CONFERENCING EXPERT

Other mobile workers in the early 2000s, like Evan, were experimenting with their PDAs and testing the limits. Evan used his PDA as his digital day planner, but he was frustrated because he could not see enough content to make this form of planning helpful for him. He also found that his PDA could not replace his laptop because it was too difficult for him to take notes and enter customer information into his customer-relationship management program. Evan explained, "I found that I could not type notes fast enough. I even tried a keyboard, but it was too bulky to carry with me and use. So I continued to use paper of some kind, but I would never transcribe it back in." Essentially, his work tools were disconnected from one another, and despite his experienced PDA use of over 2 years, he was in the process of giving up his PDA, returning to a paper day planner, and lugging his laptop with him as he traveled away from his office.

Evan was not laggard. He actually was an early adopter of technology in almost all aspects of his life. When I interviewed him, he was working as a director with a global training company. The company was rapidly expanding, and sometimes Evan had to step in to train new employees how to configure their web browsers and download the software plug-ins needed to administer his company's web conferencing–based training. "Web conferencing" describes the practice of conducting a meeting, of almost any size, using the Internet, a web browser, and an audio source like a conference call. Evan's company provided worldwide corporate training online using a web-conferencing platform. The concept of web conferencing was very new in the early 2000s, and Evan's company was responsible for rolling out many of the corporate online training programs for Fortune 500 companies.

The training company's 50 trainers worked out of their homes, and the company purchased all their needed software and hardware tools. When these training-related devices arrived at the employees' homes, they had to become comfortable using laptops from home, installing new software, coping with unreliable Internet connections, and working autonomously to conduct online training. While many of these home-based online trainers also owned a PDA, they were not always very savvy with the technology Evan's company was using for training. Evan found it frustrating that some of his trainers knew so little about technology that he had to call two members of his team to help them unbox the equipment and get it set up. But these trainers could use their PDAs, devices that many members of his training team purchased themselves. They were much easier to use—and more functional—than the company-provided hardware and software.

SENSE-MAKING AROUND ORGANIZATIONAL CONTROL AND GROWING NOTIONS OF AGENTIC CONTROL

These stories and the related data not only provide us a historical understanding of early mobile device use but also reflect a time when organizations provided most, if not all, of the communication and technology that people used at work. That era saw only limited negotiation around providing and using mobile tools because they weren't yet much of a factor, being both pricey and of limited personal use. Remember that my car phone story predates the use of personal mobiles by almost a decade. While that timeline varied around the globe, it was the late 1990s before cellular phones in the U.S. were used for more than voice-only calls. Around that time, BlackBerrys entered the business scene and business people began using these ingenious new "cellular" devices.

These early business experiences with car phones offer two key insights. As a new employee, I experienced a portable communication tool *first* through my work. Car phones were defined as *business tools*, and those companies willing to purchase them justified the expense as worth helping make field staff more productive. This example illustrates the first type of mobile control discussed here—*organizational control*—where organizations paid for these mobile devices and set the rules for their use. Yes, some employees pushed the limits of the rules; but these business tools were clearly a company's property, so no one challenged its right to control them.

These experiences also foreshadow the advantages and disadvantages of personal mobile devices that emerged in the early 2000s. For many people, whose first experiences using mobiles were in the early 2000s, it's hard to imagine a time when friends and loved ones didn't have mobiles or when people didn't have access to one another after work hours. In the early 1990s, there was no critical mass[12] of mobile-device users outside of the work teams that used them to coordinate and communicate. Today, most people take those conveniences for granted,[9,10,11] something I experienced through my work in 1990s.

EXPERIMENTING WITH PERSONAL DEVICES

Even well before there was a critical mass of portable devices and mobile tools, people like my engineer interviewee Bill were willing to purchase their own devices to give them more control over their work and data. Bill's behavior can be described as an act of individual agency. Human agency is often defined as "the ability to form goals and act."[6,7] No one ever suggested that Bill provide his own work tablet, but he unilaterally decided that using this cool new technology would help him better meet his goals. In studying technology, a human-agency perspective suggests that people's actions are not necessarily determined by a technology.[14] For example, when Bill purchased his own tablet computer, he didn't use that device in a conventional, predictable manner. He exercised his own judgment and repurposed it by adding the plastic 10″-by-12″ cover to meet the requirements of the clean room. With that modification, he both met company regulations and got to use his own, superior documenting tool. Researchers have shown that even when technologies could potentially constrain human agency, resourceful people can reinvent those systems to make them work for their situations.[3]

Organizational control over resources is also present in this data concerning Bill. The company originally paid for his Internet access in hopes that its gesture would be seen as generous and its employees would reciprocate by working a bit extra. While we don't know why the company elected to stop this practice, I suspect that many employees were as annoyed as Bill when the benefit was withdrawn. The subtle control—or norm of reciprocity[8]—the company had over Bill's behavior ended when he no longer felt a sense of moral obligation to work extra hours. Action and reaction in a context where there is human agency is another reason I describe mobile-device use as a negotiation for control. Bill's story provides an example of how this negotiation began.

The examples of early tablet and PDA use remind us that mobile connectivity—specifically to other people—is a relatively recent thing. Actually, even Evan's web-conferencing service relied heavily on landline phones and cord-based Internet to provide connections to others. At this time in mobile-device history, PDAs were *portable storage tools, not connected communication devices*. While BlackBerrys were slowly entering the mobile scene, a development I'll recount in the next chapter, many of these early mobile tools weren't used for communicating or gathering real-time data. The affordances, or material capabilities, that most workers drew upon to justify using them were these three: portability, self-organization, and information storage.

Table 1.1 pulls together the differences between organizationally provided cell phones and the early portable devices that individuals, illustrated in the data, began bringing to work. Car phones and bag phones, clunky as they seem today, were actually early-stage mobile communication devices because they were somewhat portable and were

Table 1.1. AN EARLY COMPARISON OF MOBILE TOOLS IN ORGANIZATIONS

Type of Tool	Business Tools	Personal Mobile Tools
Examples of tools	Car phones and laptops	Tablets (minicomputers) and PDAs
Ownership of tools	Provided by organization	Provided by individuals
Purpose	Connect to others in organization	Connect to data and enhance personal productivity
Type of use	Minimal need for personal use	Increasing personal use but primarily business

Note. PDA = personal digital assistant.

used to communicate, chiefly with people within the same organization. The early personal mobile tools, meanwhile, were focused on self-improvement and individual productivity. While these devices had few true communicative abilities, their use demonstrated the importance of portability and the power that individuals could have over not only their own data but also at least some data belonging to their employer. Those forerunners are quite different from what grew out of their use. Over time, these uses and ownership issues have become more complex and even paradoxical.

MOBILES AS BUSINESS AND PERSONAL ORGANIZATION TOOLS FOR KNOWLEDGE WORKERS

This chapter has established the historical context of mobiles and their early use by knowledge workers. Taken together, the stories recounted here illustrate two key concepts. First, cell phones were business tools, provided by and paid for by companies. Control over these devices rested clearly in their hands, and while there were some minor negotiations about how much money companies would spend to pay for phone bills, most of these tools could be considered organizational assets.

But these stories also reveal early attempts by individuals to use mobile tools for their own goals. Individual agency is clearly illustrated in these stories. These knowledge workers believed that their mobile tools could help them manage their impressions, establish their expertise, organize their time, improve their efficiency, integrate their leisure activities, and control their data. It was this last point—control over data—that eventually led organizations to create policies regulating mobile-device use. I'll be discussing these topics further in Chapters 3–8.

KNOWLEDGE WORKERS AND MOBILE DEVICES

I have used the term "knowledge worker" to describe any employee who regularly used the early cellular and mobile devices in their work. It's a term coined by Peter Drucker in his book *The Age of Discontinuity*,[5] where he predicted a growing need for workers who generate and use knowledge as an integral part of their employment. While the term is arguably imprecise, knowledge workers are typically considered regular creators or users of computers in addition to being contributors of content that is now regularly displayed though such ICTs as social media.[13] These workers use ICTs heavily in their cognitive work. I aim to challenge the use of this term later in the book, but for now I will bow to the lead of others and refer to these individuals as "knowledge workers."

Researchers who've studied them have found that the autonomy they're often afforded stems from their work being thought both highly skilled and self-directed.[15,19] Autonomy provides workers the flexibility to exercise their own judgment and make decisions without direct managerial involvement.[1,19] Furthermore, this autonomy, or reduction in bureaucratic control over work, is often considered a way to reinforce knowledge workers' occupational prestige in organizations.[2] This description meshes well with the early car-phone and mobile-device users I've described.

EARLY MOBILES AS BUSINESS TOOLS

The stories in this chapter illustrate the experimentation shown by many knowledge workers, who not only used the mobile tools provided at work but also began exploring new mobile tools on their own and adding them to their tool arsenal there. Strong on initiative, they sought to improve their work practices at a time when, so unlike today, they weren't yet connected to data and information was not yet available at the mere touch or two of their fingers.

But these connections to people and data became a reality in the U.S. business community during the early 2000s. Those years saw a growing use of mobile business-communication tools, and managers faced some difficult decisions about how to allocate and regulate their use. In the next chapter, I'll focus on the early struggles for control over resources and communication practices when BlackBerrys and the ability to check email on the go entered the business world.

CHAPTER 2
Negotiating Mobile Control

As long as your cell phone is on, you're available to us.
—Kjell, Company Owner

The BlackBerry had become a badge of honor and a badge of, "Hey, you're cool and you get one because we think your work is important."
—Matt, National Sales Manager

By the late 1990s to early 2000s, mobile use was expanding rapidly. Most users were still knowledge workers, but more and more they started realizing the potential of connecting to others within both their work context and their personal lives, so negotiations for control over mobile communication were bound to become more complex.

MOBILE USE IN NORWAY

I had visited Norway three times by 2005. Besides collecting part of my dissertation data there, I had either participated in or taught Qualitative Research Methods, an intensive doctoral course held in the spectacular Lofoten Islands, above the Arctic Circle. It was part of the graduate curriculum at Bodø University College and the University of Nordland, since merged and renamed Nord University. A professor there, Jan-Oddvar Sørnes, invited me to participate in the program along with my then-doctoral advisor at The University of Texas at Austin, Larry Browning. Each time I visited, I spent some 2 weeks with students from Norway, the U.S., and Europe. In addition to teaching the Qualitative Research Methods course, I taught a course on workplace technologies in Oslo, Norway, into the mid-2010s in an executive master's program.

These experiences in Norway helped me add some working knowledge to my book, knowledge of the differences in national cultures, especially in Scandinavia. For example, I was startled to see the small mobile phones that so many Norwegian students used, as early as my first visit in 2002, and how integral these devices were to their work and life. They even used their mobiles for banking and vending-machine purchases—a practice that only was seen in the U.S. nearly a full decade later. I often quizzed the people I met about the cost of using these ducky, ingenious devices as they seemed well beyond my financial reach at the time.

As part of a team of researchers interested in these cross-cultural information and communication technologies (ICTs), we collected interview data from 72 different knowledge workers in the U.S. and Norway. Our team consisted of Larry Browning, myself, and two Norwegian colleagues—Jan-Oddvar Sørnes, one of my research partners, who was also a doctoral student at the time, and his advisor, Alf-Steinar Sætre, an associate professor at Norwegian University of Science and Technology. Together, we spent the better part of 3 years collecting and analyzing our data. One portion of the data became my dissertation; another slice of the data became a book, *Information & Communication Technologies in Action: Linking Theory and Narratives of Practice*; and yet another part of this data was used for a cultural analysis.

To analyze the data using a cultural lens, our team used Geert Hofstede's prominent theory of the four dimensions of culture—power distance, uncertainty avoidance, individualism versus collectivism, and masculinity versus femininity.[4] Hofstede had collected his data during the 1970s, and to capture cultural differences, he conducted survey research using IBM managers representing over 30 countries. According to Hofstede's own data, the U.S. and Norway had looked very similar on three of the four dimensions of culture.[4,10] Both countries, for example, had scored relatively low on the "power distance" dimension, which measures the strength of the social hierarchy, since both countries value cooperation more than establishing firm hierarchical power positions between people or groups. "Uncertainty avoidance" tolerance was also similar because people from both countries showed a willingness to take risks and felt less need to avoid ambiguous or unpredictable business situations. The "individualism versus collectivism" dimension, meanwhile, distinguishes countries by examining whether they prefer individual or group actions. While Norway and the U.S. weren't that far apart on this dimension, the U.S. emerged the most individualistic of all countries included in Hofstede's original study.

Significantly, Norwegians differed the most from the U.S. on the "masculinity-versus-femininity" dimension, a finding particularly meaningful for studies of ICT use in the workplace. Countries, like the U.S., scoring high on the "masculinity" dimension value assertiveness and competitiveness and have a need to distinguish themselves by attracting notice through achievement. These countries also tend to separate work and personal life and take pride in working long hours to demonstrate the desire to excel.[4] Norwegians, on the other hand, scored high on the "femininity" dimension. Countries rating high on femininity value modesty, and they also tend to prioritize family time and personal time much more than we Americans do. This difference became obvious to me both in classroom discussions I had with my students and in personal conversations outside of class. In the MA course in Oslo, at least a quarter of my 35-person class would let me know which days they needed to leave class early to pick up their children from soccer practice. Mind you, this was communicated as a statement, not an apology; it was an important part of their lives, and it was going to happen regardless of my reaction. In the U.S., such a conversation would likely never happen because our business culture almost forces us to keep our private lives separate from work or school.

But now the rug-pull: in our analysis of the 72 interviews in our data set, where we mapped our findings on Geert Hofstede's four dimensions of culture, our research team found something surprising. The U.S. and Norway looked very similar on *all four dimensions* of culture, something counter to past research. How to explain *that*? We ultimately theorized that our study's focus on knowledge workers, who were advanced users of ICTs, had leveled the cultural differences. These workers were constantly connected to their ICTs, something never seen in the 1970s, back when Hofstede had conducted his research. In our published research paper, we concluded that ICTs blur the contrast between the dimensions of individualism versus collectivism and masculinity versus femininity.[10] While the U.S.'s individualistic and highly materialistic culture[4] had, for decades, been using many types of work tools to extend the American workday, we found that our Norwegian interviewees had started using their mobiles in a way now more and more familiar to us in the U.S. The upshot was that those mobiles had become negotiating tools that, in a tit-for-tat situation, allowed employers to coax their employees into working longer hours.

What our team did not explore was how the melding of these two cultural dimensions might also inform an understanding of organizational control over mobile communication. As I re-examined the interviews our team had collected to provide additional perspective for this book, I realized that our data revealed a bit of a Wild Wild West mentality in how Norwegian and U.S. companies experimented with using ICTs as a tool to control their workers. While "control" might be a bit hyperbolic in some situations, in the example that follows, Kjell relies heavily on the moral norm of reciprocity[3] to get additional work out of his employees in exchange for providing them a mobile device. This is in stark contrast to my personal story from Chapter 1 where my work team at Hewlett-Packard viewed cell phones as productivity tools, pure and simple. At that time, I rarely felt that my cell phone was provided with after-hours work expectations attached.

Let's turn now to see how Kjell and his Norwegian entrepreneurial software company, founded in early 2000, dealt with these issues.

Kjell, one of the company founders, was very open about why he gave every employee a mobile phone. He told them that, yes, they could also use it to call their friends, but "as long as your cell phone is on, you are available to us." Kjell's employees were predominantly programmers, and when clients wanted changes or had questions, Kjell needed immediate access to people who could meet those client needs. He believed this was a mutually beneficial arrangement because the company paid its employees' cell-phone bills as the price for having access to them. But he was also frustrated that even though he had 24/7 access, the employees used their cell phones excessively for personal use, *even during regular work hours*. Kjell needed his programmers to concentrate, but instead they were being constantly interrupted with personal messages.

Kjell tried appealing to his employees, but their behavior remained unchanged. He was concerned that productivity and quality were suffering because his workers had no uninterrupted time. To address this concern, he enacted new policies, one of which required his workers to spend at least some time at work disconnected. This presumably took care of the focus problem. But, to give as well as get, he also pledged to do a better job of respecting his employees' time off, saying that he'd now only contact them during client emergencies.

It's hard to know if Kjell's changes directly influenced productivity or perceptions of work–life balance, but he did realize that his original policy had negative unintended consequences that were exhausting to him and his workers. When I first read this interview, I assumed it was about a U.S. company, for the story it tells runs counter to many of the things that Norwegians value. Yet the growing body of research on mobiles being organizational electronic leashes seems to reflect a global trend.[1,2,6,7,8,10,13]

Kjell's company is a small one, with maybe 15 employees, so it was easy for him to observe their behavior, have team-like conversations, and make changes. He was able to engage in what is called *simple, direct control*.[1] In other narratives in this book, though, I'll show some large companies establishing policies that proved difficult to enact and made behavioral changes even harder.

WHO SHOULD GET A COMPANY BLACKBERRY?

By the early 2000s, in addition to seeing more personal mobile devices at work, many organizations struggled to decide just who should get a company cell phone, what brand to buy, and how to control these "part-corporate" devices. To better show the perspective of upper management during this time period, I want to bring in Matt, a former executive with the *Wall Street Journal* (*WSJ*). Matt's interview was captured as part of my meetings data set collected between 2008 and 2013, but his story is one of a manager struggling to control his team yet to be flexible enough to help them be competitive. Back then, he was a newspaperman through and through. After graduating with a degree in journalism, he set off to be a journalist and quickly moved into a series of sales positions. A decade later he landed in New York City, the mecca of the news business. His 360-degree view of the newspaper industry is what propelled him into the top sales position with the *WSJ*. He recounted how he and his organization wrestled with decisions concerning mobile communication.

SPENDING MONEY FOR TOYS: BLACKBERRYS

In the late 1990s, Matt recalled, America's newspaper industry was in "disbelief, especially where I worked. We thought that the Internet was not going to amount to much." Basically, he said, "we had our head in the sand," owing to a technological conservatism very different from the entrepreneurism of West Coast companies, which were rapidly advancing mobile and Internet use. Matt's clients, sensing a paradigm shift, were reallocating their advertising budgets—specifically, downsizing their print advertising because they felt like they needed to develop their websites, despite barely knowing what "websites" were. Matt's newspaper felt a tough squeeze there, and it was only getting worse.

Meanwhile, BlackBerrys were becoming the newest "new thing" for communicating with customers. But Matt explained that companies like his, which had their largest sales teams congregating in major cities, saw no need for their employees to have mobile or cellular phones. "Our office was on 45th Street," he said, "and you're making a sales call on 18th. Jump on the subway and [then] get back to the office. It's cheaper than paying for a cell-phone charge. So the people in Manhattan—we didn't feel, or the corporation didn't feel, that it was necessary."

But while the *WSJ* hadn't invested in individual cell phones, it did make some cell phones available to be checked out. Even so, there were few takers, and understandably so. Matt explained why:

> *No corporation was really willing to man their sales organization with these big $800 devices. I do remember we had a brick you could check out, I mean the thing came in one of those almost cooler-looking apparatuses. People could check [this portable phone] out and take on sales calls if they were going to far places like New Jersey or Connecticut. But it was terribly intimidating because no one really knew how to use it. And it would charge like, $5 a minute? It was an astronomically large number that scared management. So you not only had to check it out, you had to justify why you had to check it out, and you had to then account for why you were on it, because the bills would come in and it would be several hundred dollars. And several hundred dollars in the '90s was still . . . a pretty big number.*

But things changed when BlackBerrys started seriously infiltrating the corporate world around 2000. Though the *WSJ* still didn't believe that anyone actually *needed* one to do their job—after all, even most of their customers themselves didn't have one—Matt knew that his salespeople had a growing respect for the BlackBerry's utility. While visiting a customer, his salespeople often needed to call the *WSJ* home office, make a request for information to be quickly delivered to the customer, and voila!, the materials were faxed or emailed to a customer within an hour. His salespeople felt that these conversations with their *WSJ* home office staff made them more responsive to their customers' needs. Thus, they argued that they needed a BlackBerry to boost their sales.

But within a short time, the BlackBerry became more of an email tool than a phone. Matt recalled: "The big change happened when people started to realize that it was acceptable to communicate by email. That's when external communication became relevant." When Short Message Service (SMS) failed to gain popularity in the U.S., the BlackBerry, capable of both sending and receiving emails, rose to the fore, adding the first dominant mobile form of messaging through emails. Since most people now had business email addresses and since many business conversations were now conducted using email, the prevalence of email made managers start to see value in paying for the revolutionary BlackBerry.

As national sales manager, Matt was responsible for an extensive budget. He had years of budget data on office and landline phone use, and he knew how to budget for long-distance charges; but when something like the BlackBerry came along, there was no usage history. Moreover, his company combined all his telecommunications into a single budget item. He remembers his frustration in trying to decide whether BlackBerry usage was justified. The newspaper business was in a quickening downslide, so there was no new money coming in. Matt recalls his CFO coming to him and saying:

> OK, if you want BlackBerrys for your team, Matt, then you're going to take the money out of some budget. So what is that? Where's that money coming from? Do you want less people? Do you want less marketing support? Do you want less travel? OK, one of those. Take your pick and you can have what you want.

Matt reflected on the complicated decision-making he faced while wrestling with this problem:

> I had to pay for my office phones and the BlackBerrys in one bill. I would just get this number from Accounting that said, "Your telecommunications bill for the month of January was $15,000." And then how does that break out? I couldn't measure the effectiveness of usage. I'd get these single printed-out sheets of, "This salesperson spent 180 minutes on the BlackBerry. This salesperson spent 82 minutes on the BlackBerry." And then I'd start saying, "OK, what's the variation for?" I'd sit there and say, "Do I really want to give up an airline ticket to go see a client to buy a salesperson a BlackBerry?" Because that's what the trade-off was. BlackBerrys were $300 to $400, plus the monthly service fees. So all of a sudden you're looking at a $600, $700 expense per salesperson. Well, that's an airline ticket to go see a client. And no new money was being created to fund these toys.

The expense of these mobiles seemed to also drive corporate policies. For example, Matt recalls, he and his team had to sign a contract pledging that they would use their BlackBerrys only for business: "At the risk of being terminated, you would not use a BlackBerry for personal use. And the company had the right to seize the BlackBerry and look at your addresses that you used. So it was a very highly controlled environment."

FAIRNESS AND EXPECTATIONS OF WHO GETS
A COMPANY BLACKBERRY

Given the growing BlackBerry frenzy, all the salespeople in Matt's company suddenly wanted this new business tool that theoretically could make them more productive. But his bosses were dubious. "Not everybody in upper management had them," explained Matt. "There was this sense of, 'I'm not going to get involved in this.' Not everybody viewed this as a benefit. A lot of the senior people viewed it as a toy."

So Matt had to make difficult decisions. Some 20% of his salespeople were top performers. Should he present *them* BlackBerrys as a reward? Or should he give his lower performers BlackBerrys to see if it might improve their performance? Ultimately, he decided that his more remote salespeople—like those in rural Pennsylvania—were the best investment and possibly the most deserving. They didn't get to come to the central office very often, and, as road warriors, they had to spend ungodly hours in their cars, as you saw me once having to do myself in Chapter 1. So Matt's compassion trumped his other options.

Well! Almost immediately, his decision drew howls of complaint from his Manhattan-based salesforce, whose feelings were badly hurt. He, in turn, probably hurt even worse:

> My Manhattan staff whined, "Why are they getting something that we can't?" The BlackBerry had become a badge of honor and a badge of, "Hey, you're cool and you get one because we think your work is important and you need to be caught up in this technology." And you know, let's face it, technology's exciting. It was sexy and everybody wanted it. I eventually caved. All of a sudden it became indefensible to not give a Manhattan person a BlackBerry. Why fight it? They really took it personally. I would get these memos and emails from people. You know, a paragraph as to why they needed to have a BlackBerry. Everybody wanted to have those cool little blue-looking things in their pocket because they felt better about themselves.

So Matt eventually surrendered, and all of his salespeople got a BlackBerry. So also, it seemed, did everyone else in New York's supercompetitive, super-status-conscious business community, for the devices were suddenly ubiquitous. And as their price came down, people found themselves using them almost nonstop, Matt recalled. Quite ostentatiously, too: "There was a period there on the train when everybody had a clip-on [phone], and we wore them on our belt and we were constantly, like, pulling our gun."

Matt and his management couldn't help but now wonder if these were just toys that made people feel popular and needed.

UNINTENDED CONSEQUENCES OF HAVING A BOSS
IN YOUR POCKET

He also couldn't help wondering if he hadn't solved one problem—
the arming of his warriors—only to create some new ones. One of the
biggest ones—in fact, one that bothers Matt to this day—is that their
relationships utterly changed amid all these BlackBerrys. Before "BB-Day,"
people weren't as accessible. And that made for more independence, more
"breathing room," for them at all levels. In sales, it meant that check-ins
with immediate managers happened weekly, not daily or hourly, and national managers rarely talked with the front-line salesforce, so no one
felt badgered or monitored from on high. Also, there were standardized
reporting times and standardized documents to complete, and the accomplishment of sales targets was reported monthly, or even quarterly.
This meant that if some mistake were made or if something didn't go as
planned, you'd still be able to compensate for that error before the formal
reporting occurred.

The new constant access to subordinates, though, utterly changed the
power dynamic and the expected norms for immediate reporting. When
remembering this, Matt's voice tone changed. He confessed to feeling re-
morseful, and almost powerless, as he recounted his experience:

*I think that made me more present in my staff's lives. I think it put enormous pressure
on them, and I became Big Brother looking at and communicating with people who
[in the past] wouldn't have seen me except for when I came to the field once or twice
a year to interface with them. All of a sudden, now I'm in their lives every single day.
I'm sending out emails. I'm sending out texts, and asking, "Karen, what's going on
with this account in Portland, Maine? Would love your update." Now that's immediate, and my salesperson was probably sitting in Portland, Maine, and saying, "Oh
my God. My National Sales Director wants me to respond about a question and I've
never been contacted by a National Sales Director before. That is my regional and
my district manager's responsibility." That created an enormous degree, I think, of
unhealthy pressure on the sales organization. And I had enormous personnel issues—
yeah, people issues as a result of that. Because [the lower-level managers asked]
"Matt, why are you asking my salesperson a question?" [I'd respond by saying] "Well,
I have to have an answer for my boss." [And the lower-level manager would say] "Why
am I not in this mix? You know, all of a sudden you have this relationship with this
salesperson in Portland, Maine, that saw you once a year for the last three years, and
now all of a sudden you're best friends?" And in retrospect, I can tell you that not all of
the outcomes were positive. Not because I'm mean-spirited, or I'm going to get in your
business, or I have the authority and power to ask you these questions, but because the*

immediacy and the technology gave me the ability to bypass filters and I was able to go right to the source and get an answer. And that's still true today.

Matt's story provides a managerial perspective to the changing mobile landscape and the negotiation of mobile control. As national sales manager, he was stuck in the middle of these difficult decisions. His story reveals his struggles in addressing serious budgetary concerns and demands from his people. He was an integral part of the upper-management team, but he was close enough to the field to see that selling was changing at the same time that his market was declining.

THE HIDDEN PRESSURES OF REACHABILITY
AND MANAGERIAL CONTROL

Matt's internal conflict over having gained increased access to his employees through their mobiles raises an important issue concerning how and when employees are fairly expected to be available for work conversations. Sometimes these reachability expectations are present even when the organization *has not provided* the mobile device.

The following example illuminates some notions of control in the context of the advisor–advisee relationship. It features Stephanie, then my graduate student. To ensure that our little story here accurately reflects her own impressions, not just mine, I asked her to review it and edit it freely, which she did.

SENT FROM MY IPHONE: STEPHANIE'S STORY

I've been fortunate to work with many amazing students at the undergraduate, master's, and doctoral levels. But a key difference that I've found in teaching advanced graduate students is that I know all of them, being ambitious souls, will be doing social-scientific research, and they expect good training for it.

Stephanie, her actual name instead of a pseudonym, was one of my early graduate students. She started the MA program at The University of Texas and continued right on for her PhD. We knew one another quite well by the time she entered the doctoral program, and her intelligence and work ethic made her a great research partner.

At the outset, I sat Stephanie down and explained that I wanted a true research partner, not a minion who thinks her job is to stoke my ego. She was already a splendid writer when she joined our MA program at age 22, so I told her to please be critical of my own writing and challenge my ideas during the research-design process. Even though I was a relatively new professor at the time, I had already experienced both sides of the power differential inherent in the advisor–advisee relationship. I knew I had to be explicit about how I liked to conduct research because otherwise graduate students would be reluctant to provide critical feedback. Furthermore, establishing expectations for working on a research team is an important part of the mentoring/teaching process.

Stephanie immediately understood and fortunately trusted me enough to take me at my word. She edited my writing, asked for clarification on research designs, and even went out of her way to verify my use of statistical tests, despite being pretty new to statistics herself. She proved a veritable sponge—a sharp, polite, and delightful academic sponge.

One evening in the fall of 2009, I was working on a proposal document where Stephanie was my co-investigator. I had sent her an email earlier that day, and around 6 p.m. I got a response. I was then sitting at a climbing gym in Austin, Texas, waiting for my son to finish up, so I had my computer out and was still working. This particular reply from Stephanie was different. At the bottom of her email I saw the words *Sent from my iPhone*. I had recalled Stephanie telling me she was getting a new phone, but in academia, not many of our students were using mobile phones to send email in 2009, so this one caused me to smile. I immediately sent her a reply and asked her to please look up three more articles, get me some summaries, and provide ideas for how we could integrate this material into our proposal.

When I got to the office the next morning, I found a new email from her brimming with all the research results I had asked for. And of course it was top-notch, as always. I was thrilled because it meant I could finish the proposal that very morning. I went straight to work, and when I saw Stephanie later that day I thanked her profusely, telling her that because of her quick response I was able to get the proposal off and under review. She seemed equally excited as she walked over to show me her new phone, which she was really proud of. But in the middle of our chat, I realized what I had done to her. I stopped the conversation and looked at her. "Stephanie," I said, "I am very sorry. I didn't mean to put pressure on your to do all that research last night." She immediately assured me, "It wasn't a problem. I didn't have anything I was doing anyway."

I then confessed what I had unintentionally done. "That wasn't fair of me to ask you to do that. I remember seeing *Sent from my iPhone*, and

I immediately thought that you were now more accessible. I was still working at 6 p.m., and yet I never stopped to think that it was after work hours. I was actually excited that I could reach you so easily, so I took advantage of your availability."

Stephanie cheerfully insisted that I hadn't bothered her in any way, but I knew what I had done was wrong. I study mobile-device use, and I had just done to Stephanie what I was hearing people in my interviews tell me about their bosses. Whether intentional or unintentional—and I've heard both from my study participants—when someone with more power makes a request, a subordinate feels obliged to respond.

Stephanie and I have since talked about this incident openly, and she verified my recollection of it. She also confessed that she had proudly included the *Sent from my iPhone* because it proved she was an early adopter! Both she and I have used this as an example in our classes because it clearly illustrates hierarchical power and mobile-device use. I share this story with all my graduate students in particular because I know how easy it is for me to make a request and have my students move mountains to try to be responsive. I felt that same need to please back when I was in their shoes. The last thing I want to be is unreasonable. But even though I know how to recognize this behavior in others, there are still times I unintentionally and thoughtlessly put this pressure on others.

HIERARCHICAL PRESSURE AND MOBILE AFFORDANCES

I've heard similar comments from many of my study participants throughout the years I've collected data. Some interviewees have expressed frustration that their manager sends messages after work hours, and by the time they check email again the next workday, all their other team members have responded; their own absence from the after-hours electronic conversation meant they lost their say in the matter. People worry if their lack of monitoring emails or texts that arrive at supposedly off-hours will play a role in the next round of promotions or layoffs. Several people in my studies have lamented they work for global organizations. They download Skype and other web-conferencing apps so that they can leave their children's basketball games to participate in some online international meeting because 6:30 p.m. (18:30) is the only time when all their global partners are awake. By the way, some of these same people sleep with their phones on vibrate under their pillows and get up in the middle of the night to cater to their international collaborators' needs.

Examples of work intruding into personal life are well documented and constitute the bulk of the research on organizational mobile communication.[1,5,6,8,10,13] Researchers have found that many workers feel stressed that they cannot escape their constant connection to work.[1,5,6,13] Yet these same workers want and need their mobiles to do their jobs. While much of my data from knowledge workers confirms these well-documented frustrations, I also see issues of power and struggles for control played out through mobile communication in organizations. As illustrated in this chapter, some of these power struggles are overt, while others remain more subtle.

While the managerial behaviors shared here could be construed as an abuse of positional or managerial power—supervisors and managers, after all, have decision-making authority—I've tried to demonstrate that sometimes, and perhaps often, supervisors may not *deliberately* mean to intrude on their employees' personal lives. One possible explanation for why managers send messages after hours is not that they're implying that a prompt response is needed but simply that it lets them check that to-do item off their list of tasks. The Task-Closure Model of Media Choice[12] is a theoretical model proposing that some people actively choose asynchronous ICTs when others are unavailable because the act of sending the message removes that item from their list of tasks, so their stress is reduced. "Asynchronous communication" describes a situation when a message is sent using an ICT that does not relay information in real time. There is normally at least a small delay using asynchronous ICTs like email or voicemail. Even though Straub and Karahanna's (1998)[12] research was conducted 20 years ago, a quote from one of their subjects clearly explains why some people might send an email with no expectation of an immediate response. These researchers contend that when message recipients are temporally unavailable, many communicators want to bring closure to their tasks. Here's the example they provide:

> It is very important to me to call up somebody and leave a message on their machine because I'm thinking of that right now and know that I can leave it on their machine without having to talk to them. (p. 171)

Straub and Karahanna specifically note that knowledge workers feel they have brought a task to closure by sending an email, and if they doubt that closure, they can ask for an electronic receipt or use a blind carbon copy. Note that in 1998 emails were not regularly read on mobile devices except for some two-way pagers. It's quite possible that today some people send emails with the goal of closing their task and not expecting an immediate response, while other people are fully aware that the person receiving the email will likely respond quickly.

REACHABILITY LEADING TO EXPECTATIONS AND NORMS

When emails started arriving on mobile devices, there was a shift in the temporal reachability of workers, meaning that some people could access email more quickly. As I mentioned earlier, affordances are material features that don't define how people use an ICT, but they do raise a possibility for use in a specific way. One of the key affordances of mobile devices is availability, also called "accessibility."[9] With so many people having mobile devices, it's easier for people to be reached and to reach others, so they are considered available to others or simply accessible.

As BlackBerrys and other mobile devices entered the workforce in the early 2000s, several scholars studied what happened when other people began to expect their colleagues to be available to them. They found that knowledge workers often described their devices as electronic leashes,[8] things they could not escape. While workers enjoyed many of the new capabilities these devices afforded them, there were paradoxes and often negative implications of using a mobile device.[5,8,13] For example, workers from four different countries—Hong Kong, Finland, Japan, and the U.S.—described feeling both empowered and enslaved by their mobiles.[5]

A key theme derived from Matt's experience is how the affordance of mobile accessibility reduced the formalized hierarchical boundaries that had existed earlier. On the plus side, it allowed him to have one-on-one conversations with anyone in his sales team—and as often as he wished. On the minus side, the reduction of the formalized hierarchical boundaries amounted to a disruption of that hierarchy, pressured the individual salespeople, and made Matt realize that in his quest for prompt answers, he created situations where individuals lacked any time to correct their mistakes.

The example of Stephanie and *Sent from my iPhone* indicates more than the reachability affordance, but it shows how an affordance can become an expectation through norms. *Not being available* is a type of norm violation in an environment where almost everyone is available. While being unavailable might annoy a co-worker and impact trust in the working relationship, violating that norm with a supervisor can have legitimate job-security ramifications. Therefore, reachability is tricky where there are hierarchical power dynamics at play—a situation often present in organizations. Responsiveness desires and perceptions of urgency can be misinterpreted by a subordinate who feels the hidden pressure to impress or even meet the perceived expectations of a supervisor.

In examining my data, I see many instances where people sat down to do work, used their email boxes as to-do lists, and simply sent messages as a way to close their tasks. There are also several examples of people knowingly making requests outside of work hours to pressure their peers and subordinates to provide responses quickly.

But one of the cloudiest situations seen in the data involved collaborators addressing multiple tasks as part of a larger deliverable. The motives and the responsiveness become entangled because when collaborators respond immediately on the smaller tasks, the bigger task is completed faster. When working through those projects, that responsiveness is typically rewarded with verbal or written praise, not unlike how I treated Stephanie when she did the research overnight and helped me complete the bigger grant project more quickly. Responsiveness sends a symbolic message of accomplishment that hovers beneath the surface of a project.[11] In my own work on communication overload, our team found what we called an "availability–expectation–pressure pattern" that can create perceptions of overload. When someone with power, often a manager, praises a subordinate's responsiveness, it makes the pressure to be responsive more bearable, at least for the short term.

But not all collaborators or teams use mobiles as an excuse to expect team members to be constantly available to them. In her work examining differences between a footwear organization's sales team and legal team, Melissa Mazmanian[6] found that when groups think they are all using their mobiles differently, accessibility expectations don't exist, co-workers don't encroach on each other's personal time. Her findings suggest that assumptions concerning how others use technology matter, and there can be occupational, profession, job role, and industry differences surrounding availability expectations.

CHAPTER 3

Theoretical Notions of Control—A Mobile Tug-of-War

Let's pause here. The narratives shared in Chapters 1 and 2 reflect the dawn of organizational cell-phone and mobile-device use, primarily in the U.S. At that time, most cell phones were provided by organizations. That changed dramatically between 2000 and 2010. Yet these early stories anticipate many of the same tensions that people experience today: negotiating control over communication practices is reality.

These lived experiences of early work-related mobile users provide background for why mobile diffusion into organizations has been a tug-of-war. As I pulled together published research and my own data sets, I realized that the early years of mobiles in organizations (roughly 1990–2010) contain many tensions around control. Not being a critical scholar, I didn't seek to understand organizational processes by focusing on notions of power, so I didn't begin this project with that focus. Yet as I analyzed the data, I was constantly struck by the power struggles that have emerged in organizations, many of them centering on autonomy and agency—one's ability, to "form and realize one's own goals"[8,12]—while using mobile devices. True to form with qualitative data, I let the findings unearth my theoretical contributions.

While Chapter 11 develops theory more completely and integrates the data as a whole, here I'll use these early stories to introduce core concepts around control that emerged during my analyses. This chapter is simply an introduction to notions related to power and control; I hope that by setting the stage here, you can better understand how I developed the grounded theory in Chapter 11. I don't attempt to provide a comprehensive background on theories of power and control, but by directing you to relevant, existing thinking on these concepts, you'll have a lens to view the next empirical chapters and my resulting analyses.

PERSPECTIVES ON ORGANIZATIONAL CONTROL

In their 2010 book *Organizational Control*, Sim Sitkin, Laura Cardinal, and Katinka Bijlsma-Frankema review for us the history of academic research on organizational control, but they also help us see "control" as more than just a lever for *coercive* control. They argue that it is also "a source of sense-making and identity formation"[34] (p. 4). For example, organization control isn't simply about enforcing rules, but instead, control can function to unify groups by bringing people together at a common time to meet. This extended perspective meshes well with what I found as I analyzed the data for this book. Sim Sitkin and his colleagues' efforts stitch together the existing literature on organizational control and generate rich ideas to fuel future research.[34] I use their edited book extensively in this chapter to frame this work.

Two other scholars, Roger Dunbar and Matt Statler, also have a chapter in *Organizational Control*,[6] and they explain how researchers tend to approach organizational control from one of three perspectives—bureaucratic, human relations, or process. Since the arguments in this book primarily adopt the process perspective, I'll explain this view in more detail, but I'll also touch on notions of bureaucracy and classical control theories. The key assumptions of the process perspective are that control is situational, dynamic, and involved in ongoing change and adjustment. Actually, this approach to understanding control helps explain what we saw in all three stories from Chapter 2. Kjell, Matt, and I watched our own control over communication practices change, and, in the process, we all three questioned our actions (i.e., engaged in sense-making) and made adjustments.

A process perspective views control from a social, human sciences, and systems approach. Control is an integral part of working with people, and while it can be used to dominate every aspect of a person's professional life, it doesn't have to. A process perspective can be used to convey the ethical base of control[6] because it forces us to consider more than strict bureaucratic rules and resources. Control, viewed as a process, emphasizes how to create a more democratic and fair workplace, realizing that humans' intentions have a finite capacity. A person's ability to make decisions—intentionality—is limited by what Hebert Simon calls "bounded rationality," meaning that a person is not able to locate, absorb, process, and master all relevant information and, therefore, cannot identify the optimal solution.[33] As a result, people usually find it necessary to constantly adjust their understandings and goals as their view of situations change.

I use the word "negotiation" throughout this book as a descriptive term representing a communicative technique to manage conflict. This is different from the theoretical treatment of negotiation that originated from economic models. That foundational literature focused on give-and-take in disputes[31] and explained how people try to minimize their losses while maximizing gains.[15] You'll notice that in several places in this book I refer to this process as a tug-of-war, a struggle for control, and a dialectic of control. These are simply meant to explain that a two-way *negotiation process* is especially prevalent when practices around mobile communication in organizations are constantly changing. I'll explain this negotiation in detail in Chapter 11; there I link it directly to the literature on a dialectic of control.[12,21,22,23,24,28,29,30]

Since change occurs both inside and outside an organization, there's a delicate balance between formal and informal controls that evolve over time.[5] Scholars often use the distinction between "formal" and "informal" when they talk about structures—established ways of doing things—that contain both rules and organizational resources.[12] Organizational control involves more than formal rules and informal cultural norms since more subtle structures and human practices can explain how control actually functions—for example, how an organization is hierarchically designed or how it decides on holidays to recognize. In their longitudinal study of an organizational control system, Laura Cardinal and colleagues found that even when organizations change, traces of their prior formal and informal control systems remain.[5] Later, in Chapter 8, which offers a study of hospitals implementing permissive mobile policies, you can watch the shifting control systems develop over time.

In most organizations, people in high-level job roles exercise their control by regularly re-evaluating the rules they've developed that channel resources, behavior, and information flows within and outside their organization. They also determine if the rules are helping them achieve the desired outputs and goals. Furthermore, managers often assume that their understanding of situations is shared by their subordinates and others in their organization.[19] But this view of control overly focuses on upper management. Scholars who study how organizations implement planned major changes criticize a top-down approach because by ignoring the input of lower-level people, these managers create serious impediments to implementation.[16,17]

How do we avoid focusing too narrowly on these top-down approaches to understanding control? Dunbar and Statler argue that "narratives provide the medium through which organizational control is performatively enacted, implemented, and transformed through practice"[6] (p. 44). They suggest that scholars should examine organizational stories from multiple perspectives and explore how people engage in sense-making around organizational control. Using stories and examples from different perspectives, including a temporal dimension to understanding organizational control, is precisely the approach I myself use. It is through these different perspectives that we can begin to understand how the negotiation for control of communication occurs.

DEFINING COMMUNICATION, INFORMATION PROCESSING, AND TERMS RELATED TO CONTROL

I began this book by taking a historical perspective on cell-phone use because it helps show why organizations ever thought they could—and should—control personal mobile-device use. In his research examining organizational control and technology, James Beniger claims that "inseparable from the concept of control are the twin activities of information processing and reciprocal communication, complementary factors in any form of control"[2] (p. 8). While there are many definitions that try to separate information and communication, I acknowledge, like Beniger, that these two activities are closely related. If you want to dive deeply into these definitions, and get a bit frustrated in the process, try searching for differences between "data," "information," "knowledge," and "communication." People use these terms in very similar ways, and sometimes people only use one of them to represent the total process. For example, Bill Gates never mentions human communication as part of the information process.

Early in my academic career, I started calling all communication channels people used "information and communication technologies" (ICTs),[4,36,38,39] and I included face-to-face communication as a "technology." I did this because "information" and "communication" are closely entwined. To simplify these distinctions in this book, I view data as assumed facts or statistics, information as compiled data, and information processing as an individually focused activity. Communication, on the other hand, and reciprocal communication specifically are processes that actively engage multiple humans in exchanging information, ideas, and symbols, with the goal of creating meaning.[25,37]

Building on these definitions, over time, employees have garnered access to more and more company data and broad industry information through multiple ICTs like the Internet. That increased access to information magnifies the need for reciprocal communication; there are simply more opportunities for communication today. By understanding that the two activities of information processing and reciprocal communication are entwined, it becomes more sensible to take a balanced and historical view of control with respect to mobile-device use. Individuals and organizations are engaging in a negotiation process as the material features and societal norms around mobile use change over time.[18,42] Users of mobiles have simply experienced and adapted to these changes, but those adaptations include negotiations for control over work practices.

A more recent phenomenon associated with organizational control considers how computers, or non-human agents,[27] play a role in monitoring and interpreting data. Humans and non-human agents are often differentiated because humans have intentions for why they do things whereas computers don't.[27] Mobile devices are a type of non-human agent, not directly controlled by the organization; but their use is often monitored, and policies indirectly control their use. For example, today it's common for organizations to require their employees to sign an agreement specifying that if their mobile is lost or if they ever leave the company, the organization has the right to reformat their device, thus clearing all data and stored information from their device.[14] I share details about this practice, associated with bring-your-own-device-to-work policies, in Chapters 6 and 7. But humans will often interpret that practice as high-handed, especially when the device is paid for by the individual. So what could be viewed as a simple organizational practice actually provides more evidence that information and communication are entwined and embedded with power, especially around the issues of privilege, rights, and privacy. People use mobiles to address both their information and communication needs for both their work and personal lives and in doing so enact entanglements and ironies—that are often key to an interesting story.

William Ocasio and Franz Wohlgezogen recommend that we include channels when theorizing about organizational control.[26] While their definitions stray from linear models like Shannon and Weaver's information theory[32] or Berlo's sender, message, channel, receiver model,[3] they define "channels" as "anticipated, formal opportunities for communications"[26] (p. 212). Our proper focus should be on formal channels, they contend, because informal ones prove too difficult for purposive organizational control. And why? Because there's too much variation in informal channels. But wait, aren't personal mobile devices actually a type of gateway for informal communication? And doesn't the variation prominent among informal communication rightly capture a level of variety that can't be denied? My data suggests they are, so even though it might be easier to control formal organizational channels, organizations are now negotiating the control of these *more informal channels*. And most regulatory and legal advisors practically force organizations to develop policies to control them. Chapter 6 elaborates on these policies.

USING DATA TO SCAFFOLD AN UNDERSTANDING OF NEGOTIATING CONTROL

By combining the literature on organizational control and the data shared so far, we can see four forms of control related to mobile communication emerging. The first two forms of control were evident in Table 1.1 in the comparison between business cell-phone use and early personal mobile-device use. But as I mentioned there, over time, control over mobile communication became more complex. Let's examine these forms of control next.

Organizational Control

I define the first type of control observed in the data as *organizational control*. This includes organization-wide rules, policies, and norms that can shape mobile communication. With this definition, I present *organizational control* as a bureaucratic process, which is not unexpected because this type of control is focused on the entire organization, a macro-level perspective. In 1962, sociologist Richard Emerson explained bureaucratic control as evolving from simple, direct control of employee work behaviors and the physical technology controlling behavior.[7] Bureaucratic control, while diverse and not without flaws, established a hierarchy, and managers enforced rules with reward-and-punishment consequences.[7,26] My story of car-phone use at the beginning of Chapter 1 illustrates this macro-form of organizational control and mobile communication. The company provided each person a mobile communication tool, plus rules governing its use, and no one ever really questioned the organizational control over these business tools.

Agentic Control

The second form of control and mobile communication is what I term *agentic control*. It recognizes that individuals exercise their self-determination, their agency, to find mobile tools that help them accomplish their goals.

It follows that individuals play a key role in understanding control, and they're often integral to the negotiation of control. The early adopters in Chapter 1, like Bill and Gabrielle, prove my point. They began experimenting to improve their work practices by bringing their own mobiles into the organizational landscape.

Hierarchical Control

Data from managers like Kjell and Matt in Chapter 2, as well as control structures in my advisor–advisee relationship, suggest that there is a third form of control present in mobile communication. I call it *hierarchical control*, and it's closely tied to positional power. Historically, in most of the control literature, hierarchical control is assumed as a part of a job role. While I include it as a distinct form of control here, by the end of the book—Chapter 11, in particular—you'll see that it isn't distinct. It's actually an overlapping type of control that influences organizations, groups, and individuals.

Actually, all three of these forms of control—organizational, individual, and hierarchical—are, in most situations, overlapping, and sometimes they compete. For example, the national sales manager, Matt, from Chapter 2 exercised his hierarchical control when he struggled to make mobile-device decisions, and he also felt pressure from both the organization and individuals in his workforce to be frugal and fair.

Concertive Control

The final form of control seen in the data, *concertive control*, has not been clearly illustrated in this early mobile use, but you'll see it become prominent in Chapters 4–8. The idea of concertive control represents a postbureaucratic organizational type of control. It shifts the locus of control over others from managers to workers and work teams, but this is still a form of organizational control because the underlying reasons for control are to achieve organizational goals. These teams then control one another by agreeing on core values and holding one another responsible.[1,41] For example, in her research on organizational taboos, Joanne Martin shared a story of a young woman who agreed to have a caesarean before the due date of her child so that she could help her company launch a new product.[20] In his seminal work on concertive control in self-managed teams, James Barker articulated how a value consensus can evolve into normative rules that can control team members' actions more completely than any obvious bureaucratic or hierarchical control ever could.[1] As he memorably put it, borrowing a metaphor from Max Weber,[41,42] "the powerful combination of peer pressure and rational rules in the concertive system creates a new iron cage whose bars are almost invisible to the workers it incarcerates"[1] (p. 435). As for what happens to any teammate who resists the team's control, "they must be willing to risk their human dignity, being made to feel unworthy as a 'teammate'"[1] (p. 436). But remember that concertive control is a managerial strategy; management places on teams the requirement to monitor and sanction each other. We'll see this type of control present in Chapter 4 and again in Chapter 8.

RELATIONAL POWER AND MOBILES

Even though I present the idea that organizations and individuals negotiate mobile control, it's well to remember that organizations themselves are constituted by individuals. And these individuals have diverse job roles, carrying differing levels of status and information-access needs. There might be expectations and pressures associated with using a personal mobile device outside of work, but organizations, with their levels of management, wield job-security control.[11] Positional power is associated with formal authority afforded to people who hold higher positions in their organizations. Managers like Matt and Kjell have the formal positional power to directly control the resources provided to their subordinates, among them those indispensable mobile devices.

There are many examples in the data where organizations try to control mobile- communication behavior through policies, but there are also examples of managers exercising their control and enforcing those policies arbitrarily or workers viewing policy relevance disparately. In Chapter 5, for example, I'll share a data set examining janitors and how they feared for their jobs if they flouted an organizational policy, yet in that same organization, the knowledge workers, while acknowledging the policy, blithely dismissed it as something not relevant for them. And why? Because they believed the organization had no way to enforce it, or they thought they were not easily replaceable like the janitors were. In this case, job role and hierarchy clearly affected the employees' willingness to negotiate the mobile device–use policy.

In the 1960s, Emerson defined relational power as including organizational resources as an integral part of power.[7] He also stressed that power isn't necessarily something individuals or organizations inherently possess.[7] Power is a product of social relationships, and it's based on people's dependence on resources that others control. Take, for example, people carrying the title "manager." They may not be viewed as having power unless they also control resources like setting work schedules, evaluating performance, and even deciding who gets company mobile phones or reimbursed for mobile use. I include this definition of power because it reveals why some people in my data "believed" they have the ability to negotiate and ignore formal mobile policies. Power is not the same as having a specific job role. And the "zone of indifference" in Karl Weick's work claims that control is ultimately directed by the subordinate; it's only when a person accepts the control efforts, from any source, that control actually happens.[43]

ORGANIZATIONAL CONTROL–POWER RELATIONSHIP

It's important to differentiate organizational power from individual power. The latter, also called *positional power* or *relational power*, is often related to the amount of control that's associated with the position that a person holds in his or her organizational hierarchy.[11] *Organizational power*, meanwhile, is usually the result of structural characteristics, and while it can be hidden or obscured, it is not that difficult to observe.[40] The sociologist Max Weber defined power as embedded in social relations: the likelihood that one individual can accomplish an objective even if another individual resists. He also developed the idea of the bureaucratic organization as capable of becoming an "iron cage"[41] (pp. 180–181). That metaphor refers to the notion that rational, rule-based organizations that disrespect their employees can become an oppressive bureaucracy. This is what I discussed earlier in this chapter when talking about concertive control.

To better show the relationship between organizations, power, and their members, I'll provide some background on notions of organizational power. Foucault's work, most relevant to my study, focuses on concepts of disciplinary power.[10] He believed that power is omnipresent, unsteady, capable of both destructive and productive uses, and entangled with the production of knowledge. His work has shown us how surveillance, a practice seen frequently in the data I'll share on janitors, hospital workers, and customer-facing workers, can result in individuals' disciplining themselves.

While there are several different typologies that categorize power, Etzioni's (1964) definitions are derived from the type of resources used to exercise power, and they are highly relevant for explaining shifts in power.[9] He describes control resulting from physical means as coercive power, like "the use of a gun, a whip, or a lock is physical since it affects the body"[9]

(p. 59). Utilitarian power is constituted when material means are used or provided for control purposes. Material rewards include items that provide goods and services like money. Yet the final form of power, referred to as normative or social power, is derived from what he calls a "pure symbol"[9] (p. 59), one not related to physical threats or material rewards. These symbols include things like love, acceptance, prestige, and esteem.

Much research has been generated that treats the categories independently; but in reality these concepts are fluid and overlapping, and access to resources needed to wield power is always changing. Imagine being a manager trying to decide who can be more productive if supplied a mobile phone. When that manager attends a team meeting and gives all the members a shiny new mobile device, he also reminds them that he will have to take them away if their team productivity doesn't improve. He used his utilitarian power to provide the phone, harnessed normative power by providing resources to the entire team, and used his coercive power to threaten the team if productivity didn't improve.

Let's explore how organizations used all three of these bases of power between 1990 and the early 2000s when mobiles were diffusing into workplaces. In Chapter 1, I shared my story of how, in the 1990s, bag phones or cell phones were expensive and workplaces provided these communication technologies to the workers they believed needed them. Organizations exercised their utilitarian power to make workers more productive, and to that end they provided certain ones with portable phones—aka bag phones. Salespeople, executives, and other mobile workers were most likely to get them. As Matt's story revealed, an unintended consequence of providing certain employees with cell phones was the rise in normative power afforded to those workers given them. These devices came to carry high status, not to mention becoming a symbol of preferential treatment, and notions of fairness, or parity, were invoked as employees throughout the organizational world demanded their own right to be provided a mobile device. But this is not always the case. Bill, the engineer from Chapter 1, was required to be available through his pager, and he saw it not as status but as an unavoidable tether. Along the way, some organizations believed that employees were abusing their cell phones by using them excessively and racking up big bills, so they exercised coercive power in threatening reprimand if the devices were used inappropriately. This was a common occurrence across the stories I've shared thus far.

Think back to the four types of control I introduced earlier in this chapter. Now I've shown also that the three types of organizational power work in conjunction with the control mechanisms. Coercive, normative, and utilitarian types of power are meant to function at the organizational level; but as I will show in the next chapters, they also apply at the hierarchical- and concertive-control levels when mobile devices are involved.

EVIDENCE OF NEGOTIATION OF CONTROL THROUGH UTILITARIAN POWER

At this writing, it's reasonable to generalize that organizations and individuals are still actively negotiating control over any personal mobiles used at work. Organizations appear to be taking one of five general positions in this matter. I'll label them informally as organizational asset, prohibition of use, reimbursement for personal, split costs, and bring your own device.

Some organizations provide the employees they believe need mobiles with "company mobiles," or what I'm calling "organizational assets." These are either off-limits for personal use or allowed within what the company deems reasonable use. Some long-term employees in my larger data set, like Ted, the 50-year-old director of customer service for a global hospitality firm, has never owned his own mobile—and hasn't needed to. Because he travels extensively, his employer of the past 18 years has provided him virtually unlimited use of a company mobile. Over time, the specific device he's used has changed—he's gone from cellular phone to BlackBerry to his current iPhone—but he has never felt the need to purchase a separate personal mobile. He has no concept that he needs to actively negotiate anything concerning the use of his mobile phone. But his freedom from control is quite the exception in my data set.

Other organizations in the data I've collected provide certain employees an organizational mobile device with strings attached. For example, many government organizations I've studied provide a mobile, but then they forbid any and all personal use. Other organizations allow the employee to reimburse the organization for any personal use of the organizational asset. There is also a variation where the employer and employee split mobile-phone costs with some type of a monthly allowance or stipend. Sometimes these mobiles are purchased by the organization, but increasingly a company will reimburse the employee for a part of that individual's own mobile-device plan. In the U.S., these evolving shifts in mobile control have coincided with decreased costs of mobile plans and increased pressure from employees to allow flexibility in the choice of a specific device.

A final way that organizations are exerting utilitarian control with mobile devices is through a permissive bring-your-own-device-to-work policy, otherwise known as BYOD. I'll describe this type of organizational policy in detail in Chapter 6, but here I'll just summarize what the policy involves. Many organizations now have instituted policies that employees must agree to, in writing, that specify strict rules concerning how organizational data and communications passing through a personal mobile should be handled. The more recent trends in BYOD policies include requiring you to bring in your personal devices to the IT department to have encryption software and wipe-at-a-distance software installed. Encryption software protects data from easy access, and wipe-at-a-distance software, which you'll learn a fair bit more about in Chapter 6, gives employers the right to remove all data—personal and business—from a personal device if it's lost or stolen. IT departments might also install tracking systems, like GPS, and content-control software that limits access to content considered inappropriate, such as pornography.

There's a growing body of work, found predominantly in the information-systems literature, that refers to this trend as *enterprise consumerization*[13,35] since employees are bringing their own (i.e., consumer) mobile devices into the enterprise. This practice, as you can imagine, raises new concerns about organizational control. What is especially noteworthy is the informal and *individual-driven nature* of this phase of mobile adoption into organizations. This contrasts strongly with the organizationally driven adoption of bag phones, cell phones, and early mobiles. Organizations didn't need to negotiate control of those early devices because they owned them, paid the bills, and adopted them simply as another type of technology useful for increasing efficiency. Furthermore, employees had few people outside of work to call because the devices were all so expensive they were used only for important work. Having one of these devices in the 1990s was novel, as we saw in Chapter 1. These devices were often seen as both a business necessity and a benefit, especially when the company paid the cell-phone bill and granted its personal use, too.

But as mobiles became affordable and accessible, enterprise consumerization has also changed. Mobile adoption, in 2017, is now rampant on the individual level, and as the costs of mobiles have declined, members at all levels of the organizational hierarchy are jumping aboard. Some people even prefer providing their own device for work because it gives them control over the brand or type of device they choose to use. Other individuals bring their own device to work because they can use it strictly for personal reasons—their friends and family can reach them on it, whether at work or elsewhere. And the amount of organizational control over their use doesn't seem like much.

EXPANDING INTO DIVERSE CONTEXTS AND BEYOND KNOWLEDGE-WORKER JOB ROLES

Early mobile-device use was controlled predominantly by companies; they provided the resources and set the rules. Mobile proliferation created new challenges for managers who had to make tough decisions concerning who gets a mobile device and how they were supposed to manage in their new communication world. Employees were also struggling to figure out the rules and norms, but they found new freedom in the untethering they experienced.

Now that I've established a baseline understanding for early mobile use, the next chapters present detailed examples of how these forms of organizational control and power bases work in varied organizational contexts. Chapter 4 focuses on using mobiles in organizational meetings. All four types of control will appear here, and we'll see how misunderstandings around norms of mobile use develop. Chapter 5 examines how manual-labor workers—in this case, janitors—respond when their organization bans mobile use. Chapter 8 focuses on employees in a hospital who use their mobiles to coordinate patient care, while Chapter 9 examines customer-facing work. Chapter 10 pulls together these different types of workers and compares and contrasts mobile communication control to reveal four influencers: degree of autonomy in work, mobility, task variability, and the primary work-communication target. These influencers provide explanations for how perceptions of reachability and acceptability function when workers use their mobiles at work. These overarching findings also explain the mechanisms that organizations use to control their members and show how, regardless of type of job or hierarchical position, reaching others is not absolute; it's negotiated with people inside and outside of organizational life.

CHAPTER 4

Meetings as a Site to Negotiate Mobile Control

I am a constant connected soul. And the technology controls me.
                              —Tommy, Fundraiser

I have not heard our president tell us we can't, but I've heard him make little snide comments about people who do it.
                              —Sally, Senior Vice President of Operations

I'm a minion. I don't get a laptop. I don't get anything. I don't rate one. Other people have laptops, but they're the higher ups.
                              —Cordelia, Meeting Note-Taker

Ah, meetings . . .

If you're a manager, or a knowledge worker, the very word might make your nose wrinkle and your lip curl. Actually, though, while people invariably complain about meetings, most of us grudgingly accept their necessity.[26] And given the large slice of many workweeks that we sit in them, we might also appreciate how much we're being paid just to attend them.

Scholars have studied meetings in many contexts,[1,14,17,18,20,23,27,32,34,36,44] but the more recent research has turned some suppositions on their head, like people's satisfaction with meetings.[22,27,30] Not all people are unhappy with meetings, but we do like to complain about them. The recent research has also begun to unveil how people use mobile technologies in meetings.[8,9,10,32,34,36]

Wasson,[44] in one of the earlier studies of virtual meetings, found that if anyone were multitasking during them, their reputation could suffer if they missed their turn to speak or seemed unresponsive. Later, as mobile phones became increasingly commonplace at meetings, people began asking: *What are they actually doing when they're on their mobiles there?* This question raised issues of perceived incivility and rudeness,[8,9,42] plus the idea that when people see others in a meeting check their mobile, they figure it's okay for them to do the same.[36]

This chapter contains qualitative data that my team and I collected between 2008 and 2010, all of it focused on information and communication technology (ICT) use in meetings. Our 36 interviews contained a series of 12 questions, our data coming directly from the responses. The consistent responses to one question in particular were especially insightful for my present analysis on negotiating control. Here was the question, together with its lead-in: *Let's talk some more about what people are doing while they're in meetings. Who has the right to use technology in a meeting and who doesn't?*

Later, I'll share some detailed responses, but three main findings emerged from our 36 interviewees:

1) All but one person explicitly mentioned hierarchical differences. They agreed that executives and the highest-level people in the meetings had more reason, and authority, to use their BlackBerrys, iPhones, and laptops there than lower-status employees.
2) A third of them identified individuals whose jobs required them to be "on-call." But "on-call" was broadly interpreted since it was seen to cover more than just people officially required to be available during a certain time.
3) Over half of them said that people in jobs where they move around during the day—mobile workers—or travel a lot have the right to use their mobiles in meetings.

This analysis builds on past research to reveal four conclusions concerning negotiating control of mobiles in organizations. First, managers who are running meetings can establish ground rules and expect their subordinates to abide. (Not that they do, but that they can.) Second, subordinates who use mobiles in meetings are often unaware that their manager's view of them—sometimes silently disapproving—differs from their own self-flattering understanding. Third, people are sometimes quite creative in using their mobiles both to participate in meetings and to circumvent managers' ground rules. And fourth, these data reveal the fourth type of control of mobile communication—*concertive control*.[3] Discussed at the end of Chapter 3 it is a type of group-level control that can be even more powerful than more bureaucratic forms of control.[3,39] This form of control is highly norm-based, and the struggles over it often turn out to involve agentic control as well.

In the following sections, you'll meet several people I interviewed. In all cases, I used pseudonyms to share their stories, and most times, the interviewees suggested the pseudonyms I used—that's why some people have full names while others are simply referred to by a first name. First, you'll meet Olivia, a manager who's learning to use her new BlackBerry and to vary where she uses it, depending on the rules and norms she alertly infers from each meeting she attends. Because I also interviewed several of her colleagues, plus her manager, plus the senior vice president over her division, I end her story by comparing all their perspectives. Next, you'll meet Cedric, a mid-level manager at a global advertising agency. He's confident he is using his mobile appropriately, but a subsequent interview with his boss suggests otherwise. Next, you'll meet Cathy and Allison, who provide a teleconference perspective that showcases the importance of backchannel communication. Finally, you'll meet Tommy, a middle-aged fundraising executive who says that rules rarely exist in his work environment, maybe because everyone is using mobiles so incessantly that they've taken control of peoples' very lives.

NO THUMBS UNDER THE TABLE IN MY MEETINGS

Olivia, age 47, was a single mom with one child in college and another just finishing high school. As a human resources manager, she occasionally attends meetings hosted by the senior vice president (SVP) of her organization. At such times, she has to turn off her BlackBerry, for those meetings have a strict rule: *No thumbs under the table!* But turning off her BlackBerry for an entire meeting can create some challenging pressures on her. Her immediate boss, John, when not attending the meetings himself, will sometimes forget the SVP's rule and text Olivia during them. If she doesn't reply immediately, he'll start bombarding her with multiple messages via every medium possible. Hence Olivia's dilemma: which is worse—angering her boss or risking getting caught sending text messages during the SVP's meetings? Either way, it's a no-win situation for her.

When, back in 2008, I interviewed Olivia, her co-workers, her boss, and the SVP, mobile-communication devices like laptops, iPhones, and BlackBerrys had begun rapidly diffusing into organizational meetings, and people would use them to virtually "whisper" to others off-site while simultaneously listening—or trying to listen—to the proceedings. This practice seemed fairly consistent with the value that an increasingly efficiency-obsessed culture was placing on our getting more work done in less time. Magazines and television commercials during 2008 and 2009 regularly conveyed messages urging us to multitask, to clone ourselves, to not single-task, to always be on, to work anywhere, anytime. In short order, this became more than an aspiration; it became a felt obligation. Workers felt called upon to be always available for communication.

USING HER BLACKBERRY IN MEETINGS

During the time that I was studying Olivia's organization, she was promoted to communication manager. Though she'd had some ups and downs in her career, her promotion to communication manager reinvigorated her. Her previous positions had carried less responsibility and required just the standard workday, but now she said, with the pride of someone newly counting herself indispensable, that "I am basically on a leash 24 hours a day. So if there's any emergency, I have to make sure and get the information communicated." It was initially quite an adjustment for Olivia to cope with all that, but her boss proved a thoughtful mentor who taught her how to organize her busy day using Microsoft Outlook and her company-provided BlackBerry. She viewed these two tools as enabling her to accomplish many more tasks at work. Now she proudly defined herself as a "juggler" who thrives on doing multiple things at once and staying busy.

There were three key ways that Oliva used her BlackBerry in subtle, yet quite productive, ways. First, when she was in meetings and someone asked a question, she'd search the Web on her BlackBerry: "I can't tell you how many times I've gotten onto the Internet on my BlackBerry because somebody will say, 'I wonder—blah, blah, blah.' It's like, 'Oh, hang on. I'll check.'" Using a portable device to access information while in the middle of a meeting has many positive uses today as well as earlier in the 2000s. This is a type of just-in-time information access that has the potential to reshape meetings and change how decisions are made. Olivia also said that having access to that information helped her demonstrate her value during a meeting. Other people without mobiles could only ask the questions, whereas she could say, "Would you like me to check that on my BlackBerry?" People always told her yes, and, with practice, she could often find the answer in a jiff.

Besides retrieving information for colleagues in meetings, there would be the attempts of others in her office—especially her boss, John—to contact her and ask her to provide them information when they themselves were in meetings. She explained: "Now, John has emailed me and said: 'I'm in this meeting. We're discussing this. Do this, this, this, and this,' or, 'Can you get me this information?' " While her boss was one of the only people who asked her to work behind the scenes of a meeting, she predicted that this practice would increase as everyone became more familiar with the capabilities of ICTs like the Blackberry. Organizational meeting boundaries were becoming fluid because information freely flowed into and out of the meeting, often in productive ways.

Olivia also had personal productivity reasons for using her BlackBerry during meetings. For example, she'd type abbreviated notes or to-do lists. Traditionally, people brought notepads and pens for such purposes, but mobiles provided new ways to capture information and organize time. Sometimes Olivia would send herself an email in addition to making a note in her Blackberry, just to ensure that she didn't forget something important. Those redundant messages served as a fail-safe prompt.

NOT EVERYONE VIEWED MEETING MULTITASKING POSITIVELY

But not everyone in her office understood that using a BlackBerry during meetings could be productive, even as a replacement for the old notepad and pen. When tapping on hers, Olivia worried that she'd be thought "really rude." She explained: "They don't realize that what the people are typing has to do with what's going on [in the meeting]. I believe they think that others are completely distracted and talking to the wife about something else." While she admitted that personal or social messaging occasionally intruded, most of her BlackBerry use, she insisted, was to enhance her meeting and personal productivity. In my observations of her, I too found that she was on-task most of the time.

DISTRACTING ICTS IN MEETINGS

But occasionally restiveness would get the better of her. She confessed, "I feel guilty because there are times when I get bored and I'll start checking my email on my BlackBerry." She also provided insight into situations where this off-topic behavior might be more acceptable. "I usually only do it in this one particular meeting that is very, very large with 150 people," she said. "I feel a little more anonymous, although I do know that people around me can see that I'm checking it." She also noted the contagious effect on her of seeing others checking for emails: "When I see somebody looking at their Blackberry, it's like 'Oh gosh, I better check mine. Because I may have an email.'" If so, it might prove to be an urgent work request. Then again it might simply be an invitation to lunch. The people I observed in this organization didn't necessarily separate work messages from their personal ones, but most of their messages seemed to have been work-related.

THE MEETING LEADER SETS THE NORM

Observing people multitasking during meetings does seem to irk some colleagues more than others, as evidenced by both their nonverbal and verbal expressions of annoyance. Olivia explained that her boss, John, seemed more tolerant than most. He used his BlackBerry in meetings most often when he himself was the one in charge. Not only that, but he seemed to set the tone for others, subtly conveying that their multitasking was okay with him. But Olivia had personally once heard a very senior manager, Sally, the SVP, complain: "I have people in meetings that will do it under the table thinking that nobody will see it. It makes me furious." Olivia feared that the SVP might be talking about her own boss, John, so she called him and said, "John, please tell me that when you are with Sally you do not use your BlackBerry." And he replied, "Oh, no. I would never do that."

Leaders who disapprove of technology multitasking during meetings may simply want to keep everyone focused on the topic at hand. Because of the positional power they wield,[13] many of the attendees will conform. Olivia explained:

> But I can't get over worrying—and that's because I'm a worrier—what other people think when you're doing that [using BlackBerry]. It's because I know there are people here—especially the leader, who refuses to have one—completely put out by it. Just really, really put out by anybody doing anything other than completely focusing.

Every person I interviewed in this same governmental organization agreed that there was one meeting where no one dared use a BlackBerry: the SVP's meeting. Sally was a strong, high-level leader in a large governmental organization. In her mid-60s, she was the only female SVP in this organization, and the VPs who reported to her were almost all males in their 50s and 60s. She always wore a full suit, and her grooming exuded professionalism. Starting her meetings at 7 o'clock every morning, she described her work life by saying, "I live in meetings." Her reputation was one of efficiency and competence; people respected her and seemed to trust her.

When I interviewed Sally, she quickly told me the same story about no thumbs under the tables that I had heard from everyone on her staff. "That is something I let my people know they cannot do that. I find it rude, and there is a way that people do this [she role-plays people holding a BlackBerry under the table] and you know exactly what they are doing."

Now Sally was by no means a Luddite. She had her own BlackBerry with her at all times and gave me many examples of how her mobile technologies made her and her staff more efficient and organized. She explained, "I [always] take my BlackBerry with me, and if we are waiting for the meeting, I'll check email. I get bored easily, and I like to stay up to date, so I use my BlackBerry."

It appears, then, that her issues with BlackBerrys and laptops centered solely on notions of respect and her belief that people couldn't do two things simultaneously—or at least do them properly. As the boss, she insisted on having her subordinates' full focus: "I am not spending my time in a meeting if everybody is not paying attention." She also believed that it was a sign of professionalism, and she aspired to model a respectful meeting environment: "The directors are aware that I'm their boss's boss. I would hope they take that professional style back to their own staff." But she was aware that some of her staff occasionally had urgent issues, so she didn't mind if people had to leave her meeting to take a call; but she resented the sneaky thumbs under the table. She conceded, though, that she wasn't as strict when contractors—not her employees—attended her meetings: "There is one group that we work with, and they travel all the time, so they are only occasionally at my meetings. That is one group that I have not slapped on their hands."

WORKAROUNDS

During my observations of Sally's meetings, her no-thumbs-under-the-table rule worked most of the time, but there could be some amusing exceptions. For example, in the spring of 2009, I observed one of her monthly meetings with 40 of her top managers. We were located in an auditorium-style room—three rows of chairs and tables, with two aisles between them. Sally began speaking, and everyone gave her full attention. But as she transitioned to another speaker, she momentarily turned her back on us to help that next speaker find some slides on the computer. Instantly, at least 25 BlackBerrys came out from under the tables, and thumbs began flying! Then, as Sally turned around to introduce the speaker, the devices just as instantly disappeared. This happened three times during the hour-and-a-half meeting.

At one point, maybe an hour into the meeting, Sally was talking once again, and as she turned around to point to her slide, I noticed a piece of folded paper fall on the floor in the aisle between opposing seats. A man in his early 60s quickly reached down to retrieve it just as Sally turned around to address us again. The man looked slightly shaken and like maybe he was hiding something, but without missing a beat he resumed acting like he was giving Sally his undivided attention. When Sally turned her back the next time, he grabbed the paper from his lap, read it, snickered, and whispered to another man in his 60s across the aisle, "That sounds great for lunch." These were two vice presidents in a very large organization who resorted to acting like middle-schoolers. Though literally honoring Sally's rule, they passed notes as an alternative in order to coordinate their lunch plans.

Sally conceded that her hard line on BlackBerry use in meetings wasn't as clear of a line for either her peers or her own boss, the organization's president. She mentioned other executives using their BlackBerrys in high-level meetings, especially the director of information technology. But she suspected that the president didn't fully approve: "I have not heard our president tell us we can't, but I've heard him make little snide comments about people who do it."

EXPECTATION OF RESPONSIVENESS

Olivia's job required her to attend many meetings, and with people throughout the organization. She tried to use those attendees and managers as a gauge to help her determine the acceptability of her Blackberry use. But this wasn't always easy. She struggled with two major decisions. First, in meetings where it was unclear as to the acceptability of multitasking, she couldn't decide whether to sit obediently and pretend to listen to what was often irrelevant information or to use her BlackBerry to stay productive, productivity being hugely important to her. Second, now that her co-workers and manager knew that she used her BlackBerry religiously, they expected her to respond quickly. They didn't necessarily know her whereabouts, yet it didn't matter. They still expected a fast response.

This was also the situation with Olivia's co-worker Andy. He explained:

So, today as I was sitting on the PT [physical therapy] table with the electrode plugged into my back, here I am on my BlackBerry, emailing back and forth to people at work. I live and breathe my BlackBerry. It's very nice because you stay connected, but it certainly is an evil because people know you are connected.

My VP really knows I'm connected. So I'm sitting at my house at 8:30 at night and he's still emailing stuff—and it's business. We're doing business. So to kind of be on-call. You're on-call. This thing strapped to your hip really does do that for you.

ANDY'S VIEW OF MEETING BLACKBERRY USE

Andy also attended many of the same meetings as Olivia, but he had a slightly different view of when mobile use was acceptable. "One of the things we have established in most meetings," he said, "is kind of media etiquette. Especially for people who are above my pay grade when I'm in their meetings, I don't dare look at my BlackBerry." He extended this understanding to the meetings of his boss, John, as well. While Olivia thought it was fine to use her BlackBerry in John's meetings, Andy disagreed:

Basically John doesn't like people on the Blackberry, but I've been in meetings where people's cell phones ring and people are looking at their BlackBerrys. Sometimes I'll put a kind of disclaimer out to people saying I'm waiting for an important call or I've got a message that I need to respond to, so I may be checking my BlackBerry in this meeting. As long as you set it up, people are okay with it.

Andy also said that people who overuse their BlackBerrys in his meetings or others' meetings annoy him as well. "It detracts from meetings," he explained. "I think some people walk around with BlackBerrys just because it makes them look like they're—I don't want to say in a power position, because maybe they *are* in a power position—but they feel like because they have a BlackBerry, that gives them exclusive rights to keep on looking at it." Andy's examples provide additional insight into this organization whose managers were struggling to be responsive, polite, and efficient and to demonstrate these behaviors by using or refraining from using their mobiles.

My research team and I spent over 50 hours observing meetings in this governmental organization, and we also interviewed 22 managers and their subordinates. The data shared above are representative of what we found throughout this organization. There was strong evidence of managerial control, concertive control, and agentic control but very few organization-wide mobile policies. Some managers laid down explicit rules governing mobile use in meetings, and their employees were either unfathomably ignorant, faithfully obedient, or sneakily inclined to circumvent the rules. Approximately two-thirds of the people interviewed said flatly that there was a norm of reachability associated with having a BlackBerry. While the organization paid for these devices at the time of our study and expected its employees to reimburse it for personal use, the norms appeared to form at the workgroup level. These norms were very strong in some teams, as illustrated by Andy's prompt, nearly reflexive responses to team members even during his physical therapy session. Finally, agentic control over mobile-device use in meetings was also present. Olivia observed situations and made her own decisions concerning when and where she could use her mobile and still be viewed as being professional. Futhermore, some employees were actively enhancing the impression others had of them by using their mobiles to push meeting agendas forward by capturing detailed notes.

CEDRIC DOES IT, BUT NOT HIS BOSS

My meetings research team also spent time in an international advertising firm, DG&G, to learn more about how they used their BlackBerrys in meetings. Cedric, age 30, was a mid-level manager at DG&G charged with devising the creative strategy for both a prominent cruise line and a large non-profit. Overseeing 10 designers, he was always on the go, averaging 25 meetings on any given day. "I basically run around and go to meetings and make sure that the plates are spinning," he said drolly.

In every meeting, Cedric was on his BlackBerry, but he also protected his creative staff to give them a quiet, uninterrupted work environment. "There is not a meeting I can think of that is so important that a BlackBerry couldn't rattle," he said. "Meetings are not sacrosanct to me. What is sacrosanct to me in this business is creative time." Although he himself viewed his BlackBerry as indispensable, he discouraged the rest of his creative department from using it:

> I urge creative people not to listen to BlackBerrys and not to check their email too much because it interrupts what they do. What they do is think, and they're paid to think, and thinking happens only in great big bursts of sustained creativity, which are hard to come by if you're always checking your email or fooling around on your BlackBerry.

THE VIEW OF THE CHIEF TECHNOLOGY OFFICER

But Cedric needed to be available to his clients, so he viewed his BlackBerry and laptop as lifelines. Ann Marie, chief technology officer (CTO) at DG&G, explained that a meeting without the presence of technology was "a rare situation." Furthermore, she explained that its use had both positive and negative aspects:

> I think that what I've seen is two levels of things happening in meetings. The first is when multiple people are interacting with one technology. For example, they're doing collaborative editing or review of a presentation on a laptop computer. The other situation, however, is when there haven't been any ground rules established as to how technology should be used and people are still answering emails and conducting free-form business.

Interestingly, the ubiquity of technology within DG&G was Ann Marie's doing. As CTO, her job was to implement new ways of using technology for developing advertising campaigns. Recently, her team focused on creating "a mobile workforce" by supplying employees with the proper resources—chiefly laptops and cell phones—to meet their clients' needs. "We have enabled as many people as we can to become mobile with their technologies," she said. "Once employees fire up their laptops, they have access to all corporate resources: instant messaging, email, video conferencing, intranet, etc." But while this should be a good thing, Ann Marie admitted that it could sometimes be detrimental. Her solution? "I think it's important for the person who's conducting the meeting to lay some groundwork as to how they want the meeting to work," she said. "Depending on their meeting practices and the importance of the agenda, the leader of the meeting should announce whether communicative technology should be out in the open, quickly glanced at, or temporarily put away." The CTO placed the responsibility for establishing the meeting ground rules squarely on the meeting leader.

THE VIEW OF THE PRESIDENT AND CHIEF OPERATING OFFICER

David, the president and chief operating officer (COO) of DG&G for the past 5 years, had a long history with the agency, including having worked as an account director for 12 years. Now barely 40, he was accountable for the day-to-day operations and management of over 500 employees working on 17 different accounts around the globe. Employees constantly wanted to meet with him because he gave the final approval for any budget- or content-related decision regarding a client's business. That inevitably involved plenty of ICT use. And yet he himself didn't like to use a Blackberry or computer in meetings. "I find that it's rude, and so I tend to not check that in a meeting," he said. "I think it's inappropriate."

Yet he constantly watched every member of his Leadership Council— 16 senior-level employees, including Cedric—bring either a BlackBerry or a computer into meetings, expressly to send and receive email. Though David, as I said, used neither mobile device himself there, he took no action against the persistent multitasking of his employees. "I'm not against multitasking, but meetings would be more efficient if people would come prepared rather than try to multitask," he told me. "It sort of drags the whole process down. Multitasking in meetings is detrimental not only because it prevents attendees from focusing on the agenda," he said, "but also because it impairs their ability to listen."

But outside of meetings, David was an enthusiastic supporter of BlackBerrys and other mobile technologies. "They're good for triage or on the road or in between meetings," he said, as well as for managing the flow of information. He often checked his own BlackBerry in between meetings, but he emphasized the importance of not reflexively jumping on every new message. For David, the problem with BlackBerrys was that they seemed to have become prioritized over face-to-face communication: "I think people somehow have lost sight of the fact that while technology can be an accelerator for performance, instead they use it as a way to communicate." In other words, while technology is helpful in starting the dialogue or relationship between two or more people, it shouldn't be allowed to *become* the relationship. After all, David explained, "The advertising business is all about forming a relationship between the client and the consumer," not between a pair of ICTs.

I still remember working with this interview at the time it was collected and thinking that as the COO of DG&G David had a very balanced, insightful perspective on mobile technology. But what shocked me was learning that he never shared these perspectives with his staff. Indeed, he never set ground rules for meetings, and his staff continued naïvely using their BlackBerrys there. But his comments suggested that he silently judged their behaviors. I was left to wonder why he never shared his view with them and how many other leaders shared his views. I offer two speculative explanations. First, David may have assumed that he and his staff had a shared understanding about meeting etiquette and, since the norms changed gradually, he never consciously established formal rules. The other possibility is a bit more cynical. He may have deliberately withheld his views as a way to express his power. He stood in judgment while some of his employees never figured out how to read his mind.

MASTERING THE BACKCHANNEL IN TELECONFERENCE MEETINGS

Some people rarely attend in-person meetings, and instead, they live in the online meeting world. Cathy, a fairly young but already burned-out team leader in a Fortune 50 company, was one such manager. In a matter-of-fact voice she said, "I have meetings from 8 a.m. to 8 p.m. almost every single day." Cathy's whole job, it appeared, was essentially to attend meetings—and, worse still, most of them were back-to-back. They generally relied on a teleconference mechanism like Livemeeting or Netmeeting, and they ranged from 5 to 50 attendees. She said she received meeting invites through Microsoft Outlook, accepted the ones she believed she should attend, and then joined them via phone or computer. "When you are on that many meetings," she told us, "mobile devices become an integral part of how you join meetings when you are not in front of a computer."

As the team leader, Cathy confided, "I get invited, to be blunt, like a CYA [cover your ass], to make sure—'Oh, well, she was there. She signed off on this.'" But just because she accepted an invite didn't mean that she stayed for the entire meeting. As she grew into her position, she became bolder about asking the person who invited her about the objectives, why she was needed, and if there were a way that she could attend only part of the meeting. She also learned to delegate. "I'll have somebody from my team join, and I'll ask them to give me a report back and let me know if I need to follow up on something," Cathy explained. She found this was helpful in managing her own time, but "It's not useful for a lot of my team members' time, and they get frustrated. So I have to balance that, too. I don't want to burn somebody else out, especially creative types that don't really like meetings."

MULTITASKING IN A TELECONFERENCE

Multitasking and multicommunicating though mobile devices works differently on a teleconference than in a face-to-face meeting. We found that on a teleconference the attendees are multicommunicating much more frequently. In Cathy's case, she explained that "part of my job responsibilities is being there 24/7." So she often needed to have "backchannel" conversations (i.e., ones that the entire group never hears or knows are going on). Cathy might need to put the teleconference on mute and simultaneously make a phone call to some colleague to collect information she needs for the group conversation. The first category of backchannel conversation that Cathy explained was much like coaching people behind the scenes:

> [Backchannel conversations can be] very productive conversations, like, "Am I doing okay?" "Is the tone right?" or "Do I need to speed up?" My boss also messages me to say "Don't forget to mention this." Or a lot of times, in a teleconference, you don't know who's talking, and vice presidents, for example, assume that you do [know their voices]. And they'll just start speaking. A lot of times, you need to check with your boss and say, "Who is this? How should I address them?"

Cathy also explained that there were tactical questions that happened through the backchannels of these meetings:

> You join a call late and there are 50 people on the call. You don't want to disrupt the call, but you don't have the passcode to get in the LiveMeeting. Or you didn't get the LiveMeeting link or you didn't get the presentation. So you message somebody that you know is on the call and say, "Hey, can you shoot this over to me?" Or, "What's the number?"

Finally, people used the backchannels to vent, with colleagues saying things like, "This is stupid!" or "Why am I here?"

Taken together, all these backchannel conversations, even the productive ones, become distractions that disconnect people from the meeting, she said. Some of these conversations were urgent, but many of them could have waited. Cathy explained that it's "hard when you're on a meeting and you're trying to focus and you're getting lots of—I call them 'fireworks' because our windows blink on the bottom of the page. So when I'm on the call, I have 50 of them down there going *blink, blink, blink, blink, blink.*" Cathy also explained that organizational power played a key role in how much she was willing to let others distract her. She called this "a pecking order." Whenever she herself organized a meeting, she only let other executives get her attention during it through backchannels. But when it was a meeting of all peers, "we're not going to have any qualms about multitasking through the meeting."

ALLISON

Allison, a middle-aged marketing manager with a Fortune 50 company, echoed many of Cathy's comments. She also spent her days sitting through one teleconference after another, and while she was not managing a large team like Cathy, she did work remotely almost every day. In her company, only executives and salespeople were given BlackBerrys and iPhones, but the one backchannel tool that her team used all the time was instant messenger (IM): "Definitely, IM is part of our culture. And when it started I really wondered, do I really want to be interrupted all the time? Now I couldn't live without it. Because we're all remote, we're working in our homes or away from our primary colleagues."

Allison's company had been struggling financially, and staff cutbacks meant that everyone was doing more work than in the past. She mentioned her own workload at least 10 times in her one-hour interview. She used that workload to justify the constant multitasking people did while they attended meetings: "Yeah, I think everybody knows it happens because of the workload. There's no way we can handle this workload if we give 100% attention to something that isn't our #1 priority. If it's not your #1 priority at that moment, then you're doing something else."

Hierarchical considerations are a bit different in online meetings compared to face-to-face ones, but managers still rely on their subordinates to get them needed information. One of the biggest differences, though, is that, online, people can be double- or triple-booked, meaning that they have accepted invitations to attend multiple meetings happening simultaneously. Allison shed light on how people navigate this tricky challenge:

> There are situations where people get double- or triple-booked. So they'll start on a call, go off to the other call for a little while, come back, and continue. Sometimes they get caught. Sometimes they don't. That happened yesterday with my manager. She left, came back, and just as she was coming back, somebody was summarizing by saying that I had a really good comment. [My manager] Same-Timed me and said, "I had to leave for 10 minutes. What did you say?" I told her. Nobody else knew she had two other meetings at the same time and she was trying to split her time.

The prior data were gathered between 2008 and 2010, a time when organizations and individuals were establishing and testing the rules of mobile use in meetings. Almost all the data my team gathered during those years included examples of heavy meeting multitasking and multicommunicating by knowledge workers since that was the focus of my study. But along the way, we gathered a few divergent cases that offered an alternative perspective. At the end of this chapter, I'll share a counterexample of an administrative assistant whose job was to take the minutes during meetings. Her telling comments set the stage for moving the mobiles-at-work discussion beyond knowledge workers and into a different type of negotiation for mobile-communication control. But before I share her story, let me update this meetings chapter to explain what happens in the later 2010s.

TODAY, WE ALL USE MOBILES IN MEETINGS BECAUSE WE USE THEM IN OUR LIVES

Tommy is currently a middle-aged fundraising director who lived through the early years of mobiles in meetings: He now opines: "Generally speaking, I don't think it matters. I think that's what technology's done. I think we are in a constant state of communication, and because we're in a constant state of communication, even I can't pay as much attention as I would like to." Tommy acknowledged that just about everyone is multitasking and multicommunicating in meetings, but he was also frustrated with his own behavior and that of others:

> What's really troubling is the people who just walk into a meeting anywhere and will automatically sit there and start doing it [using their mobile]. They have no degree of understanding of what that's doing to the context of the meeting and what that's doing to the person running the meeting. And I do it. I mean, I get in these administrative committee meetings and they start talking about things that have no relevance to me whatsoever. I'm sitting there. "OK, let me check what's going on in my emails." Disrespectful, but nonetheless we all do it.

Tommy provided some context for this meeting behavior, explaining that there was almost no place where he and others aren't checking their texts and social media and sending emails. "We're at a basketball game—one of the biggest games that the university will play this calendar year. And *all four* of my colleagues and I are on our iPhones!" he said in open astonishment. Even on dates, Tommy had to turn his iPhone off or leave it in the car for fear that he would check email:

> I am scared to death I'm going to start doing that [checking work email]. Because I'm habitual. It's a habit. If I'm not engaged in a good conversation, if I'm remotely bored, if I'm multitasking in my mind, there's no doubt I would pull this thing out to see who wants me. Who wants to talk to me? That's important. Somebody who wants to talk to me? It's mind-numbing and it's fascinating to me. Then you sit down and you look at this thing and you bitch because your battery's draining and you go into a panic mode. "Oh my God. I only have 59% left of battery and it's 10 a.m. What am I going to do? What am I going to do? I've got to get to the car. I've got to plug it in. I've got to plug in devices in my office. I've got to plug in devices in my car." I mean, I am a constant

connected soul. And the technology controls me. If people are disciplined, technology
can be an asset. I'm not sure I'm disciplined enough for technology to be an asset.
I think the technology runs me.

Tommy's comments reflect much of the contemporary research on mobile devices, meetings, and knowledge workers. Individuals are becoming so wedded to their mobile devices that they doubt their capacity for agentic control. Do they really own their time and life or do their seductive devices? But that's apparently a moot point, for people won't—or feel like they can't—give them up because they're the nexus to all parts of their lives. People may simply lack the self-discipline needed to establish boundaries and create their own rules to use mobiles.

Next, I will unpack these narratives and link them to existing research on mobiles and meetings.

MISUNDERSTANDINGS, WORKAROUNDS, AND KNOWLEDGE WORKERS NEGOTIATING FOR CONTROL

When I tell people that I study meetings, they immediately say, "Yuck! Why?" I think it might be because I spent a decade in industry prior to my academic career, and I attended lots of meetings—some great, some not so great. So, for better or worse, I became something of a connoisseur, or at least a wised-up veteran. For example, I loved sales meetings with my customers, even the difficult and uncertain negotiating ones, because we got things done. I had objectives ahead of time, and the adrenaline rush of being the ring leader amidst moments of sheer chaos was exciting. But internal meetings with colleagues and managers? Hardly the same. There, I was in my 20s sitting with people at least 10 years older, and I had virtually no power or status. I often felt pressure to "follow the rules," but no one ever explained the rules. The only way I knew rules existed were when a manager would grab me after the meeting and tell me to speak up more or to be patient and follow the lead of my more experienced colleagues. I often felt the deck was stacked against a young, driven, fast-paced woman.

So, to look properly professional, and to keep awake, I took notes—lots and lots of notes. At first I used paper and pen, and then I moved to a laptop, where, as a touch-typist, I was fast enough that I could type almost every word people said. Yes, this was a bit of an escape from the pressure I felt to perform, and it did foreshadow my future career in research; but it also made me a resource. Much like Olivia in this chapter and Bill in

Chapter 1, I'd have people turning to me during and after meetings to ask me for details since I had virtually kept the minutes. I also watched others and told myself that I could learn how to "behave" in meetings from taking notes not only on content but also on others' meeting behaviors.

But what my note-taking really did for me was help me pay attention. I've always found it hard to listen and be actively engaged when I'm just sitting there, twiddling my thumbs. I often tell my students that if they come into my office, I might take notes during our one-on-one meetings because it helps me focus on them.

So later, when people started bringing their BlackBerrys into meetings and using them for extracurricular activities, like catching up on email, I couldn't believe my eyes. I had spent a decade trying to overcome my weaknesses in paying attention and I wanted to understand the magical powers these people possessed that seemingly allowed them to split their attention yet somehow remain tuned in.

While the worker comments I've quoted in this chapter haven't revealed any magical powers, they have provided a wider lens on meeting behaviors and how rules and norms developed around mobile-device use. These examples are a small part of the over 50 interviews on organizational meetings that my teams and I collected between 2007 and 2016. The findings from my early observations and interviews prompted me to conduct several quantitative studies on meetings[32,34,36] and have helped me develop a measurement scale on multicommunicating meeting behaviors.[32] The stories in this chapter also further illustrate how mobile-communication negotiation is constituted and how it changes in different situations.

MISUNDERSTANDINGS AROUND ACCEPTABILITY OF MEETING MULTITASKING NORMS

One of the biggest takeaways from the qualitative data in this chapter is that we can't read people's minds concerning how they view others' use of mobile devices in meetings. (Remember David, for example?) But even without formal rules, people think they can somehow decipher whether this behavior is acceptable.

These conclusions from the qualitative data support what Jenn Davis and I found in our quantitative study of mobile use in meetings.[36] We used the social influence model,[15] a perspective partially derived from social learning theory,[2] to look at communication overload, group norms, and co-worker influences on mobile-device use in meetings. Our survey respondents represented a host of industries and professions, such as engineering, finance, utilities, advertising, healthcare, and government organizations. We also had a mix of managers and non-managers, and roughly half of the people had been in their current position between 1 and 6 years. Even though the sample was relatively small (119 participants), the views represented a wide range of organizational members.

We predicted that a main reason people use their mobiles in a meeting is they feel overloaded with work obligations and need to use the meeting time to catch up. We had suspected this from the over 30 interviews we had collected before conducting our survey study. But here was the surprise: we found that regardless of whether people felt overloaded with communication, it didn't significantly influence how much multitasking they did on their mobiles in meetings. (Keep in mind that this was self-reported data, so this is what people told us influenced their meeting mobile use.)

Two things, however, did markedly influence whether people used their mobiles to multitask there: *seeing others do it in meetings and sensing that there was a norm in the meeting that tolerated mobile use.* By "markedly," I mean that those two variables explained 41% of the variance in people's likelihood to use their mobile in a meeting, and that was after accounting for their experience engaging in these behaviors. It's uncommon for a social-science model to explain that much of human behavior, so we felt comfortable making the claim that observed mobile-use behavior and perceived norms are primary reasons people use mobiles in meetings.

Once again, even in this quantitative study, people thought they could read the minds of others and make an informed decision about using their mobiles in meetings. This misunderstanding is important because organizational meetings have political dynamics at play.[29,40] There will always be individuals trying to show their co-workers and managers how much they know or how hard they work, and others who are demonstrating their ability to lead and make decisions. While past research has identified different types of meetings with different goals[18,27,29] and that using a mobile in meetings is likely related to certain meeting types, the political ramifications of meeting behavior are invariably often present.[18,29]

MULTICOMMUNICATING

This practice, mentioned earlier, involves people using technology to conduct at least two near-simultaneous conversations,[24] for example, by phone and email. The use of "near-simultaneous" in the definition is deliberate. When people engage in conversations or do two tasks together, they are often quickly alternating between the two, so it's difficult to claim that true simultaneity exists.[24,31,33] Scholars have distinguished this concept from "multitasking" by explaining that carrying on the former, which involves conversing with others, is often more cognitively taxing than doing multiple independent tasks nearly simultaneously.[24] Even though it's common knowledge that true simultaneity rarely exists, people often use "simultaneous" as a shortcut to help distinguish multitasking from single-tasking, conducting one task followed by another in succession.

But multicommunicating does share two important features with multitasking: speed and time. In the academic literature, multitasking has both a speed dimension (i.e., people think they are more efficient when they do multiple tasks at the same time) and a time dimension (i.e., multiple tasks happen as simultaneously as they can instead of our doing one task at a time).[6,16] Furthermore, multitasking can be broken up into two timescales: people can complete multiple tasks simultaneously, and they can complete multiple tasks in succession.[33] People perceive the speed at which they are multitasking as faster when they are engaged in multiple activities simultaneously.[33]

Multicommunicating has a similar nuanced meaning, and in meetings we have a fairly good idea of the different ways that people multicommunicate.[32] Multicommunicating consists of five major activities that people might engage in during meetings: (1) they ask questions and respond to those of others as a way to improve their understanding of meeting content, (2) they try to influence others, (3) they will blow off steam by joking or making sarcastic comments, (4) they may support one another by providing encouragement, and (5) they may wish to be available to others off-site while participating in meetings.

Multicommunicating can be a productive activity. In some workgroups, when participants combine their backchannel communication with their ongoing meeting activities, they can resolve issues and have fewer follow-up meetings.[11] Research suggests that when people carry on multiple conversations about the same topic, the extra information can enhance the overall conversation.[42] But multicommunicating can also create problems. When people combine conversations during a meeting, they can experience high levels of cognitive load and their decisions can be lower-quality because people gather data quickly and then rush the decision.[11] Also, as we've seen, some people find these multiple-conversation practices distracting,[25] error-ridden,[11,43,44] and downright rude.[7]

MULTICOMMUNICATING AND NORMS

So what are the norms of multicommunicating, and how do they influence our perceptions of others? "Norms" are guidelines that help us identify, in a given context, whether behaviors are appropriate.[5] Reinsch and colleagues[24] explain, "If a person senses that the norm for productivity outweighs the norm for full attention or immediate responses, he or she is more likely to multicommunicate" (p. 397). But this depends on the norms in a given organization and within specific workgroups. Regardless of managerial status, workers who follow organizational norms for communication-technology use are often rated higher by their supervisors than those who flout them.[41]

But norms are perceptual. Some people are better at grasping them than others, and it takes newcomers and groups a while to develop a perspective on them.[24,38,44]

Let me now summarize the narrative data presented so far in this chapter to better show how misunderstandings about multicommunicating and multitasking norms develop.

EXAMPLES FROM THE DATA

Our data corroborates several key findings from prior research, but it also reveals some new explanations. Olivia regularly multicommunicated while in meetings, especially when she was seeking additional information for herself or for others. In their theoretical work on multicommunicating, Reinsch and colleagues[24] argue that such information-conveyance tasks are often interpreted favorably because they signal that an individual is both accessible and thorough (i.e., willing and able to gather additional information).

But at least 10 people in our data set made comments like, "We can't tell what people are doing on those devices." Many people, it turns out, are suspicious of *all* mobile-device use; and because they can't tell if the use is appropriately productive, they make assumptions. Their assumptions are typically based on one or more of several things: job role, hierarchical level, perceptions of others in the meeting, and type of meeting. These assumptions might be wrong, though, especially because we had so many conflicting comments in the data. Some interviewees seemed to think that people higher in the hierarchy are busier than people at lower levels, so those higher-ups have to multitask. But that is not necessarily what I see in the data. There are no firm rules to guide these behaviors.

The data also illustrates that interpreting organizational norms for using mobiles in meetings is much harder than we might imagine, as in the following examples:

1) We can't watch others' behavior and automatically assume that the same behavior is appropriate for us. Recall John, the manager at the governmental organization. He was on his mobile devices constantly during the meetings he ran, but his subordinate, Andy, said that John didn't like it when others weren't giving him their undivided attention.

2) We can't assume that just because peers share a norm, such as, *it's okay to use mobiles in meetings*, a higher-level manager shares it too. In the advertising agency, Cedric explained that all the mid-level managers multicommunicated constantly in meetings, yet privately the COO, David, objected to this behavior.

3) Hierarchy should be considered before multicommunicating. Olivia shared her practice of actively observing the hierarchy to decide whether she should and could multicommunicate. Andy said that when he attended meetings run by senior managers, he kept his BlackBerry hidden. Cathy said that when communicating to more senior managers, she needed to be ready to speak up at all times, so she avoided multicommunicating.

FORMAL POLICIES ON MOBILES IN MEETINGS

Only one person in our data set, the SVP, Sally, had a formal policy against the use of mobiles in her meetings. Because she articulated this emphatically, every person we interviewed in her organization knew her rule. But there were many people who hedged concerning rules of mobiles in other meetings. We'd hear comments like "Oh, there's a rule—well, I've never heard him *say* that—but I think . . ." or "I don't think it's a problem to use my BlackBerry in a meeting, but I probably won't use it *all* the time."

While our team was collecting this data, several studies and news reports emerged on the topic of formal rules and policies. For example, one study on meetings in work teams showed that managers and meeting leaders forbade laptop use because they wanted attendees to pay close attention to meeting content.[10] In March of 2008, ABC News carried a prime-time report on what it termed "continuous partial attention." They said that organizations faced some new employee issues now that smartphones and laptops had become ubiquitous. Several companies went "laptop-less" by banning electronic devices, and their employees had a tough time adjusting to disconnecting during meetings.[21] Yet some people claimed their meetings were shorter and more productive without the distraction of technology.[10]

JOB ROLE MATTERS

Job-role differences further complicate these misunderstandings because people in certain job roles enjoy unspoken and undisputed permission to be constantly attending to their mobile devices during all types of meetings. I was able to corroborate this myself in the governmental organization we studied, where I attended several meetings and interviewed the chief crisis communication officer, Amanda. During one of the meetings where I sat next to her, I noticed her BlackBerry constantly lighting up with messages arriving through several different channels. After six messages, she grabbed her phone, slipped out of her seat, and moved quickly toward the door, speaking softly as she left. During my interview with her later, she explained that when a journalist calls about a breaking situation, she has to take the call immediately or risk being thought "unresponsive."

The problem in this sort of situation arises as other colleagues notice Amanda's behavior. Though many of them knew exactly why she took the call, seeing her on her mobile still prompted them to reflexively check their own messages. In one of my quantitative studies on meeting multitasking, my team found that a main reason people say they use their mobile in meetings is that they see others doing it.[36] I also observed a related situation where Amanda took a call in a larger 40-person meeting. Not everyone in that meeting knew her job role, so it's quite likely that they wondered why she was emboldened to just step out. Was there some emergency? Was she bored? Was she angry?

WORKAROUNDS TO FORMAL MEETING RULES

Even with knowledge workers, many were busy hiding their devices under the table and even passing notes to communicate in meetings where mobiles were forbidden. I can still remember the look on that 65-year-old vice president's face as he dropped the note that had been passed to him while Sally's back was turned. Workers are creative. Sometimes just sneaky, too. Rules seemingly invite workarounds. Still, when enunciated emphatically, they also clarify expected behavior.

RULES ESTABLISH CLEAR EXPECTATIONS

From the analyses in this chapter, it should be obvious that people with positional power are best situated to set mobile device–use rules. But many leaders—perhaps most leaders—fail to establish them explicitly. This leads to situations where people simply assume the governing norms. But they're often mistaken, and they never know that their behavior is being tsk-tsked by their peers and by their managers. Just observing others is no substitute for having direct conversations among work teams to reach agreements or to establish rules. These days, when I teach my students about the culture of meetings, I warn them about misunderstanding the norms and how important it is to ask a manager his or her preferences. I still wish that meeting leaders would start their meetings with ground rules that include mobile device–use expectations. Ground rules, along with well-designed agendas, have long been recognized as vital for creating more productive meeting environments.[26,35]

EVIDENCE OF CONCERTIVE CONTROL

Earlier in this chapter I discussed a large governmental organization and a large advertising firm, DG&G. In both, besides collecting interview data, my team and I spent enough time simply observing to see the power that peer groups had on mobile-device use in meetings and beyond the workday. Andy's story of being on his BlackBerry while getting treated at a PT office is one example. In addition, Cedric, the creative manager, had his views on his need to use his BlackBerry in meetings to enhance his productivity constantly reinforced by his peers on the Leadership Council. They had taken the mobile affordance of availability[28] to a new level. Several teams we studied constantly reinforced and punished other members until they all behaved as if being available was the group norm, which then became a powerful group expectation.

Let me advance this argument a bit further. In recent work reconceptualizing communication overload in light of the growing norm of constant connectedness, I worked with my co-authors to create a formative model that examined what, exactly, constituted communication overload. While our findings supported past research on the quality and quantity of messages, and the pervasive sense of being overwhelmed, we also identified what we term an "availability–expectation–pressure pattern."[37] People needed to keep connected with others, and they felt a responsibility to do so. Our study supports suggestions by Christian

Licoppe who believed that if connectedness became an expectation, it could induce a "dialectic of normative constraint and internalized discipline in which presence and absence, availability and unavailability, will be regulated in a game of expectations, obligations, and constraints"[19] (p. 153). In other words, people will feel an internal pressure to make themselves be more present, and over time, this pressure will lead to expectations.

In more recent work from 2016, Joseph Bayer, Scott Campbell, and Rich Ling[4] push this argument further and claim that people are expected to be available for communication through their mobiles at all times. The data I've shared in this chapter suggests that the group pressure form of concertive control, along with hierarchical control, played key roles in virtually forcing workers to be always on, and hence always available, for messages from managers and peers.

Thus far, most of the data I've shared has been from more traditional knowledge-work professions. And that's not surprising, for almost all of the research on multitasking and multicommunication in meetings has been conducted on ones that are ICT-intense and often include lots of people who bring their own devices into the meetings and use them. But not everyone attending meetings operates from the always-on, constantly connected, knowledge-worker perspective. It's time to meet one of those exceptions.

CORDELIA: TAKING MEETING MINUTES IN THE POLICE DEPARTMENT

I'm a minion. I don't get a laptop. I don't get anything. I don't rate one. Other people have laptops, but they're the higher-ups.

Consider the perspective of people attending workplace meetings who don't actively participate but instead work in the background taking notes. Such a one was Cordelia. "I am a temp," she told us. "So I am at the lowest echelon of the chain, which I enjoy. But being at the lowest echelon of the chain, I take minutes." Why did she enjoy her secretarial role? "Well," she explained, "a temp worker, where I work, they get the weekends off and then they have flex hours."

Cordelia worked as an administrative assistant in her city's police department, and she was genuinely happy with her job. She watched, observed, and took notes in almost every meeting at the department. No one had ever asked her perspective on these meetings, so when my team interviewed her, she leaped at the chance to share her opinions. She began by explaining who normally attended them:

> Leaders. So you have the chief, the assistant chief, two captains, and the head administrator—okay, five people. This meeting could probably best be done in email. I'm just the minutes person, and you [could] send me an email with everything you want to get across. And then they could be accomplishing another job while reading this email.

But the chief wanted his people face-to-face in order to bond, she told us. That was the idea, anyway. But Cordelia didn't see much bonding going on during these meetings. Here was her own theory for why the police department had so many meetings rather than simple email exchanges:

> If you're a captain and you can't be there, you have to send one of your people to take your place, to speak for you. Let me tell you a little bit. This might help out. The higher-ups are in their mid- to late 50s. We have some people in the higher-ups that are in their 60s to 70s. So for them, the way they've worked, all this time has probably not been through email. Their communication, for most of their lives, has been meetings.

Cordelia might have been the meeting note-taker, but she had a lot of wisdom and life experiences for a young woman in her late 20s. She also used various ICTs in her administrative job, outside of taking meeting notes, and in her personal life. But in meetings, she used a pad and paper. How come? we asked her. Why not a laptop? Her response: "I'm a minion. I don't get a laptop. I don't get anything. I don't rate one. Other people have laptops, but they're the higher-ups. They have laptops." So why do they get them? we asked. She replied: "Well, so they can go home and do work. I think that's what that's all about."

But Cordelia didn't see anyone use laptops in meetings, and only rarely BlackBerrys or iPhones either. When asked if having a laptop in meetings would help her do her job, she thought for a bit and said, "Some of the acronyms, I could look up. If I had a laptop, I could just look them up without asking people what in the world they were talking about. Some people use words you've never heard of. Especially if you're taking minutes, you want to know what they're talking about so you can make it make sense to you." But she didn't necessarily believe that having a laptop would make the meetings more productive. This was likely a combination of her personal preference and the meeting norms in the police department.

She was a bit appalled when we asked her why she and others in the meetings didn't ever multitask in meetings. "That's rude!" she exclaimed.

"Why, that is *so* rude." This response seemed to fit the culture of her workplace. This was not a high-tech organization; if anything, it was an organization that wanted to be higher-tech but was struggling to accomplish that goal.

We explained that there was a catchphrase being thrown around in workplaces these days called "always on." We asked her how she would relate her experience in the workplace with this phrase. She replied:

> Okay. We're not. The people I work with in my office are not. The police department is always on. Of course, it's a police department! But my department is not. We're just Monday to Friday from 7 to 5, sometimes 7 to 6. That's it, though. We go home. We don't bring our work home with us. Nobody in the admin section has laptops. We all leave it at work. We go home. We spend time with our families. Or do whatever. We definitely have that distinction. We always get holidays off. That's always nice.

Cordelia had had other jobs in the past, like when she was in the U.S. Marine Corps, where she didn't take notes but where she did have to attend lots of meetings. These came with no advance notice, and she'd have to sit or stand for hours at a time. "I only had something to say about 1% of the time," she recalled, "and it was related to my job. It was the only thing that pertained to me. It was more of a waste of time than writing the minutes." When we asked her if she could multitask in those meetings, her response revealed why she felt so strongly that being in a meeting and not giving one's undivided attention was rude: "No. Definitely not, because the Marines would probably kill you for not paying attention to the whole [meeting]. 'Pay attention to your elders and your superiors and listen to what they're saying.'" After learning about her past, including the fact that military life in the U.S. is supremely hierarchical, our team could understand why she couldn't fathom that anyone would so rudely risk using a mobile device in a meeting while others were talking.

CORDELIA'S EXPERIENCES MOVE US BEYOND KNOWLEDGE WORKERS

Cordelia's experience as an administrative note-taker provides a welcome perspective. Even today, not everyone works in an organization, or a workgroup, where people have mobiles at their fingertips. And not everyone *wants* to be a knowledge worker, especially when it often means working way more hours than they are nominally expected to work. Being nonexempt from overtime pay—that is, receiving no pay beyond the 40-hour workweek—is desirable for many people because it also relieves them of overtime and the headaches thereof. Well, usually, anyway. Furthermore, some people have no desire to integrate their work, personal lives, and devices. Understanding people's past experiences and their views on their "place in the hierarchy" helped open our minds to the views of people in roles not traditionally considered to be those of knowledge workers.

Cordelia's story is the first I've shared that introduces a broader perspective on mobile-device use at work. Back in the early 2000s, you'll recall, organizations didn't provide mobile devices like laptops, BlackBerrys, personal digital assistants, or iPhones to employees who weren't considered mobile knowledge workers. And in some organizations, they constituted the bulk of the workforce. These workers are often categorized as "blue collar," "clerical," "manual labor," "retail," and "service providers." On the surface, it's fairly easy to overstate differences between knowledge workers and these others, holding less knowledge-intensive jobs. And while having categories makes comparisons easier, it also obscures some of the information- and knowledge-generating work of non–knowledge workers.

As mentioned in Chapter 1, knowledge workers often use computers to "do" their cognitive work. It's rarely routine work, and they tend to enjoy autonomy in it.[12] But what about this other "group" of workers? What happens when the cost of mobiles drops and workers ineligible for an employer-sponsored mobile device are able to buy their own devices? It's easy to conclude that some workers like, say, a floor cleaner wouldn't need computer technology and other mobile devices to "do" their work. But people forget that work is more than physical labor. It involves coordination, working in teams, learning new things, and being reachable in case of emergencies. The data shared in the next three chapters invites all of us to rethink the assumptions we hold about work, power, control, and differences between stationary and mobile work.

CHAPTER 5
Trust, Understanding, and Mobile Control in Manual Work

Cordelia, the blunt-talking secretary you just met in the last chapter, offered us a mobile-communication perspective quite different from that of more traditional knowledge workers. Her employer, the city's police department, didn't provide her with a laptop or smartphone, but that really didn't bother her. She owned her own mobile phone, and it was fully under her control, which was exactly how she liked it. And she actually preferred being an hourly clerical worker, paid for every hour she worked and then free of all work obligations once home. All she really needed for her job, she was given: a desktop computer, landline phone, and access to a fax machine.

When she wasn't taking notes in meetings, she was summarizing those meeting notes and arranging the next set of meetings. Cordelia worked in a small, open-office environment with six other secretaries, each with his or her own desk, located right next to one another—close enough to hear one another cough, see the projects on each other's computers, and know who was on task and who wasn't. Cordelia characterized her work environment as "very relaxed. If you don't have work, you can do whatever. . . . Nobody cares if you go on the Internet throughout your workday. They understand that staring at a computer screen [means] you need a break. And it's okay to get up and go outside for 10 minutes. That's fine."

Yet for all that informality and trust, her work team appeared highly productive. Unusually team-like, too. During our observations, we noticed that they all seemed to get along well and had similar interests. Said Cordelia: "Everyone I work with is very family-oriented and very religiously oriented. The meshing is very good—the relationships between co-workers are good." We also noticed that they seemed to understand that getting their job done had to come before handling any personal messages. "You don't want to abuse [the flexibility]," she explained. "There's a fine line. You have to ride the line." Her rule of thumb for riding the line was straightforward: "If it has something to do with work, it's automatically responded to. If it's from a friend, and I have nothing else going on, then I will respond to it. So, that's the way it works."

In this unusually lenient environment, Cordelia had delineated her own rules for how she used her personal mobile device and various work-related communication channels. The instant messaging (IM) feature that came with her email? It got reserved for personal use. "My IM is for my friends. None of my coworkers. See, this is my job," she explained. And for email? There, she didn't hesitate to combine her personal and work communication. But her idea of consolidating email messages was quite different from that of most knowledge workers included in the data sets I've discussed in this book. She used her *personal* email for everything, including work:

> *Everybody has the same kind of email, except for me. I didn't get a department email because I didn't want a department email. When they asked if I wanted an email, I said, "No, I already have an email address. Just use it." My email is cooler. My email has more options to do things. Like it has the chat thing. I have larger storage capacity. I can send multiple pictures, videos. It's private. They can't go back and look at my emails.*

The police department went along with Cordelia's preference, but my interview team was curious as to why she wanted to have *all* her communication funneled through her personal mobile phone and email account. So we asked her, and she was quick to explain: "Because when I was in the Marines, I had an email account where they could look at it whenever they wanted to, and I didn't like that. So I definitely didn't want to be in that situation again." She shared a bit about her military experiences, and she made it clear that she was tired of being controlled and having no privacy.

Interestingly, even in her trusting, permissive work environment, Cordelia prized her privacy. She wanted absolute control over her communication, and she held out for a way to make that happen. What a reasonable perspective on a humane work culture! Her team had earned their manager's total trust, a difficult thing to do in many workplaces.

Seven years later, I wonder if anyone in her department still enjoys that flexibility and autonomy. Nowadays, it's a high challenge for even broadminded organizations to adapt to the information and communication technology whims of their varied employees. I'm also stuck by the contrast between the permissive work environment that Cordelia experienced and Delilah's experience when her manager flicked her a nickel and told her to be a team player. By the way, they both worked in the same police department—but with different job roles and radically different managers.

CYBERSLACKING AND EMPLOYEE REACTIONS

"Cyberslacking" is a term used to describe how people wastefully use technologies at work for non-work-related tasks and amusements.[38] Editors with the *Oxford English Dictionary* acknowledged this term in 2003, a time when the prefix "cyber-" was being added to many terms to indicate activities happening on the Internet. "Cyberloafing" is a related word; both "slack" and "loaf," in this context, refer to workers engaged in activities not related to their actual work.[8] Mobile devices present a tremendous temptation in the workplace because people have gotten accustomed to being available and connected to others at all times,[22,23] even during their work hours. While workers have used company computers and Internet access inappropriately for years now, mobiles have introduced a host of new challenges for organizations to manage.[3] Sneaking in a little online shopping during work hours is just a single example of how employees cyberslack.

One of the challenges mobile devices introduce is the growing norm of connectedness.[22,24] I've mentioned it elsewhere in this book, but it's especially relevant to the issue of cyberslacking. Quite frankly, it goes well beyond the individual in his or her workplace; other people want *and expect* them to be available, so there's felt reciprocity involved. Texting friends and loved ones and posting a personal update on social media can be driven, at least in part, by the need to stay connected to others.

Another big challenge concerns device ownership. Nowadays, mobile devices are often purchased by the employee and represent a type of personal property.[32] The privacy that carried was precisely why Cordelia, for example, chose to send and receive all her email on her personal mobile phone. She was basically in charge of her own policy-making. When technologies are company-owned, it's much easier for an organization to enforce policies concerning the appropriate use of those technologies because, quite often, organizations monitor how their own resources are used,[11] something Cordelia knew all too well from her previous job in the military.

Finally, these devices are portable, and many can fit easily in a pocket or a small bag. Unlike, say, laptop computers, their small size helps them virtually disappear in clothing.

These days, mobiles are found in nearly every kind of work and workplace. Let me share some of these diverse people and environments that other scholars have already studied.

Minu Thomas and Sun Sun Lim treated us to a particularly striking study: the mobile use, in Singapore, by Indian and Filipino maids. These migrant workers, it turned out, purchased their mobile phones to stay in contact with their friends and distant family and to further their future job opportunities.[37] In short, their mobile phones were both emotional support tools and career capital–enhancing tools. Thomas and Lim also found that when these migrant workers signed contracts with their employers, those contracts carefully spelled out how their phones could be used.

In another study, this one examining security guards and other migrant workers in Beijing, Ke Yang found that guard duty involves lots of waiting around to see if anything happens, so these workers were often bored and consequently sought refuge in their mobile phones, which they brought to work and used either to text or to play games with their friends.[40] Many jobs have this ebb and flow between waiting and actively working, and often the transition is quick and unexpected. For example, a security guard might sit at a desk for 3 hours with no visitors during his night shift, and then, with no warning, three men could come running past him and barrel up the stairs, prompting his immediate pursuit. Customer-service jobs often show a similar ebb and flow, particularly if the worker isn't consistently facing customers. Concierges at hotels, information-desk personnel, and even flight attendants are just some of the many workers who experience significant "waiting."

These examples, together with other research studies, raise important issues concerning workers' control over their own working environment. Unlike knowledge workers who can switch tasks, take breaks on a whim, and work fairly autonomously, clerical and manual-labor workers are often narrowly constrained and subject to close oversight by managers, whose entire job is indeed to manage them.[29] In often boring or routine jobs like these, mobile phones can help pass the time and give employees a way to escape the monotony[7] through activities that employers could call cyberslacking.

EMPLOYER REACTIONS

While workers might view their mobiles as simply a harmless way to pass time, many employers think otherwise, for an employee to play games or indulge in other non-work-related activities while being paid to perform a specific job is often viewed as both costly and morally unacceptable by employers.[16,38] And using mobile devices for such purposes seems, for some reason, especially egregious. For example, after she had finished her beverage service, I noticed a United Airlines flight attendant coloring a sketch of some sort as she sat on the jump seat in the back of the plane. I couldn't resist asking her about it. After we chatted a bit about our shared enjoyment of mindlessly coloring, she opened up: it helped her, she said, to stay off her mobile phone. You see, she said, the company has this policy where flight attendants are never, ever to use their personal mobile on the airplane because "customers" will see them. So, as there are no private places for flight attendants on airplanes, and as she needed a break on long, 6-hour flights like this one to Hawaii, she had taken up coloring—at least until they told her she couldn't do that, either.

Organizations have responded to the rise in cyberslacking by introducing Internet use policies,[30] placing limits on employee privacy,[11] and sometimes restricting mobile-device use altogether.[13,34,35] Because it's so hard to tell *what* people are doing when they are tapping or swiping away on their mobiles, it tends to make employers suspicious. And there is very little research examining *how* workers use technologies for personal use at work,[38] so organizations are experimenting, hoping to find ways to address what they see as a real productivity problem.

In the past decade of my research, I've seen a rise in the number of mobile-device policies that restrict use. Early conversations about these policies centered on knowledge workers and their meeting behaviors that distracted them from whatever was being discussed.[33] But now, in addition to establishing these formal and information policies, organizations are posting signs forbidding use.

Some organizations even assign individuals a place to put their mobile when they enter the working area. I took this photo of one such holder—a makeshift from a closet shoe-organizer (Figure 5.1).

The most common type of restrictive policy involves employees with direct customer contact. Most people say that it isn't possible to provide excellent customer service if they are *seen* (as in *caught*) using a mobile phone. The word "seen" is important because, as I will explore in Chapter 9, while most workers agree with this general restriction, they are also very creative in how they hide to stay out of customer view. That lets them stay connected with their loved ones while still honoring company policy.

Figure 5.1. An image of a mobile device holder

CONTROLLING CYBERSLACKING WITH A POLICY

The data for the rest of this chapter comes from a case study of a big janitorial-supply company where I led a small team of graduate students to collect data from 2010 to 2012. This company didn't provide janitorial supplies; mostly, it supplied janitors themselves, sending them out to whatever firms or organizations in the area needed their service. Janitors, or building cleaners, of course, are manual-labor workers. They use their hands and heavy equipment to sweep, polish, dust, mop, and remove rubbish. There are quite a few janitors worldwide, and in the U.S. in 2014 there were 2.3 million janitors, a number expected to grow 6% in the next decade.[1]

Most of the employees in this company were either janitors or managers, the latter ranging from supervisors to the vice president of operations. Besides its manual-labor workforce, the company boasted an active human resources (HR) department that provided training, onboarding—also known as new employee orientation—and employee-benefit services. Upper management, HR, information technology, marketing, and sales— all played important roles in the company, and, throughout their own ranks, at least, all their jobs resembled knowledge-worker roles. That is to say, these people, unlike the janitors, were fairly autonomous, used the Internet to conduct their daily work, and were responsible for developing new knowledge for the company.

In 2009, the senior-level managers in this company convened to discuss some recent complaints they had received concerning their janitors. Tenants in the buildings they cleaned had reported seeing several janitors on their mobile phones chatting away in the hallways while they should have been on the clock. The managers had, in fact, certainly noticed that more and more of their workers were bringing their personal mobiles to work, and these recent complaints made them believe they needed to address this growing concern. But they also knew that by allowing their employees to bring their personal devices to work, those same devices might prove invaluable in an emergency situation. So, what to do?

Well, they eventually implemented a policy they believed would allow for flexible interpretation and enforcement. Organizations, one finds, can either develop policies that are explicit and meant to control behavior in all circumstances or create policies using principles of what's called "strategic ambiguity."[12] Eric Eisenberg has defined that term as an organizational practice where messages, rules, and policies are kept deliberately vague. This might sound odd—after all, people regularly complain about communication being unclear—but past research has shown that it's actually a common organizational practice, for it allows supervisors more flexibility than if the policies were overtly clear.[12,31] Furthermore, such policies can be helpful because they allow various people, with diverse goals, to embrace and understand the messages, even if they are ambiguous.[12]

The senior managers in this janitorial-supply company wanted to curb cyberslacking, improve worker productivity, and allow workers the flexibility of using their mobile devices when emergencies arose. To accomplish these goals, senior managers created a policy that workers signed on paper or clicked through electronically, stating that personal mobile devices could only be used during emergencies. Knowledge workers read this policy and viewed it as more of a *guideline*. They never imagined that the policy applied to devices they used regularly for work, and one HR trainer I spoke with had no idea that a policy even existed! This trainer didn't regularly work with the janitors, but he did train other employees in the company on the computer technologies they used, so his ignorance was stunning to us. They interpreted the spirit of the policy and viewed the inclusion of "emergencies" as ambiguous enough for them to essentially ignore.

The janitors, meanwhile, who weren't in managerial roles believed they needed to interpret the policy literally to avoid the risk of being fired. Emergencies, for them, were rare events, situations identified by their managers and often handled through managerial decision-making practices. This literal interpretation meant that many janitors didn't carry their mobiles with them at work—a problem when actual emergencies and even last-minute schedule changes arose. The policy was interpreted differently depending on the job role of the individual.[35]

NO MOBILE PHONE IF YOU'RE A JANITOR

There has to be another way—I mean, we aren't in the eighth grade, so note-leaving isn't really the greatest.
　　—Salvador, a janitor commenting on the policy banning mobile devices

Janitors are the almost-invisible backbone of most buildings today, the night workforce. They swoop into rooms and other spaces, tidy up, and disappear. And even when other people are actively working in those buildings, janitors are often on-call to clean up unexpected messes. A visitor trips and spills her coffee all over the stairwell, a colleague gets a stomach bug and doesn't quite make it to the restroom, and who comes to the rescue? The janitors, of course. At night, janitors get out the vacuums and heavy floor polishers, wash the blackboards, clean the desktops and tabletops, climb up ladders to dust in places well beyond anyone's reach—the list goes on.

I was lucky to get to know quite a few janitors who worked for this big company. Based in one of the largest cities in the U.S., it provided janitorial services for approximately 75 buildings in a 3-square-mile range and employed over 200 janitors. The company had first invited me in to do a series of studies theme-based around an organization-wide communication and engagement survey. It proved as educational for me as for the organization itself. I was gratified to learn that their janitors were generally happy with their jobs and with the company itself; furthermore, many of them had a family legacy of working for this firm.

But there were also things I learned about this type of work that were disturbing. These things compelled me to continue my research there. I aimed to learn more about this understudied group of workers who did manual labor on 8-hour shifts, typically at night, five times a week.

One Wednesday evening around 8:50 p.m., my team was just finishing up a survey we had conducted on-site when I was approached by an older gentleman I will call Daniel. He appeared to be in his 60s, quite weathered, and slightly stooped. He asked me if I had a minute to talk about the survey. I said "Sure," so, for a bit of privacy, we found ourselves some nearby seats in the 500-person auditorium.

He said that he liked the survey but confided that he hoped his boss would make some changes that could make him a lot happier. "What sorts of changes?" I asked. Well, he said, it was already just a week before Easter, and he was frustrated that his boss wouldn't let him have Good Friday off as a holiday. He seemed to know a lot about the company's vacation and holiday policy, and the way he described the situation made me wonder if his boss was out of line there. Daniel said that he'd requested time off over 2 months before Easter because all of his family planned to meet at his house to celebrate. This would be no small get-together. He told me about his five children, his 14 grandchildren, his wife, and his mother, who would all be together to celebrate. But he wouldn't be able to join them because his boss told his entire team they needed to work that day since the buildings would be empty.

He bluntly asked me what I thought he should do. I still remember feeling queasy about this request because I'm not an intervention researcher, but I knew a bit about his company. He had already talked with his boss— actually three times, he said—so I suggested he ask someone in Human Resources if they could help him negotiate the time off. He replied: "I think we have one of those, but I work night shift. The person I ride with gets me to work right before my shift starts at 8 p.m. Then I leave at 4:30 a.m. I'm not here when HR is." So I suggested he email his representative. He told me he didn't have email and didn't use a computer. Then, embarrassed, he also admitted that he couldn't spell most things, or read. He spoke English, but he had no other way to communicate. In short, he was functionally illiterate. The only way he did the survey, I discovered, was that he had had a colleague quietly read every question to him, then circle the number indicating each response.

I felt acutely uncomfortable—wanting so badly to help but feeling like my hands were tied. Then he suggested that we could use the U.S. mail. He tore off a sheet of paper from one of my unused surveys and wrote his name and address on it. I in turn agreed to find out the name of his HR rep and send that back to him through the same mail. He would then get a friend to write that person a note for him to see if he could meet with her during his shift.

I did find the rep's name and mailed it to him, but I never heard the outcome. On Friday, April 22 that year, I wondered if he got to spend time with his family or if he celebrated what was a religious holiday for him working with his team. By the way, this happened in 2011, so it was not that long ago. Since that day, when I celebrate Easter, I think of him. I myself also rarely get Good Friday off from my work because I work at a public university, but I'm certain that if I had a special event I needed to attend that day, I could find someone to cover for me. Daniel didn't have that flexibility.

This story touched me because I felt helpless. I couldn't use technological solutions to solve his temporal dilemma. I share Daniel's story because it's important for people interested in understanding communication technology at work to realize that other people don't necessarily use these tools the same way we do. This story reflects the life and work realities of many hourly, labor, and clerical workers. It also sets the stage for us to better understand why banning mobile devices, for this type of workforce, might be interpreted differently than if the employees had been knowledge workers.

Let's now see how this group of janitors coped with a mobile-device ban that only applied to non-supervisor-level janitors.[13,34,35]

ACCESS TO INFORMATION ON THE JOB

The high-level managers in this janitorial-supply company, all of whom, of course, were knowledge workers, assumed that front-line janitors had no need to access the Internet or use mobile devices to do their jobs. These managers believed that mobile devices were a distraction, so they banned their use by the janitorial staff during work hours.

"I signed a paper that said I'm not allowed to use a cell phone," said Jimmy, a janitor marking 12 years' experience with the company. Jimmy, a participant in our focus group, explained that he recently transferred within the company, and at his previous job he was unaware that there was a ban on mobile devices. He struck me as a conscientious employee who didn't break rules and who appeared worried that he had been out of line in his former job. He didn't question authority, and he didn't complain about the rules. I'm sure he wasn't unique.

But this wasn't the case with several other janitors in the focus group. They were openly critical of the policy, and in some cases they unapologetically explained how they broke the rules. Chris was one of the scofflaws. Among the youngest janitors on the crew at age 26, he had been with the team for less than a year, but he felt like he knew everyone because his father had worked on the same crew before he retired. Chris told us:

> I know there is a policy, but I use my iPad every day at work. I have back problems, and a lot of this equipment is heavy. There are some great YouTube videos that show people how to lift properly and protect their backs.

As Chris relayed his story during the focus group, I caught several pairs of eyes rolling. The more experienced crew members actively tried to ignore him, along with his comments. One older gentleman who was sitting next to him pointedly turned his body around so his back faced Chris. As I watched the reactions in this particular focus group, it was hard to know if they were afraid that management might learn that one of their crew members was breaking the rules or if these older crew members saw Chris as the young, overanxious technology nerd in their group. I suspect that his peers didn't like him very much and saw him as a slacker who got the job purely as a legacy. After all, he could have easily consulted his iPad at home instead of at work.

It's also possible that the more seasoned janitors were reacting to an unspoken norm of staying healthy and not getting hurt at work. Compared to his peers, Chris appeared decidedly overweight. When he sat down in the chair, his body spilled out in all directions. Being only 26 and verbalizing that he had back pain could have been taboo in this environment. After all, the janitors in this organization began their shift with stretching and light exercise. They needed to be ready to move heavy equipment and do physical labor during much of their time at work.

The company provided weekly safety education, so being safe on the job was a top priority there. The breakroom bulletin boards were papered with infographics containing photos of how to properly lift heavy items, use the floor polisher, and pour cleaning products into the mopping buckets. All of these safety briefs were in both English and Spanish.

One time that I visited, two janitors, Alma and Elizabeth, shared details from their most recent training course on reading material safety data sheets (MSDS) and warning labels. Elizabeth proudly picked up a bottle of cleaning fluid and showed me the warning label. She explained that the cleaner contained harsh chemicals and that the picture depicting a person donning gloves meant that she herself needed to wear gloves when using this cleaner. Her co-worker, Alma, spoke only Spanish, so with my limited ability to speak and understand Spanish, I tried to ask her how she read those labels because they were only provided in English. Elizabeth helped me talk with her. Alma looked uncomfortable, and then she motioned to me and acted like she was putting on glasses. Elizabeth immediately jumped in and explained that Alma needed her reading glasses to see those pictures and that she had left her glasses in her locker while she was mopping the floors. Her glasses were in the same locker where she kept her mobile phone while she worked. The only answer I got to my question was from Elizabeth, who said that part of her job was to translate for her colleagues who couldn't read English.

After that observation I did a quick Internet search and realized that there were translations in over 30 different languages for the warning labels and the corresponding MSDS. There was also at least one mobile app that these workers could have used to translate this safety data, but they were banned from using their mobile devices.

During my observations with this group, I heard very few complaints related to the physicality required to do the job, and when workers needed clarification related to safety, they limited their conversations to other peers they trusted. I never learned the real reason the focus group shunned Chris and his acknowledgment of rule-breaking even though his iPad use was actually to enhance workplace safety—assuming, of course, that he was sincere.

But Chris wasn't the only janitor who bent the "no mobiles" rule. In another focus group, Mateo openly admitted, "We hide to do it, because the manager isn't going to walk three blocks to come find me to tell me to do some small thing." Hiding in huge, often unoccupied buildings wasn't hard. But they still knew it was risking their jobs when they made those decisions to break or bend the rules.

Another reason some people felt like they needed to break the rules was for their loved ones. Sometimes their family needed to reach them, and that could be difficult with their late-night work schedules. Alejandra explained, "If it's something very important, send a text, [but] maybe the person can't get the text because they're working two shifts or something." Working multiple jobs wasn't uncommon in this workforce. Alejandra said that sometimes she and her family used a system to prioritize messages. They moved beyond simply texting and added a call as well as left a voicemail. Seeing three messages, sent through different channels, signified the urgent need for a response.

Janitorial staff who work in multiple buildings can be considered mobile workers because their work doesn't involve a single location. In truth, they're always on the move. And it's quite common for them to need the help of other team members or supervisors to complete their tasks, yet their team is often spread between floors and buildings. Furthermore, many janitorial tasks are time-sensitive: they need to be completed at night or at times when there are few people around who might slip on wet floors and possibly get hurt. Supervisors often instructed their employees to work in pairs or small teams, but it's very common for one person to need to stay behind the group when finishing up a one-person task. For the night shift, this means being alone on a floor or in a building while working with equipment that can be very loud.

Before the ban on mobile devices at work, janitors often texted a colleague requesting help, and someone would arrive within minutes. Now the janitors had to stop their task and physically track down other workers. Here's how one janitor described this common situation:

> There is no solution besides walking upstairs, pushing the elevator back down to see the person on the first floor, but that's a complete waste of time, and it's not worth it. You're, like, I'm going to wait for a break.

Waiting for a break might work sometimes, but there were other times when crew members needed to reach their colleagues more immediately. Even though many of the janitors had a mobile device in their pocket, if they followed the letter of the policy, they couldn't pull it out for a quick text or call. One focus-group member, Alejandra, explained that she was embarrassed because her only option was to "go to many buildings to ask permission to borrow the [landline] phone because I'm not allowed to use my personal cell phone." Alejandra also described her frustrations interacting with the building's receptionists, who were often annoyed at being interrupted by a janitor. Her comments revealed the sad truth that many people disrespect the profession of others, especially when it involves manual labor. Ironically, in this organization, the janitors were full-time employees with company benefits, whereas most of the receptionists in the building were temps or part-time workers. Yet there were several comments made in focus groups suggesting that the receptionists thought themselves superior and would look for any excuse to get the janitors in trouble.

SAFETY AND EMERGENCY COMMUNICATION CONCERNS

One of the most complex issues resulting from the mobile-device ban involved reaching the janitors with safety and emergency information. For some time now, researchers have recognized that mobiles serve core functions like safety and security,[23] and they are also important for notifying all organizational members about emergencies.[32] So imagine their frustration when these workers didn't receive timely notifications of important information. Lacking access to computers at work, and without their mobiles, they often received emails only after their shift ended and they were at home. That's assuming, of course, they even had a home computer *and* someone in their family who checked their email.

Evacuations are an especially noteworthy type of emergency that janitorial workers can encounter. Many janitors work around office buildings that have flammable chemicals. Even dental and doctors' offices fit this category. At night, if the security guard spots an unauthorized person, he can hit an alarm and everyone, including janitors, evacuates. Yet fairly often emergency situations don't trigger audible alarms. Instead, text messages or emails are sent to employees.[32] In these cases, employees with mobile devices learn details of the situation instantly. Not so, of course, for the janitors without devices handy. One of them, Hector, a janitor, had developed a reliable strategy of decision-making during emergencies, even though he kept his mobile locked in his car while he was at work:

> I use my eyes. When lots of people are moving in the same direction, I don't hesitate to follow them. I can ask other people to tell me what is happening while we are evacuating.

But keep in mind that this janitorial company's mobile policy contained an exception: during emergencies, employees *could* use their devices. But that solved one problem while creating others. For example, some employees admitted to us that if they ever got caught using their device illegally, they would try to avoid punishment by claiming they thought there was an emergency. Also, as we've already seen, many of these workers couldn't risk having their manager catch them with their mobiles, for it risked their being fired, so they kept them stowed in their cars or lockers—which meant, of course, that when an emergency happened, they had no device readily available. In effect, they were stuck in information holes[34] and were completely reliant on others, or, like Hector, having to use their own eyes to help them decide how to behave.

José, a janitor who once experienced a multibuilding emergency evacuation, described his supervisor's situation during that evacuation: she "couldn't get a response from all the employees, so she was worried. When she evacuated, she wasn't sure if all the employees got the message or not."[13] In his own team, he said, there was added pressure to reach all crew members because they spoke three different languages and the supervisor spoke only English.

José's comments provide context for the findings I share next concerning the four main issues that employees in this janitorial-supply company face during an emergency:

1) Trust between supervisors and front-line janitors.
2) Inconsistent interpretation of rules.
3) Language barriers.
4) Computer literacy and access.

Besides these four major issues that dance around issues of control negotiations between janitors and supervisors, the supervisors themselves are in what appears a no-win situation. They are sandwiched between the janitors, who have almost no mobile access, and their own managers, who are essentially autonomous knowledge workers.

Let's examine the janitors' issues first.

TRUST AND SHARING MOBILE NUMBERS WITH SUPERVISORS

In this organization, many janitors aren't willing to share their personal mobile numbers with their supervisors. Why? Because they fear they might be tricked into answering their mobile when on work time—a "gotcha" situation inviting prompt punishment. Other janitors—quite a few, actually, because this was mentioned in every focus group we conducted—believe that their mobiles are their personal property and no one from work should have a right to contact them through a device not owned by their work. Fundamentally, these issues seem to revolve around trust, privacy, and cost.

Mariana was a middle-aged crew leader with 14 years' experience working at this organization. Her wise comment summed up these concerns: "Many people don't give out their numbers because they don't want us to know anything about them."

Supervisors of all levels in this company were responsible for every member of their crews at all times, especially during emergencies. Two different supervisors in our focus groups, Javier and Bella, shared their strategies for reaching everyone in a crisis. Because many of the work teams trusted one another, the supervisors learned how to leverage that group-level trust. Javier said:

> There are some people who give out their number, and others don't want to do it. So then I go to the one who has given me the number, and I say, "Notify your co-workers and those that are near you and let them know to get on their way over here."

Another supervisor, Bella, had a similar strategy:

> Since I have different buildings, I have at least a telephone number for one supervisor in [each] building, and I call that person and I say, "Gather everyone because there's an emergency. If you find everyone, bring them over here. If you don't, then I'm on my way there."

INCONSISTENT INTERPRETATION OF RULES

In every focus group, janitors complained that supervisors weren't consistent in how they interpreted rules. The janitors knew this because many of them were close friends, some of whom might have a different supervisor. (The typical crew size here was about seven people.) Also, with the average tenure for these janitors being over 10 years, it was likely that they had moved around some within the company. For example, Julio, a janitor who had worked for several different supervisors, explained, "Some [supervisors] don't give out complete information." Other members of Julio's focus group chimed in that they never received training notices—and that was a big deal, considering that additional training was a precondition for promotion. The janitors were also concerned that different supervisors provided completely different instructions on bad-weather days. Four different janitors expressed frustration that certain supervisors required them to work when bad weather made the roads unsafe, while other supervisors gave their employees the day off.

One janitor from our Spanish-speaking focus group explained what happened once during a blizzard:

> I'm going to tell you something. Look, not all supervisors act the same. Do you understand me? I'm saying it because I've had several who don't act the same. This one says, "No, it's all going to be fine. Your head is going to turn white from the snow, but that's not a bad thing." And then you call another one and he says, "Oh, yes, it's turning ugly. If you want to leave, leave."

Another older man in the same focus group added:

In my building, we couldn't leave either. And then I skidded all over the road

By examining all the focus groups, observations, and informal conversations in this organization, we learned that the problems associated with supervisors' inconsistent decision-making were indeed real—not only real but occasionally downright imperiling. For example, many of the janitors shared rides to work with one another and made carpooling decisions based on where they all lived, so if a carpool had four people in it, all four could have a different supervisor. So when one supervisor let his or her employees leave work, if one of them owned the car that was part of a carpool, that janitor ended up stranding the workers whose supervisors wouldn't let them leave. Remember, these janitors worked shifts, so that could mean that someone was stranded at night, without a ride home, in the middle of a blizzard.

LANGUAGE BARRIERS

This was a multicultural workforce with no hiring requirement of a high school diploma. However, all employees had to be U.S. citizens or have legal documents to work in the U.S., and the organization carefully monitored this requirement. Slightly over half of the supervisors spoke only English, approximately 30% of the workers spoke only Spanish, and another 10% of the workers only spoke a language other than Spanish or English. The organization had a strategy of placing at least one bilingual worker on any team with members who spoke no English. But this was tricky because sometimes that bilingual worker was sick or felt encumbered with multiple jobs, including translation.

Many supervisors and managers had thought that they informed their employees of something important only to later hear complaints that, no, they were never told. To head off that problem, this company now printed a sheet of paper with all the employees' names on it and had them sign saying that they'd been informed. But some workers felt pressured to sign, and some didn't even know what they were signing or didn't fully understand what was being communicated. Hear the frustration of one janitor in our Spanish-speaking focus group when trying to set his friends straight:

"What are you signing? You don't even know what. . . ." That's what I would say to my co-workers [when they say], "We're signing here?" And later on [my supervisor

would] say, "Look, you signed." But if you didn't even understand what was said to you because they were speaking English, he was just speaking to himself. And that's the thing: sometimes you understand nothing. Some understand just a little and some nothing, and they just say, "What did he say?" and you have to ask others.

COMPUTER LITERACY AND COMPUTER ACCESS

A common added complication in this workforce was their lack of computer literacy and access to computers and the Internet. At work, there was just one computer in the supervisor's office, and during breaks, janitors could ask to use it if they knew how to. But that meant asking a supervisor to get off the computer for a while. Most janitors said they needed a good reason to make that request, and the only reason considered valid was the need to complete a time card. In this organization, all the hours people worked were recorded on the computer, so all employees were trained to complete their time card online. But many of the janitors didn't have a computer at home, and even if they did, their skills were inadequate. Here's an example of what it was like for one of the janitors at home:

> [For many of my coworkers], their children use it, but they don't. Even my husband doesn't know how to use the computer. He has email but he asks me to check it. "Learn it, I tell him!" And not just him. There are many people who don't know and don't want to learn. They depend on their children. And sometimes the children say, "I don't have time, I'll show you later."

WHAT WORKS COMMUNICATING UP DOESN'T EXIST COMMUNICATING DOWN

Supervisors, as well as the managers above them, got to operate under different rules, as Salvador, a janitor, explained: "The one that has authorization to use a cell phone is the supervisor, who carries one belonging to [XYZ] Janitorial Services. The supervisor is the only one, and the manager [also] uses a beeper." Front-line supervisors were in the awkward position of being both the constant conduit for their crew and always accessible to their manager. These supervisors were in an unbalanced communicative media state because the devices they used to communicate with their manager didn't work with subordinates, who were banned from using their mobile devices. To further complicate this situation, executives and senior managers were completely unaware of what it's like to have subordinates

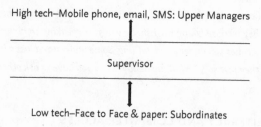

Figure 5.2. Supervisor's communication sandwich situation

who are unreachable unless they find them and talk face-to-face. Upper managers simply picked up their mobile and reached the front-line supervisors at their own whim.

Figure 5.2 illustrates the supervisor's communication sandwich situation. I use the sandwich metaphor and provide a visual because this finding was so unexpected and unique for many types of workers today. Essentially, supervisors experienced a deluxe club sandwich when communicating up to their managers; there were choices in their bread, and it could be artisan or multigrain. But to their subordinates, there were few options; it was day-old white bread.

Several supervisors expressed frustration with the dual demands of communicating in their job role. For supervisors, mobiles were their most important communication tool. They had no choice but to receive emails, texts, and calls on those devices because they were often walking around, checking on their crews. Several supervisors explained that their managers assumed they weren't doing their job properly when they didn't return emails quickly or answer every call on their mobile. So supervisors were in the frustrating situation of being a slave to their mobile devices while also needing to be constantly available for face-to-face conversations.

In addition to dual communication needs, supervisors had another burden resulting from their being the main information conduit for their workers. Supervisors regularly received emails from on high about staff development opportunities, policy changes, and organizational updates. But they couldn't just forward those emails to their crew. No, these supervisors had to either meet with their team face-to-face or post the information on bulletin boards in the break rooms. Typically, the janitors were left off email distribution lists because the company knew they had no email access at work.

Having to prioritize which information to share with their team was only part of the challenge for the supervisors. Quite often, as discussed earlier in this chapter, they had at least one subordinate who spoke a language foreign to them. While researchers have demonstrated the value of using mobile devices to translate messages between languages,[4,6,19] the restrictive mobile-use policies in this janitorial organization precluded translating English words into, say, Spanish or Chinese. Instead, the supervisors relied on face-to-face communication and asked their subordinates to translate for one another. Subordinates got frustrated with their supervisors because they believed that information was being filtered more than it should be and that supervisors were inconsistent in their decision-making. Placing this much responsibility on supervisors could create resentment and suspicion for their entire work crew.

Not knowing how to reach all subordinates during times of crisis placed a huge emotional burden on the supervisors—a burden whose expression had to somehow be managed. Arlie Hochschild used the term "emotional labor,"[18] to describe that management. It helps explain—and, for that matter, even acknowledge—the strategies that workers find themselves using to regulate and display their emotions.[7] High levels of emotional labor negatively affect organizations and work teams because they lead to stress, job dissatisfaction, and burnout.[7] The supervisors in this janitorial-supply company faced high levels of emotional labor as a normal part of their job.

CONSEQUENCES OF A BAN ON MOBILE USE AT WORK

The stories in this chapter reveal the complexities involved when an organization tries to address cyberslacking in manual-labor workers. The control dynamics and the negotiations for control were different in this environment because the janitors had less autonomy. Yet they found ways to push back, and I suspect that over time supervisors realized they had to allow their teams flexibility in interpreting the policy because they needed to coordinate to reach their goals. We found that policies aren't apt to be interpreted uniformly across an organization (if indeed they were even meant to, given the advantages of "strategic ambiguity"). We also found that organizational dynamics like trust influenced mobile use and that stricter control over mobiles didn't necessarily improve productivity; indeed, it could be counterproductive.

DECREASED PRODUCTIVITY

While senior managers initiated the mobile-device ban to overcome cyberslacking and increase their workers' productivity, ironically, it sometimes had the opposite effect. Many workers said they now had the perfect excuse to sit down, take a break, and wait for help to arrive.[35] These workers had been using their mobiles to coordinate their activities by calling or texting a colleague for assistance. After the ban, they felt inefficient and blamed the policy for causing them to lose their communication lifeline. Without their mobile, these workers simply gave up. They were frustrated that they often couldn't complete their tasks, so ultimately the policy ended up being their excuse to do less work, in part almost in retaliation.

BANS REINFORCE EXISTING ORGANIZATIONAL POWER STRUCTURES

Did senior management in this organization know that banning mobiles had negatively affected productivity? The data my team collected suggests that in fact they had virtually no knowledge of the daily practices of their front-line staff, especially their use of mobiles at work. How to account for such appalling ignorance? Did they live in a bubble? Apparently. They didn't know, for example, that the janitors texted their colleagues to help them move heavy equipment and look up MSDS about the chemicals they were using. They didn't realize that mobile phones can be flashlights, translators, text magnifiers, and a lifeline to information during emergency situations. These janitors' mobiles *were* their information and communication connection beyond their supervisor, and while, yes, some of the time they were surfing the Internet or talking to family, they also used them for actual work.

In some ways, management's reaction was primarily to quell the grumblings occasionally heard from clients in the buildings who saw janitors on their phone and assumed they were cyberslacking. Managers assumed, just like those clients, that janitors didn't need access to work information through their mobile, so they must be goofing off.

Sometimes inventing a work policy is easier than spending the time to truly understand actual work practices, and my data suggests that senior management took this path of least resistance.

But I suspect that at least the supervisors, just one level up from their team members, knew what was going on. The problem was, they had no power to change the situation. We had limited independent data from them as they were often in the same focus groups as our janitors and thus not completely free to talk candidly, so I've had to rely on that limited data and my observations to make this claim. The supervisors in this organization might have had managerial responsibilities, but they didn't have the formal positional power necessarily to control resources (e.g., policy interpretations and Internet access) that could be helpful for their subordinates.[20,28] They, too, had to live within the rules that upper management made.

Recent mobile scholarship suggests that mobiles can liberate individuals by changing relational power structures and providing access to information and people.[5,39] Indeed, over a decade of research in interpersonal contexts supports these claims.[21,23] But in the workplace, as well as in other organizational contexts, there are considerations beyond the control of an individual. What about policies? Can they change individual behavior? Can they liberate individuals? Unfortunately, my research shows that the policies discussed here neither change nor liberate. These policies target lower worker groups in organizations and, by design or not, serve to keep them marginalized from getting access to the information and social connections needed for them to advance professionally.

Banning mobile devices appears to be a managerial control mechanism that reinforces an unfortunate stereotype, namely, that labor workers need only their hands and backs, not access to computers and the Internet, to do their jobs.[2,29] But this quite ignores the reality that many organizational functions, like basic employee benefits and human resources, have migrated to the Internet.[36] Workers without access to the Internet can't sign up for healthcare and other worker benefits, a fact I saw first-hand when I studied this organization. Recall Daniel, the night-shift janitor who couldn't find a way to meet with his HR representative. Furthermore, certain types of mobile access can help people build their work-related social networks,[26] another key activity in advancing in a career.

Many researchers have found that mobile devices offer a unique way for people to access the Internet because they are less expensive than computers and legacy Internet services. In addition, researchers have found that workplace computer and Internet use can have positive spill-over effects in people's personal lives. These technologies provide workers a safe place to learn about computers, try new software programs, and take these new skills back to their homes to teach family members.[25] By banning mobile use at work, organizations are simply reinforcing the existing organizational hierarchy and ensuring that lower-hierarchy workers can't move above their current levels.

LIMITING ADVANCEMENT OPPORTUNITIES AT WORK

As the use of personal mobile devices at work continues to become a global trend,[14] we need to better understand mobile use in these environments.

"Digital inequality," a concept that has developed over the past decade, describes unequal access to technology as a society-level issue including the many demographic differences between who has access to computers and the Internet and who doesn't.[17] More recently, these concepts have been applied to mobile devices and the various capabilities people have on their specific mobiles.[9,26] Katy Pearce and Ron Rice have found that people with more basic mobile access experience a form of digital inequality that isn't present in advanced users of smartphones.[26] For example, people whose devices have slow Internet speeds are less likely to use applications that require downloads or fast screen refreshing.

What's missing from the digital-inequality research, though, is examining how it plays out in the workplace. Besides the types of worker inequalities that surfaced in the studies I've explored here, organizations themselves can also suffer when their employees experience digital inequality. For one thing, it can affect workforce stability. In the janitor study, the non-supervisor employees reported feeling that their exclusion from mobiles was both unfair and stupid. In the academic literature, the concept of "organizational justice"[15] describes this situation well because for people to feel an injustice, they must be able to compare their lot to that of others. Organizations provide that means. When workers compare their situation and feel disadvantaged, they can experience what's been called "relative deprivation."[27] Feeling deprived relative to others in your company or organization can be detrimental for organizational progress because you tend to voice your objections more, resist the deprivation, and in some cases ultimately quit in disgust.[27,41] Making matters worse, that resentment can become contagious. No organization thrives on mutinous workers.

QUESTIONING KNOWLEDGE WORK

Prior to this chapter, I used data from people I've called "knowledge workers" to construct a perspective on organizational control of mobile communication. I adopted the term "knowledge workers" from the popular press and academic literature, both of which now like to differentiate workers who primarily use and develop knowledge (once called "white-collar workers") from their more "blue-collar" counterparts, now designated "manual workers"[10] or "labor workers."

This distinction permeates much of the information-science literature as well as the managerial literature. I'd like to believe it's a heuristic, and by classifying workers this way, or by job role, it makes organizational technology-use decisions easier. But the stories of the janitors in this chapter raise issues that challenge this knowledge/manual worker segmentation as simplistic. Didn't Chris, the young janitor who used the iPad, access, use, and potentially generate knowledge as he found ways to safely lift heavy equipment? What about the conversations the two female janitors had about using MSDS to understand how to use the chemicals for cleaning? And what about the janitorial team members who doubtless shared best practices with each other from day one on the job, all of them having been "brought along" and corrected or cautioned by their more experienced mates? Is it not possible that these changes in practices are a form of knowledge creation? I plan to revisit these issues in the next few chapters.

CONCLUSION

As we leave the janitors, I invite you to question the job description I chose for them, "manual workers." Is this really accurate? Consider a comment made by Cindy, a janitor with 8 years' experience. In the focus group, she reminded all her co-workers that the reason they have to ask a receptionist to use a landline phone is because their "clients might see [them using the landline phones in private offices] and complain." Even in night-shift janitorial work, which takes place while most buildings are empty, customer-service principles seem to be present. Clients, customers, and the people around us shape our decisions to use mobile devices even when there are no formal policies. When we bring our mobiles into organizations, is mobile use always an individual choice? On the surface it's easy to say, "I need to make a phone call," but this chapter should make us all question the judgments others make depending on the actual device—mobile or landline—we choose when we place that call. It should also make everyone who currently enjoys the freedom of using mobiles at work think twice about whether people around them enjoy that same privilege.

CHAPTER 6
BYOD Policies as a Negotiable Control Lever ... or Not

So far, the data in this book has demonstrated two binary approaches that organizations and managers have taken concerning how personal mobile devices should be used at work: ignore them or ban them. In the late 1990s, organizations typically ignored them because the devices weren't yet widespread and were primarily used by individuals for their own private needs. In the past chapter, I illustrated how organizations can ban a large part of their workforce from ever using personal mobiles at work. That particular policy was really meant to curb cyberslacking,[21,65] but the janitors felt like they had to interpret the policy in absolute terms, so many of them ended up leaving their devices in their lockers or cars.

But, with smart phones becoming ever more ubiquitous and habit-forming, a third approach began making headway in the early twenty-first century: organizations began allowing workers to provide their own personal devices for work use. This represented a radical change in how people used information and communication technologies (ICTs) and accessed information in organizations, and it turned out to be a rather complicated issue. For example, mobile devices might handle the transmission of proprietary organizational data, but those same devices are apt to play an integral role in workplace communication and coordination.

The historical perspective shared earlier in this book reminds us that before the proliferation of personal mobile devices, *organizations* themselves provided, and controlled, almost all of the technology resources. The world changed when mobiles came to work. The entwinement of information, communication, and technology created a far more complex organizational environment, making it inevitable that we'd see emerging wholly new types of negotiations for control over mobile communication.[4] Let's explore these issues further in this chapter.

MANAGING ENTERPRISE CONSUMERIZATION

"Enterprise consumerization," also called "IT consumerization," are terms often used to describe how technologies purchased by "enterprises" (i.e., organizations or companies) became consumer products.[24,31,54] These terms have been around since personal computers were introduced in the 1970s and 1980s, but it wasn't until consumer technologies became inexpensive that the use of the terms exploded. Their affordability, combined with their expansive functionality, meant that employees not only began bringing these handy devices to work but also began using them to access organizational data. Information-technology (IT) and information-systems (IS) personnel thus had to quickly address what essentially had become an invasion of their secured networks.

That's when bring-your-own-device-to-work (BYOD) policies were born. The idea of allowing employees to bring their own technology began appearing in popular-press online blogs and magazines directed at chief information officers starting around 2008. They focused primarily on solving the problem of keeping data secure; policies laying out the dos and don'ts are often how organizations approach these issues. Many types of employees began using organizational IT resources to access, share, and store data. These uses ranged from accessing customer databases to simply logging onto a personal social-media site using the company's Wi-Fi. The way they accessed these organizational resources was often through a personal mobile device, and BYOD was an organizational reaction to what emerged out of this enterprise consumerization.

FREE CONTROL

BYOD policies function a bit differently than many other types of organizational control. Let's examine the work of Aurelie Leclercq-Vandelannoitte and colleagues,[33] who make us consider that *getting what we think we want might be at the heart of the problems we now face when we use ICTs at work.* While Leclercq-Vandelannoitte and colleagues studied knowledge workers, and some of their findings are specific to more autonomous forms of work,

I find their conceptual idea of "free control" helpful in describing this complex form of control associated with BYOD policies.[33] They identified four characteristics of free control:

1) Shift in the location of authority. Organizational members participated in creating this new form of control by providing their own devices and being satisfied with the constraining rules.
2) Emergence of a time-related system. People moved freely outside the organizational boundaries and worked anytime and anywhere.
3) Trust-based control. When the organization they studied allowed people to provide their own devices, it built trust.
4) Unawareness of the control being exercised. Employees became totally involved with their work, used mobile tools to pursue their goals, and experienced what these researchers called "coercive autonomy" (p. 552).[33]

In their study of a consulting company, they began by explaining that organizational surveillance and control practices have changed considerably now that mobile devices are embedded in organizations. They grounded their arguments in Foucault's work, which likened organizational control to a prison with bounded enclosures and prisoners aware that they are always observable. Called the "panopticon metaphor,"[18] it has been used to dramatize the idea that in the quest for improving productivity, employees are often watched and controlled. But mobile devices have erased the notion of fixed organizational boundaries, and thus there are now expanded options for organizational control. Leclercq-Vandelannoitte and colleagues explain that "unlike hierarchical surveillance based on constant visibility by a superior authority, free control involves more distributed control, relying on an information network through which voluntary participants build the means of their own control" (p. 554).[33]

BYOD policies allow workers not only to have flexibility in choosing their devices but also to "voluntarily" participate in being controlled. Furthermore, those same individuals have supplied the physical means—mobile devices—that allow organizations to monitor their behavior and, in some cases, directly control their personal devices by remotely wiping them clean.

This is just one, rather cynical, perspective, relying on critical scholarship's premises, and it's quite possible that many organizations have not been so calculating in their rollout of BYOD. Perhaps some IT managers will read this argument and realize that, without meaning to, they have systems in place that resemble Leclercq-Vandelannoitte and colleagues' notion of free control.[33] It's potentially the most powerful form of organizational control because it lurks in the background, so employees simply forget it exists.

I view free control as the organization-level equivalent of the group-level phenomenon of concertive control. It, too, operates behind the scenes and is often more powerful than overt power structures.[61] There are also elements of concertive control that function within free control. For example, the "work anytime, anywhere" portion of free control can be reinforced and perpetuated by concertive control. But concertive control is more localized because it's based on group norms.[61] Free control seems rather more insidious; employees think they have freedom, but instead control is omnipresent in the form of surveillance and ultimately as the final decision-maker in who "owns" data and personal devices.

Let's turn to other forms of control seen in BYOD that relate to prior chapters. There's considerable evidence that managerial control is woven in and around BYOD policies because, in some companies, it's managers who have to "sign off" on their employees' participating in a BYOD program. Those same managers have difficult decisions to make sometimes because even if they want to be inclusive and allow all their employees to participate, they simply cannot afford running the risk of having a non-exempt employee check email after hours. Selectively allowing participation might be a self-protective mechanism more than a discriminatory practice.

Agentic control is also apparent in BYOD but only with employees who've been allowed to participate in the program. These employees have the personal responsibility to set their own boundaries, and they'll need to because the norms of connectedness can compel, or at least tempt, people to work at all hours. There is also agentic control involved when individuals decide which specific mobile tools to purchase for their work use. But there is also an element of awareness that makes this form of control murky. For example, if someone has no idea that the mobile version of a piece of software contains limited functionality, it's hard to claim that this is an issue of agentic control.

In all these forms of control, negotiation is playing a role, but it shifts depending on the circumstance. With free control,[33] employees may think they won the negotiation by getting to choose their devices, but in the process, many new micro-negotiations have emerged. Now people are negotiating for work–life sanity, and that has reached the level of governments, like that of France, getting involved.

As a communication researcher, I don't typically get involved in the intricacies of IT policies. I find the jargon unnecessarily confusing because I am more focused on using technology for my own goals, not understanding the latest advancements in security protocols. But as my research started uncovering issues involving these policies, I realized that there are many incontestably important communication-related concerns in BYOD policies—and indeed in IT consumerization in general. Furthermore, most of the people issues surrounding these policies have yet to be studied.

What has appeared in many popular-press reports has focused on best practices and aggregated data on BYOD trends. For example, researchers working for the IT/IS industry collected data from 882 professionals, mostly in IT jobs, who represented diverse industries, company sizes, and career levels and compiled it in the document *BYOD & Mobile Security: 2016 Spotlight Report*.[52] The report found that companies with BYOD believed the three biggest advantages were that they increased employee mobility, improved productivity, and enhanced satisfaction. Workers are happier and more productive if they can use their own mobile devices on the go. One caveat to consider is that the data in this report, and many others, were collected from IT professionals, so it's hard to know if their views reflect how diverse groups of employees actually interpret and use BYOD.

The two chief BYOD concerns expressed by the IT professionals responding to the survey in *BYOD & Mobile Security: 2016 Spotlight Report* were security and employee privacy.[52] The report contained, among other things, survey questions on expenditures for data security. It appears that companies are spending a lot on security, possibly even more than they'd have spent if they had provided company-owned devices to employees. Protecting personal devices against malware and unauthorized network access has proved difficult.

So IT and IS groups, in conjunction with corporate lawyers, created policies, and employees would have to click the boxes or sign the documents saying they'd agree to them. But in reality, people do a lot of things with these same personal devices—and in lots of less-than-secure places! For example, while standing in line at the grocery store one day, I heard a woman say to her 7-year-old son, "Are you playing Minecraft on my phone again?" Three minutes earlier I had watched her son reach into her purse to pull out the phone, then type in a password and hide behind the grocery cart to feed his game addiction. The mom did nothing to stop him, but she was fully aware that he was using her mobile phone. And in using her device, he most likely accessed an unsecured public Wi-Fi.

And here's an example that everyone can relate to. Sitting in a Starbucks in early 2017, I counted 14 of the 15 people, most dressed in business attire, accessing the free Wi-Fi and sipping their coffee. People deliberately seek out restaurants and shopping centers that offer Wi-Fi because it helps them stay connected, and it might be where they get at least some of their work done. In an article reviewing existing data on just where people do their work, Felstead, Jewson, and Walters explain, "Office work is being carried out in a variety of different places—in the home, in an assortment of locations within the office and in 'third places' such as the train, the car, and the plane—that for some constitute a mosaic of contrasting sites"[17] (p. 428).

My point is that many people use their mobile on less-secure public networks, and they tend to feel only slightly obligated to keep it secure, like they would organizational property.[40] These examples likely ring true for many people who have clicked those corporate boxes agreeing to abide by their companies' policies. How likely is it that these public networks meet the security requirements in BYOD policies? Yet these same personal devices will often carry proprietary information that no company wants tapped into. And these are all concerns being raised by IT and human resource (HR) professionals.[43,71]

The survey in *BYOD & Mobile Security: 2016 Spotlight Report* also asked what happens when employees leave their company. This is a relevant question because when people are terminated or voluntarily quit, they might still have company data stored on their personal mobile device. Only 34% of the organizations whose IT professionals participated in this survey actually wiped the data from devices 100% of the time, and 14% of the organizations never wiped the devices.[52] I will discuss data-wiping later in this chapter because while it seems organizationally necessary, it is also highly controversial and can be viewed as a personal-privacy issue. Furthermore, if employees had problems using their personal mobile for work, company IT departments rarely helped. Only 15% of the companies offered support for all devices, and 23% of them provided no help when employees had BYOD issues.[52] This means that many employees who agree to use their own devices also give the company permission to wipe all data when they leave, and if they have problems with their devices, well, they're on their own to find help.

These BYOD policies often leave some employees out—like we saw with the janitors in Chapter 5. Results of this survey indicated that BYOD was available to all employees in 40% of the companies and was selectively available to certain job roles in 32% of the companies.[52] Most often the job roles included in the policy are knowledge-worker positions.

In addition to mobile devices, IT consumerization has opened the general-access gate wider, meaning that workers are bringing in with them lots of new technologies and downloading the latest mobile applications (apps). The trend now is toward BYOA (bring your own application) and even BYOE (bring your own everything).[37,55] Jane McConnell, a Europe-based consultant who has followed the BYO trends for the past 3 years, raises some nuanced considerations relevant to certain industries and types of workers in her 2016 article in *Harvard Business Review*.[37] She claims that high-performing consumer-oriented organizations with mobile employees (e.g., those in sales or consulting) acknowledge that their customer-facing employees currently have difficulty finding the information they need to effectively collaborate with their myriad stakeholders. These employees thrive when they are on the cutting edge of efficiency; it gives them the competitive edge. Furthermore, such employees often develop closer relationships with their customers than with members of their employing organization. After all, they spend their days with their customers, not in the office. As a result, they are more likely to sidestep official policies if those policies don't help them reach their efficiency and effectiveness goals. This group of employees will find ways to push the envelope of mobile resources, such as using apps and cloud services to help them do their job.[37]

ACADEMIC RESEARCH ON IT CONSUMERIZATION AND BYOD

Most of the research on IT consumerization has focused on policy, liability, legal, and usability issues within organizations. In short, it has offered more of a macro, or big-picture, organization-level perspective. When examining how individual workers are using ICTs that either they or their employer provides, the academic literature often focuses exclusively on knowledge workers or on IT departments. Furthermore, most of the knowledge-worker research has focused on work–life issues that appear to be of global concern.[30,39,40,41,67,68,69] A notable exception is the work of Carsten Sørensen, a researcher in information systems and innovation at the London School of Economics and Political Science. He's studied ICTs since the late 1980s and his book *Enterprise Mobility: Tiny Technology with Global Impact on Work*, published in 2011, provides a thoughtful account of mobile use at work that spans occupations such as police officers and delivery drivers.[54] He focused on mobility, and while he's situated in IS, his examples and use of literature reflect an impressive breadth of interdisciplinary research. I'll share more of his research in the final chapters of this book because he developed a comprehensive model that links work paradoxes and mobile affordances with workplace performance.[54]

Beyond academic research that's appeared in books, there's a growing interest in IT consumerization appearing in research journals. I've shared related research on work–life considerations in prior chapters, so let's examine some of the more nuanced research findings specifically addressing BYOD and IT consumerization next.

IT CONSUMERIZATION DIFFERENT FROM ORGANIZATIONAL TECHNOLOGY USE

Carter and Petter[8] used established ICT-use theories like the *technology acceptance model*[63,64] (TAM) to see if consumer technologies might function differently than organizationally supplied ICTs. TAM is a highly cited ICT-use theory that often highlights the important role that perceived usefulness and social influences—or how others around you use ICTs—play in how people use ICTs.[63,64] You might remember in Chapter 4, which talked about meetings, that social influences also played a pivotal role in people's use of ICTs in meetings. But Carter and Petter's study found something different: habit and "facilitating conditions" (having the resources, knowledge, and help from others needed to use a mobile Internet) affected how people used their personal devices, not usefulness and social influences.[8]

Carter and Petter suggest that "IT consumerization is fundamentally different from acceptance and use of organizational technologies" (p. 4623) because people are already comfortable using their own devices and they have fairly well-established practices.[8] Essentially, their work-related use becomes a matter of two things: personal habit and whether they have the training to use the mobile Internet—a resource often provided but also restricted by a BYOD policy. If companies assume that their workers need little or no training in using personal mobiles, this could be a problem; employees might not use their mobiles frequently enough to get their work accomplished. Even though habitual mobile use is a growing research topic,[2] we know very little about how people come to understand how to use personal mobiles. Therefore, there remain many opportunities for further research into the entwined nature of information, communication, and mobile use.

Another way to study IT consumerization is to focus on how different IT departments are dealing with it. Put yourself in their shoes. Within just a few years, IT and IS departments had to respond to this growing invasion of their secure networks that they prided themselves on creating and maintaining. One team of researchers, led by Hope Koch, has done a nice job of outlining three approaches used by IT.[28,29] The first is what she calls "discriminating," meaning that the organization provides the devices to specific individuals in specific job roles, as long as the managers of those employees agree they should have a device. The second approach, more reactive and dubbed "firefighting," involves IT departments scrambling to put policies in place to cope with the fact that their employees are bringing devices to work. The third approach, which Koch dubs "innovating," is where IT staffers actively seek ways to encourage employees to use their mobiles, the idea being that advancements like mobile apps can actively move the company forward.[28]

Viewing individual workers as the most capable part of an organization to innovate with their mobile devices offers a progressive perspective that is catching on, but it's in the early stages.[32,36,51] Sebastian Köffer and his colleagues developed a model that compared individuals' innovation behaviors when using enterprise IT versus using their own consumer devices. When they tested their model, they found that giving employees permission to use their personal devices made them more likely to be innovative than if they had used an enterprise ICT.

One industry experiencing considerable innovation within BYOD is healthcare. I cover this topic in depth in Chapter 8, but let me share a couple of examples here. Sarah Marshall studied how The Ottawa Hospital initially purchased iPads for their physicians and residents, and the staff used these devices in innovative ways to help them achieve timely patient care.[36] In her research, as well as my team's study of how healthcare workers used mobile devices in a pediatric hospital in the U.S., innovative practices seem to emerge faster than formal and informal policies.[59] Even in healthcare, a highly regulated industry where violations of patient privacy can get people fired, workers are experimenting with consumer devices that improve their work practices.

Schmitz, Teng, and Webb offer one of the first theoretical models that assumes workers will adapt their mobiles and take advantage of rapid advancements with what they call "malleable technology."[51] For example, people can use their mobile phones as flashlights, and they can also download mobile apps that are helpful for their job but unknown to IT departments or management. They build their model using the group-level *adaptive structuration theory* (AST),[11] but then they show how AST can be used to study individuals. Their table A1 compiles the literature on adaptation concepts in the IS field into a three-page list that is quite helpful for people wanting to investigate these behaviors further. They successfully remind us that technologies aren't fixed things—users interact and adapt them to meet their needs.

One caution in interpreting these findings is warranted. The research has yet to dig deeply into these innovative behaviors to see their impact on the organization. Currently, most of this research—like that in other fields, such as electronic healthcare records use[1]—is focusing on individuals' perspectives. These adaptations can turn into innovations that diffuse and serve productive or destructive purposes. In my work with Ashley Barrett studying the diffusion of electronic health records, we found that healthcare workers felt more positive about using the system when they created workarounds.[1] But that was studied at an individual level. Those workarounds could create problems with patient safety, data-sharing, or governmental mandates. The next step with innovation research will be to link these individual innovative behaviors to organizational outcomes to see the bigger impact of these adaptations.

Zachary Steelman and colleagues published an article in *MIS Quarterly Executive* that provides a comprehensive overview of the different approaches that three big organizations—Cisco, Wal-Mart, and the Arkansas Department of Information Systems—took during their BYOD policy development.[55] These researchers identified four waves of BYOD implementation and were curious to learn how the companies had handled each wave. In all three organizations, they found that, pre-BYOD, employees were using their personal mobiles to work around the traditional systems, even though the organizations provided all the ICTs for their work. Cisco identified the employees who bypassed the organizationally sanctioned system as "rogue" employees, yet by 2014, just 6 years later, Cisco was allowing everybody considerable flexibility in hopes of helping them become innovative and more productive. Ah, but with this flexibility came a high level of monitoring by IT; personal devices were required to have software downloaded to them that gave the company access. Should you want to better understand how these roll-outs occurred, I recommend that you get a copy of their article. It's clearly written and provides a solid historical comparison of different types of organizations and their IT philosophies.

EXAMINING BYOD POLICIES

So what do these policies look like? I'll share some examples because even though you yourself may have routinely clicked "Agree" after quickly scrolling through the maddening legalese of your employer's policy, you may be ignorant of all that you agreed to. Let's examine a sample provided by the Society for Human Resource Management, or SHRM.[14] Note that IT and HR departments are increasingly partnering on IT/people issues,[56] and the fact that a national HR organization has this template online is further evidence that disparate organizational units are having to learn from each other how best to address BYOD.

The key headers in their sample policy include the following:

- Device protocols
- Restrictions on authorized use
- Privacy/company access
- Company stipend
- Lost, stolen, hacked, or damaged equipment
- Termination of employment
- Violations of policy

Their template includes some etiquette guidelines like quieting the phone or turning it off during meetings.[14] It also suggests that employees limit their mobile use while on work time, and it explicitly says that if a manager suspects cyberslacking, he or she can ask to see an employee's bill to determine exactly when the mobile use occurred—on company time or not. There are also paragraphs about installing mobile device–management software to protect against malware, add security, and enable company access to the personal device, when needed. Some of those needed circumstances include when the device is lost, when the employee leaves the organization, and routine monitoring of communications happening through the device to determine if the use was appropriate. Finally, safety considerations, like driving and using a personal device, should be spelled out, and many organizations now agree that any type of mobile use behind the wheel shouldn't be tolerated.[14,15,45]

I chose this particular BYOD template because it was representative of examples I've seen online. Also, and most blessedly, it uses fairly clear language. Many of these policies contain so much jargon that it would take someone with an IT degree or plenty of spare time to look up definitions of terms, to understand their agreement. Want a good challenge? See if you can understand the policies at your own company the next time you have to take online training or click the button confirming you read one of the policies. I should warn you, though, that reading the policy might make you a bit paranoid. I'll share some of those reactions later in this chapter.

My university, The University of Texas at Austin, has numerous documents that have changed yearly and reflect BYOD-related considerations. The 2017 policy for portable and remote computing is fairly easy to read, with minimal jargon, and the cybersecurity training is almost entertaining. But even a clear BYOD policy is difficult to navigate. For example, one of the requirements is that personally owned devices that store or create "confidential university data" must be encrypted. Users must then navigate to a different document to understand the types of data used at our university and what constitutes "confidential" data. I also suspect that people are unclear what is meant by "encrypted" data. By the way, I've taken my most recent compliance training, and I paid attention, so I know these definitions—at least until they change the rules.

At the University of Michigan, meanwhile, their data-security guidelines for research ethics and compliance state the following:

> M+Google Mail and Calendar services may not be used to collect, store, or transmit confidential or sensitive human subjects research data. For a list of allowed and restricted services when storing/transmitting sensitive identifiable data, see . . .

In my personal experience, it can be very hard to convince some students, who've put everything in the cloud, often using GoogleDocs, that these locations aren't appropriate or approved by the university to store research data. And while I tend to be very conservative and use whatever storage system is approved by the university, when I collaborate beyond UT-Austin, I often offer my system as a way to maintain some control over keeping data safe and following our policies.[10]

The simplest example I've found of a university's storage-usage policy is Temple University's Tech Policies Website.[60] First, they define different types of data classification—confidential, secure—using a color-coded system. Then, the color codes are embedded into the guidelines that explain things like this: "for sensitive and unrestricted data, GMAIL is approved if people use encrypted files."

The examples I've provided aren't meant to be comprehensive but simply to illustrate the complexity involved in trying to follow BYOD and their related storage policies. It's easy to use an iPhone to check GMAIL and send a colleague a data file, but is that approved? In some organizations, using a personal GMAIL account is problematic, and depending on the type of data in the file, the attachment might need to be encrypted.

REMOTE WIPE

A common part of many BYOD participation agreements is a data-wipe agreement. These agreements give an organization the right to remotely remove all company data when the employee leaves the organization or if the device is lost or stolen.[35] The ability to wipe data isn't a new part of these agreements, and it isn't necessarily restricted to any particular country. For example, in 2012, Volvo, France, had the legal right, and ability, to remotely wipe company data from its employees' personal devices.[66] But you can see the problem with such an agreement: unless IT departments can somehow distinguish organizational data from personal data, they might end up legally wiping *all* data—including personal—from your mobile device. For many employees, this means that if they lose their personal mobile and it contains company data, they can also end up losing all their personal contacts along with the latest photos of their family. It also means that the company will install software or have some form of access to their device, to make the wipe possible.

It was policies like this, combined with rights for privacy, that led the education unions in Minnesota to aggressively fight a plan, originally going into effect in May 2016, that would have allowed the University of Minnesota to "inspect" personal devices if their employees used them for work.[50] As I traced through the public documents on this case, I found the issue intriguing on two levels. First, many private and public corporations have similar "inspection" clauses in their BYOD policies; after all, they retain the right to completely wipe all data from the device if needed. The vendors selling BYOD-related enterprise security software are quick to recommend that companies download mobile device–management software to company assets as well as to protect their employees' personal devices from malware.[25]

Second, this was a case where unions became involved to protect the privacy rights of its members. As you'll see later in this chapter, I haven't found cases where unions have advocated that their members must be allowed to keep their mobile devices on them at all times—something that would've countered the mobile ban on the janitors discussed in Chapter 5. These areas of communication privacy and access to personal devices are ripe for exploration and will likely be tested in courts around the globe.

GLOBAL CHALLENGES

For multinational organizations, one of the biggest issues with BYOD concerns countries' varying laws. For example, in the U.S., work-related email is considered the property of the employer, but in Europe and Canada, it's considered the property of the employee.[24] Furthermore, when organizations implement these policies, they might need to consider differences between state laws in the U.S., work council laws in Europe, and labor union considerations.[22,35,46] In the UK, The Centre for the Protection of National Infrastructure published its own guidelines concerning BYOD policies, and it mentions the vulnerability of public-sector organizations in particular.[7] Policies vary considerably between organizations, and public entities often have different rules from private organizations, as Niehaves and colleagues found in their study of a German public institution.[47] In Canada, the Office of the Privacy Commissioner of Canada partnered with their information and privacy groups in British Columbia and Alberta to provide their set of recommendations on BYOD.[48]

In examining these documents, it's clear that cultural differences play a role in what motivated the creation of these official papers and whether they target public- or private-sector organizations. In early 2017, France took these policies to a new level by implementing what was called a "right to disconnect" that applied to all companies with over 50 employees.[19,20,45,46,70] At this point in its history, France was focused on finding ways to create better work–life balance for its citizens. It had recently reduced their standard workweek to 35 hours,[70] and this law was a way to ensure that workers were paid fairly for their time and had their private time protected.[45] Benoit Hamon, a French legislator at the time, explained the goal of the law to the British Broadcast Channel. He described it as a way to help employees who "leave the office, but they don't leave their work. They remain attached by a kind of electronic leash—like a dog."[45] By the way, the concept of an electronic leash—and related terms like "Crackberries"[41]—was recognized in the early 2000s, and its problems and merits often appear in published research.[26] One way organizations have already tried to control their members' responses to this law is to automate replies. For example, an article in *Time* reported that the KEDGE Business School sends an automatic email at 7 p.m. that informs employees that email is "out of schedule," a message reminding people to wait until the next workday begins to send messages.[70]

But will this law work? Countless popular-press articles feature interviews with a host of workers and managers saying they hope it works because they are overworked. Yet other articles suggest that this is just a Band-Aid covering larger social problems and a desire to overly control French people despite the fact that the world is changing.[70] When I read about the policy, I found it fascinating, but I also had my doubts concerning how to regulate work behaviors that are increasingly integrated with private life. After all, mobiles have created a number of paradoxes because being available all the time is both desirable and undesirable, depending on the circumstances.[26] An article in the *Telegraph* mentions the common practice in France (and I suspect around the globe) of taking a couple hours off in the late afternoon between 3 and 5 p.m. to pick up kids from school and cook dinner, something difficult to do before we had mobile devices.[20] The *Atlantic* ran an article in late 2016 about Tristan Harris, a former Google employee who blames technology companies for getting people so addicted to their phones.[5] He's creating systems to help people become aware of how tech companies design this addictive software and how people can break their bad habits. But this is proving hard to do.

Legislating connections to others, even work connections, might help set the stage for groups of people, working under the same rules, to agree to stop sending emails in the evening, but this is complicated. Being available constantly is now considered a norm.[42] Some people merge their work and personal email accounts, while others need to collaborate beyond a single time zone.

Then there is concertive control.[61] I've mentioned this before, but it is fairly common for members of a workgroup to establish their own internal norms and hold one another accountable.[57] If a group's norms aim to use the law to disconnect from work, the rule might work for some teams. But it is equally plausible for workgroups—especially those on tight deadlines—to convince one another to collaborate off the monitored email grid. Remember the story of Stephanie and *Sent from my iPhone* from Chapter 2? I could've just as easily sent her a text message, instead of an email, asking her to work on our grant. However, I do hope that if this type of policy had existed at that time, I would have thought twice before bothering her on a Friday night.

BEYOND DATA SECURITY CONCERNS

While most of the current popular press and research literature on BYOD policies focuses on keeping data secure in organizations, these policies also involve departments other than IT. For example, in an interview with Randy Nunez, a senior network engineer with Ford Motor Company's Mobile Computing IT Enterprise Technology Research Division, Nunez explained, "We created a cross-functional workgroup; and it wasn't only IT folks, but we had folks from auditing, from legal, from HR—groups that would be impacted by this [policy]."[62] There is a growing realization that there is more to BYOD than designing access systems that protect organizational data. People also matter.

HUMAN RESOURCES AND LABOR LAW CONCERNS

We are only beginning to acknowledge and study the impact that BYOD policies have on human-resource concerns. In my team's work published in the *Encyclopedia of Information Science and Technology* (2014), Stephanie Dailey and I highlight the increasing changes that HR departments face now that ICTs are such an integral part of work.[56] We explain how HR often works closely with IT, public relations, and legal departments to handle their expanded, often overlapping, responsibilities.

One of my research teams explained the changes in HR by developing the notion that organizations have become translucent.[58] We built on past organizational communication research demonstrating that organizations don't necessarily have defined boundaries where communication occurs either outside or inside the organization.[38] We chose the word "translucent" because it reflects the reality that communication no longer happens inside a contained organization. Today, people unaffiliated with a company can still observe, communicate, and exchange information with organizational members—often through various ICTs, both personal and company-owned. The growth in social media and how employees interact with it at work, in addition to more formally sanctioned social-media organizational use, further complicate the translucency of organizational activities. Is the factory worker who posts a comment about his or her employer on social media acting as a private individual or as a representative of the organization? These are challenging people, privacy, and control issues.

One area where HR is getting involved is with BYOD policies and communication with non-exempt workers. These employees are defined as staff who are paid an hourly wage and are eligible to receive overtime if they work beyond their contracted hours. Exempt workers, meanwhile, are salaried employees who cannot receive overtime pay. If hourly personnel receive work-related text messages and emails when they are technically "off the clock," this could create lawsuits and requirements for issuing back pay for undeclared overtime.[27] In 2014, this very issue was tested in court (*Mohammadi v. Nwabuisi*), and the employer had to provide back pay.[44] Some legal advisors recommend either forbidding non-exempt workers to participate in these BYOD programs or clearly specifying that they cannot use their devices outside of work hours.[35] The SHRM BYOD template I discussed earlier in this chapter includes language concerning non-exempt workers.[14] Yet is excluding non-exempt employees from participating in BYOD practices fair? Some consultants acknowledge there is value in a BYOD policy for hourly workers and entry-level employees. These workers typically don't receive company devices, but they need access to information on the job.[27] This isn't unlike the challenge my team saw with the janitors discussed in Chapter 5. Many companies are wrestling with these exact issues because, in many ways, BYOD is also enabling work to continue 24 hours a day.

UNIONS AND LABOR LAWS

In addition to encountering problems with hourly workers, legal scholars, like Patrick Beisell, are now discussing the challenges of BYOD in light of outdated perceptions of work occurring at a fixed place and labor laws being outdated.[3] Today many employees don't go to a single location for work; people telework or drive to multiple job sites.[17] Beisell's research explains the complexities involved when union organizers, union members, and management use email to exchange protected information.[3] He raises important issues concerning how communication occurs and how information is shared through contemporary ICTs.

His arguments prompted me to explore the academic literature on unions and mobile devices. Neither I nor the several colleagues I contacted about it could find even a single study where unions are advocating that their members be allowed to carry mobiles with them at work. But I did find evidence that mobile-device use is being considered in union worker agreements. For example, in the Building Construction Agreement between the Mechanical Contractors Association of Metropolitan Washington, Inc., and Steamfitters Local Union No. 602 of the United Association, this is what their policy says concerning mobile devices:

> 26. the personal use of electronic devices (cell phones, pagers, MP3 players, boomboxes, IPODs) during work hours is strictly prohibited except as qualified herein. [This prohibition applies to use on job sites, in pre-fab shops and in company vehicles.] Personal use of cell phones, pagers and texting devices during normal working hours is permitted in the case of an emergency. In addition, personal use of cell phones, pagers and texting devices is permitted during the break and lunch periods. (pp. 4–5)[6]

When I read this union agreement, I immediately thought of the policy implemented with the janitors I discussed in Chapter 5. The agreement they signed was very similar. It, too, carried an exception made for emergency situations, breaks, and lunch. Note that this union document extends the notion of mobile communication to include personal devices that can broadcast or play music. The union documents also specifically mention prohibiting the use of these devices in company vehicles, in pre-fab shops, and at job sites.[6] It's likely that these three contexts fall inside the range of what is defined as "their workspaces," contexts where safety is of high importance.

In May of 2015, The National Safety Council of the U.S. created a document promoting a comprehensive ban on mobile-device use in vehicles.[15] It argued that this is important from a liability perspective, and it identified organizations with strong safety cultures as leading the way. I also found this to be the case in my research. Several global oil companies have strict policies that apply to their own employees and contractors working for their company.[45] The National Safety Council document also shares several detailed stories of what happens when organizational employees are using a mobile device while driving and someone is harmed or killed. Not only are these stories terribly sad, but they drive home the message that organizational liability for an employee's negligence with mobiles is real.

POTENTIAL DEVICE DIVIDES RESULTING FROM BYOD AND BYOE

The BYOD literature often touts the notion that workers want the flexibility to bring to work the devices they already use in their personal lives. Furthermore, when people use the devices they like and know, training time is shortened, they need to carry fewer devices, and some people claim that this will prompt individuals to keep their devices updated.[35] This along with data security and potential cost savings on devices are dominant narratives that have driven organizations to implement BYOD.

But scholars and practitioners are beginning to recognize additional hidden challenges to these policies. First, they aren't necessarily saving organizations money. There are added costs due to the installation of software that protects the devices and organizational data called "mobile device management tools."[27,52] In addition, permissive BYOD policies create new dilemmas for employees since now they must make decisions about the best ICTs to choose to accomplish their work.[55] Many of these issues are more communicative and organizational than they are necessarily IT issues. For example:

- Some employees will not be innovative in their choice of technology because they aren't early adopters. These employees will continue using what they have because their current solution is good enough.

- Some employees can't afford the devices and apps that would make them more productive.
- Employees who began using devices for personal use may not understand how to transition to business use or how to combine personal and business use.

As organizations shift onto their employees the responsibility for choosing which devices and applications to bring to work, it elevates the importance of revisiting a body of literature often omitted in organizational technology use, namely, *digital inequality*. Considerable research representing different disciplines has focused on the subject.[9,12,13,23,34,49] "Digital inequality" means that not everyone has equal access or the abilities to use digital tools. There are several well-documented types of digital inequality, most of which focus on sociodemographic influences that make it easier for some people to have Internet access and allow them to engage in different activities on the Internet. Furthermore, contemporary researchers in this field discuss these inequalities as being on a continuum, in a hierarchy, and being multifaceted.[9,13,34] While a review of the literature is beyond the scope of this book (see Hargittai & Hsieh, 2013,[23] for a summary), the idea of a device divide is highly relevant in organizations considering implementing BYOD or even BYOE policies.

DEVICE DIVIDES RESEARCH

Think about the different ways that you use (or have used) personal computers and your mobile devices. Some have keyboards, larger screens, apps, and different software. Katy Pearce and Ronald Rice used the differences in the "affordances" of devices—that is to say, their capabilities—as a way to compare mobile and personal computer Internet users.[49] They were interested in seeing how device use and access affect the types of activities people engage in with their various devices. They used a sample in Armenia, a country with recent Internet adoption, high education levels, high poverty, and a considerable proportion of mobile-only online users. This allowed them to examine their digital-divide questions across different types of device. They found that sociodemographic factors had the largest influence of use but that device type also had some important influences.[49]

The speculative findings from their study that are most relevant to the arguments I advance in this book are that these differences in device activities could impact people's careers. A 2015 Pew report that focused on people looking for jobs found additional support for these scholars' claims.[53] In their survey, people with a lower education level or without a current job were more likely to use a mobile device to access the Internet.[53] So mobile devices certainly have expanded the number of people who can access the Web, but now we are realizing that people need more than access. Participants in the Pew study identified several concerns, like filling out employment forms online and creating résumés, that suggest that small screens and websites that aren't optimized for data entry could further show that a device divide exists and has genuine impacts.

While it's hard to make broad-brush claims that all consumptive or entertaining use of media is categorically unproductive, some Internet activities certainly can be more career-enhancing. For example, scholars have argued that information-seeking activities "offer users more chances and resources in moving forward in their career, work, education, and societal position"[12] (p. 509). Zillien and Hargittai identified activities like seeking job, political, financial, and health information online as career capital–enhancing.[72]

Imagine an employer who has a BYOE policy, and an employee of the company decides to do all her work activities through a small mobile-phone device. This means that she doesn't need to invest in a lot of computer hardware; she has her mobile phone and is ready to start her job. In a related example, imagine an employee who has experienced hard-drive failure on his older computer. Instead of paying to have it repaired, he decides to transfer all his work to his mobile-phone device. These practices might work fine for individuals in certain types of jobs, but I worry about limiting people's understanding of the possibilities of using different devices that offer affordances to enhance their productivity.

BYOD AND NEGOTIATING FOR CONTROL

Most of this chapter is centered on utilitarian power (control over resources)[16] exercised through organizational control (BYOD policies). These are policies, created by organizations, meant to keep their data secure given an increasingly mobile workforce. But quite often, organizations position these policies as responding to employees' wants, and arguably, they're right; after all, before BYOD, employees were flouting ICT-use guidelines and using whatever devices they preferred, organizationally sanctioned or not.

But consider this: the notion of free control reminds us that what we think we want—permission to bring the devices we choose—can also be used to control our behavior. And we often are unaware that this is a form of control. As Beniger reminds us: information processing and reciprocal communication are both inseparable from control.[4]

Furthermore, with BYOD people must educate themselves as to the capabilities of different mobile devices. That will be an important part of the next chapter, where I share data collected from college students as their internships began requiring them to provide more and more of their mobile tools. The chapter following that one examines a permissive—almost evangelical—BYOD policy implemented in a hospital eager to coordinate care among its varied providers. There, the affordances of the mobile technologies used across disparate jobs were only relevant if people were aware they existed. It's hard to send a text message unless you know a person's name and have a way to contact that person. I end this section of the book with a chapter comparing mobile use at work across a number of diverse industries—everyone from retail clerks to fast-food workers. Every worker needs access to information and the ability to communicate, but some of them negotiate differently than others.

CHAPTER 7

BYOD Challenges for New College Graduates

My laptop's just about dead. I need to get a job to get a new one.
—Graduating Senior, '17

Sure, I've used Excel, but it isn't that helpful. All those columns and rows mean I have to scroll and scroll and scroll on my phone.
—Abigail, Graduating Senior, '16

While a few students walk into class with the latest gadgets on their wrists and in their hands, that's not necessarily the norm. Many college students lack the money to upgrade their mobile devices regularly while they're in college. And some students try to get by without purchasing a laptop, so their mobile phones or tablets become their writing and computing resources. Looking around my classrooms in 2017, I see many iPhones, but most of them aren't the latest version. I also see Android devices and even one flip phone, quite a few Mac laptops, some tablets, and an occasional PC laptop. I'm entering my 14th year in the college classroom, and I've taught classes at two different public undergraduate institutions, The University of Texas at Austin and Texas State University, so I have a well-rounded understanding of the financial situations facing many of these young people.

When I share bring-your-own-device-to-work (BYOD) research with my undergraduates, they seem interested but still unaware that they will likely face these types of policies when they transition into the workforce full-time. In the prior chapter, I explained that BYOD is an organizational reaction, in the form of policies, which resulted from the influx of consumer products—specifically mobile devices—that employees started bringing to work. In this way, BYOD is one of the major outcomes of what is called "enterprise consumerization" or "IT consumerization."[2,3,10] While writing this chapter I went into class on January 19, 2017, and asked my students how many of them had held a job or an internship; all of them raised their hands. Then I asked how many had heard of a BYOD policy or an "acceptable technology use" policy; no hands came up. Even after a discussion surrounding this concept, all I saw was blank stares. They simply had no idea if they had ever signed an agreement or received training on using their personal devices for work purposes.

One sees many claims in the popular-press BYOD literature that young people have driven at least part of the BYOD trend,[5,7] but the data are speculative. My experience working with and studying this age demographic for the past decade causes me to question some of these assumptions. I agree that mobile-phone preferences are fairly well cemented by the time young people enter work, and often if they use one manufacturer's mobile phone, they also use other portable devices from the same brand. Apple Computer is the classic example in 2017 because students who use iPhones get to connect seamlessly to iTunes, and that in turn leads them to understand how to use Mac computers.

But are these early life choices of mobile communication and computing tools always the best solution for young people to stick with as they enter work? Furthermore, do they know how to use these tools effectively, or are they simply getting by? There are socioeconomic factors, workplace-exposure factors, and personal/professional experience factors that make me worry about how equitable a BYOD/bring-your-own-everything policy might be for a new college graduate. Let me share the data I've collected from these students, and then we can revisit the questions I raise here.

DATA FROM STUDENTS ENROLLED IN INTERNSHIPS

I was one of two professors teaching the UT-Austin Communication Studies Internship course between 2009 and 2016. In classrooms of 30-60 upper-division students, we saw them approximately once a week, and they spent the rest of their classroom hours in their internships. Students averaged 10 hours a week working part-time during their semester with us. Some of them interned with established or start-up companies that needed help ranging from managing social media to more traditional activities, such as public relations, human resources, sales, and marketing communications.

Other students, primarily our political communication ones, interned at the Texas State Capital or worked on political campaigns. The final group of students interned with non-profit organizations working in fundraising and often wearing many different hats.

My colleague Dawna Ballard designed the original version of this course, and when I joined her in teaching it, I adopted many of her original goals. We wanted to expose these juniors and seniors to things they needed to know for transitioning between college and career. We also provided them exercises designed to help them reflect on the career they wanted and the type of work environment that could meet their specific goals. These topics are important for our majors because communication studies both allows career flexibility and demands that students choose how to apply their education to a specific career.

As part of the assignments in this course, students applied the readings to their internships and wrote three reflection papers during the semester. Meanwhile, I created surveys for them that captured their work experiences over the entire semester, then shared the results with them at the end. My surveys allowed me to collect good data on the following topics:

1) Communication technology use at work
2) Overload perceptions over time
3) Job satisfaction over time
4) Multitasking and work-style preferences

The reflection papers, class discussions, and survey data—all three have guided me in raising the concerns around BYOD for new college graduates. Let me begin by sharing the survey data, which will provide a longitudinal perspective on how college interns used their personal mobile devices at work. Realize that these data were collected for educational purposes, so the questions varied a bit from year to year and were designed to meet the specific needs of the students. But, together, the data reveal several patterns.

EXPECTATIONS FOR BRINGING DEVICES TO INTERNSHIPS

In 2012, a class discussion emerged about managers' expectations that they could contact students on their personal mobile phones. Approximately half of the 44 students enrolled in the course that spring were involved in unpaid internships—a fairly common practice, especially at non-profits. Students in paid and unpaid internships were concerned that they were expected to use their minutes for work. (Data plans were too expensive for most people to use in 2012, so minutes were purchased for talk and text time only.) After two conversations in class around these issues, I created a quick survey asking students how often this was occurring. I had students circle the number, on a scale of 1 (meaning "Never") to 5 (meaning "Always") that represented how often these things occurred. Table 7.1 shows the average scores.

Several findings emerge here. First, the standard deviations are quite large, indicating the students vary a lot in how they responded to these questions. Most of these students believed they were expected to provide their own mobile phone at work (3.57 on a 1–5 scale), and almost half of the students were expected to provide their own laptop (2.95 on a 1–5 scale). In class discussions I learned that some students didn't mind at all; they had enough minutes that this wasn't costing them anything extra. Other students viewed providing their own device as helpful in making a positive impression on their manager. But some students were confused when their managers sent them texts or phoned them, especially when they were off the clock. We had open discussions in class concerning what I call "expectation-setting conversations." For students who didn't have the minutes available to use at work, I encouraged them to explain the situation to their managers and see if they could get that cost covered. In my years of working with young adults, I've found they need a framework and a pep talk to encourage them to converse with their managers, especially when the content's delicate. I suspect that most students never had those conversations because they didn't want to bring up anything problematic.

Table 7.1. QUESTIONS ASKED IN 2012 TO 44 STUDENTS IN INTERNSHIPS

	Average	Standard deviation
How often does your manager contact you by text?	2.38	2.05
How often does your manager contact you on your mobile phone?	2.68	1.93
To what extent do you choose to use your personal mobile for work?	2.38	1.80
To what extent are you expected to use your own laptop at work?	2.95	1.60
To what extent are you expected to provide your own mobile at work?	3.57	1.74
To what extent are you expected to provide your own Internet access at work?	1.95	1.05

This is a population that feels vulnerable; they're learning the ropes, and they don't want to ruffle any feathers in the process.

WHAT ICTs DID STUDENTS USE AT THEIR INTERNSHIP?

Starting in 2011 and then again in 2013, 2014, and 2016, I asked students about their use of information and communication technologies (ICTs) at work. In 2011, only 50% of them reported using their personal mobile there, but by 2013, students couldn't tell me what device they used for work as opposed to non-work. Most of the students' monthly service plans had changed by that time, and they had enough minutes that they were no longer concerned about using them for their internship. As you look at the data in Table 7.2, realize that many of the questions remained the same during the years I used this survey, but most recently, I started asking questions early in the semester and then again at the end. I was curious to see if their use patterns changed during a single semester. My sample size was never large enough to make statistical-significance claims, but the consistency of students' responses leads me to believe that they were able to provide fairly accurate responses when reporting their use. Almost always students would physically pull out their mobiles during the survey and use the data in their phone to report the exact number of their personal texts and emails sent per day. The data in the tables reflects absolute numbers (e.g., "How many did you send?"), percentages relative to all students responding, and averages. T1 means "time one" and happened early in the semester, and T2 means "time two," later in the semester.

Several patterns emerge from this data. First, work emails and phone calls have declined over time. Work texts have remained about the same, while personal text messages have increased. These aren't necessarily unexpected findings. Even though the composition of the internship classes varies from year to year, the types of internships students participate in have remained the same, except for one area. The growth in social-media internships exploded in 2016. Yet that doesn't seem to have affected the general ICTs that students use in their internships. Conversations in class and my observations of students strongly suggested that they were using more social media and apps in 2015 and 2016, but I didn't ask those specific questions.

One unexpected finding is that the number of students reporting access to their mobiles during their internship has decreased. There's one potential explanation for that decline. Some students' mobile use may be restricted while they are working at their internships. The data I share in

Table 7.2. ICTS USED IN INTERNSHIPS OVER TIME

Year (spring)	2011	2013	2014	2016
Number of participants	49	39	34	42
	ICT questions			
People with daily access to a mobile phone at work	100%	97.40%	91.10%	85.70%
People with mobile phone reimbursed by work	0%	0%	0%	0%
People whose mobile phone is a smartphone	91.80%	100%	100%	100%
People whose mobile phone can text	100%	100%	100%	100%
	Messages sent			
Number of work-related emails sent per day T1	10.21	12.03	9.05	8.64
Number of work-related emails sent per day T2		9.58	9.79	7.2
Average of T1 and T2 work emails per day	**10.21**	**10.81**	**9.42**	**7.92**
Number of work-related phone calls made per day T1	6.46	6.49	11.66	2.86
Number of work-related phone calls made per day T2		4.32	8.97	3.45
Average of T1 and T2 Work phone call per day	**6.46**	**5.41**	**10.32**	**3.16**
Number of work-related text messages sent per day T1		4.23	3.5	3.69
Number of work-related text message sent per day T2		4.97	3.18	3.2
Average of T1 and T2 work text messages per day		**4.6**	**3.34**	**3.45**
Number of personal text messages sent per day T1		35.37	48.83	73.09
Number of personal text messages sent per day T2	43.6	43.84	50.21	50.8
Average of T1 and T2 personal text messages per day	**43.6**	**39.61**	**49.52**	**61.95**

Chapter 9 could speak to this trend because in some jobs—especially customer service—mobiles are often put away during work. Several students did mention in class and in their reflection papers that their supervisors didn't like it when they were on their mobiles. Over time, this has become a more difficult habit to control, and that could explain the downward trend.

WORK AND PERSONAL ICT USE VARIES

In 2013, I collected data at two points in time that directly compared students' personal and work ICT use. I made this addition because we had several class discussions concerning students' dislike of email when compared to text messaging. Students seemed to prefer the spontaneity of text messaging; email was cumbersome, so they only used it when they didn't have a mobile number for one of their contacts. These discussions in class clearly supported what had been shared in other mobile literature,[1] but there were no direct comparisons between work (internships, in this case) and personal use. The other important conversation emerging in my classes at this time was students' ignorance of the professional norms governing using email in a work context. I actually had a class discussion on this very topic and even conducted some research to help me better teach about workplace email.[11] So, true to form, I created a survey to learn if students were expected to use email more at work than in their personal lives. The numbers reported in Table 7.3 are actual quantities.

Table 7.3 shows direct comparisons between personal and work use of various ICTs. In their internships, students sent twice as many emails and made almost twice as many phone calls as they did in their personal lives. At work they were interacting with more people who were not in their mobile phone's contact list. Email was a more professional form of contacting co-workers, managers, and customers. Furthermore, conversations in class suggested that students who were in customer-facing roles were using both of these communication modes much more than students who worked in an office and had internal customers. Despite the growing norm of using text messaging as a replacement for actual phone calls, when working with those external customers, texting was still a bit too casual for use in these developing professional relationships. So while the average doubled, some students experienced even higher needs to use email and the phone.

Text messaging not only followed the opposite pattern but was highly skewed toward personal texts. Students used text messaging in their personal lives 8.6 times more often than they did at work. The data demonstrates that students in these college classes used their mobile

Table 7.3. 2013 DATA COMPARING PERSONAL AND WORK COMMUNICATION TECHNOLOGY USE

Personal Use of Mobile ICTs			Work Use of Mobile ICTs
Personal emails sent per day T1	5	12.03	Work-related emails sent per day T1
Personal emails sent per day T2	5.63	9.58	Work-related emails sent per day T2
Average personal emails per day	**5.315**	**10.805**	**Average work emails per day**
Personal phone calls made per day T1	3.63	6.49	Work-related phone calls made per day T1
Personal phone calls made per day T2	3.92	4.32	Work-related phone calls made per day T2
Average personal phone calls per day	**3.775**	**5.405**	**Average work phone calls per day**
Personal texts sent per day T1	35.37	4.23	Work-related texts sent per day T1
Personal texts sent per day T2	43.84	4.97	Work-related texts sent per day T2
Average personal texts per day	**39.61**	**4.6**	**Average work texts sent per day**

devices and communicated with others differently depending on if they were working or not.

REFLECTION PAPER COMMENTS AND BYOD

In addition to the survey data, I learned a lot from the students' reflection papers, where they elaborated on their core learnings and the challenges they faced at their internships. Two themes related to BYOD stand out from the papers submitted.

Employers Expected Students to Know How to Use the Software at Their Workplace

Sometimes students were expected to know how to use generic software like Microsoft Excel, Microsoft PowerPoint, or social-media platforms like Twitter. But quite often, what the internship employer thought was "standard" was actually highly variable between industries and organizations. This included software like business analytics, customer relationship management, website design, and graphics design tools.

Many students had no exposure to these specific tools and only limited experience with more standard tools, especially Excel. I came to learn that sometimes they downloaded mobile versions of the software just to get by. Remember in Chapter 7 when I shared the literature on device divides? Pearce and Rice found significant differences between people using a mobile and a laptop to access the Internet.[8] These are college students who experienced that same device divide, and it hurt them at work. Let me re-share one of the quotes that began this chapter:

Sure, I've used Excel, but it isn't that helpful. All those columns and rows mean I have to scroll and scroll and scroll on my phone.
—Abigail, Graduating Senior, '16

Abigail was the tall young woman who made this comment about Excel. She was always garbed in an oversized sweatshirt and shorts so short that it made me wonder if she really had shorts on at all. It was the style around 2016, but I still found it an odd trend. When Abigail approached me, pulled out her mobile, and questioned the comments I had just made in class about Excel being wonderful at handling many rows and columns of data, I was puzzled. I still remember looking at her, confused. Then it dawned on me: she had never seen Excel on a computer screen! In our department, at that time, few students took classes where they learned what I've heard people call "standard Microsoft software." I knew this was important for my students, so I'd mention free online courses they could take to get those skills. It never crossed my mind that they were trying to take those online tutorials on the tiny screens of their phones. No wonder she thought Excel was frustrating and useless! I took her into my office and showed her what it looked like on a normal desktop screen. I also explained that I don't even like to use my laptop when I work in Excel or other spreadsheet programs. She nodded and looked at me like I had just done a magic trick. On the desktop she could see how Excel actually looked. Then she commented that she might want to learn the program using a shared computer in our library. She didn't have a desktop, a reasonably sized monitor, or a laptop. The library was her best option.

Employers Assumed Their Interns Had a Constant Connection to the Internet

The second theme, related to BYOD, that students discussed in their reflection papers was their frustration with needing to "do work"—most often requiring an Internet connection—outside of work hours. For example, I had an ambitious student, Samantha, who was taking 18 credit hours— 3 more than the 15 credit hours, or five classes, our students normally take. Barely 5 feet tall, she'd come to class straight from her marketing internship with a high-tech company during her lunch on Wednesdays, always sharply dressed. Meanwhile, she was partially supporting herself through college by working at an Olive Garden restaurant most Friday evenings and two shifts on Saturday. After studying all day Sunday, she needed downtime on Monday, so she negotiated her internship hours to be Tuesday 8 a.m.–11 a.m. and Wednesday 8 a.m.–4 p.m., with a 1.5-hour break for lunch on those Wednesdays so that she could come to campus and attend our class. A month into the semester, she came to me frustrated. Her co-workers at the high-tech company had gotten mad when they emailed her a project late Wednesday afternoon and she didn't even open that email to start the project until the following Tuesday morning upon returning to work. She worried that her boss was also mad and that this might affect the evaluation he'd complete for her to earn course credit.

I shared my "expectation-setting conversation" strategy with her, and she actually followed through by meeting with her manager. They renegotiated her work hours and added Friday morning to her schedule. It wasn't ideal for Samantha; but she was the only part-time worker in her office, and she couldn't figure out any other way to be viewed as a team player without being physically available at least 3 days a week. By the way, her evaluation was fine; she completed all 18 hours that semester, and she graduated the following year.

CLASS DISCUSSION RELATED TO BYOD

During the 6 years I taught this course, most students had fairly neutral views on BYOD-related issues. What I saw as the biggest issue many of them faced, oddly enough, was *using* the technology they themselves already owned. For example, many students using a Mac laptop would forget that they needed an adaptor to connect to most projection systems, so they'd arrive in class frustrated that our classroom audiovisual system wouldn't work. Some students used Keynote to design their presentation, and then when the classroom only had a PC, the presentation wouldn't run or the fonts would change. There are subtle differences between Microsoft PowerPoint and Keynote, but they are enough to really mess up a student trying to design a presentation using layouts and fonts that meet class-specific grading criteria. Many students didn't understand how to create versions of their presentations, like with an Adobe PDF, that would remain stable across platforms.

I also learned from my students that I needed to shift some of my teaching norms. For example, I used to routinely specify page numbers from textbooks for students to read. But some students started buying online versions of their books, and they'd say the page numbers were different on their Kindle, iPad, or iPhone. And of course that was the device they'd bring to class. Getting us all on the same page now requires some collaboration.

Discussions concerning costs of technology typically emerged in class when we covered salary requirements and budgeting for communication and entertainment technology. This is one of those practical lectures where I'd show a blank Excel spreadsheet, ask the students to tell me how much they spend in each category, and at the end, show them how much money they needed to earn to support themselves. The cost of mobile technology always came up in this discussion. While several students shared their concerns out loud in class, more spoke with me privately about the burden of providing their own devices. These are some of the comments I heard more than once:

1) "I don't have enough minutes/data on my cell-phone plan/data-access plan to use my personal mobile device for work."
2) "I don't own a laptop. I have to come to campus to access computers, and now that I have an internship, I'm having to do my work using computers on campus as well."
3) "My Internet connection isn't very fast in my apartment, and I work from home. I have to leave my apartment and find a place that gets Wi-Fi to do my work."
4) "My team uses an app to communicate, and I don't have enough memory on my phone to download it."
5) "My laptop's about dead, and I can't wait to get a job so I can get new technology."
6) "My parents expect me to start paying for my own technology and Internet access when I graduate."

Today, I have conversations with many of my graduating seniors when they get job offers. I remind them to ask if their employer will provide mobile devices or give them an allowance. Students are often surprised that they need to ask about this because they assume that employers know they are recent college graduates and probably don't have the latest technologies. Increasingly, I advise my students to negotiate a start-up communication technology allowance to help them get their career underway in the most productive way possible. I also mention that many larger companies, knowing this is an issue for a new college graduate, make such an offer without the student having to ask.

EDWARDO, THE INNOVATOR

Innovation, along with the flexibility that employees have with BYOD, is highly relevant in the current information-technology (IT) and information-systems academic literature.[4,6,9] Not all of my students are going to need handholding to use their devices productively in the workplace. Edwardo, a student I had in 2009, is a great example of the young adults who will lead the way in innovating with their mobile devices at work. Edwardo was a slim young man with a short, military-type buzz cut and blazing eyes that mirrored his intense personality. He sat in the front row of my class, and while everyone else was talking about getting iPhones, he showed me his Android device. I think he was learning how to write code for it, and he wasn't even a computer science major—he was a communication major.

While a student at UT-Austin, Edwardo already had his own company, and he was using mobile tools that no one in the class had heard of. It was fun to have him in class and learn from him. I still remember him coming to see me when he landed a coveted position with a major computer company. He went into sales, and I bet he's done well. He will certainly be that mobile employee who will push his IT department and cleverly work around inefficient systems.

SUMMARIZING BYOD CONCERNS FOR THE NEW COLLEGE GRADUATE AND NEW EMPLOYEE

While many of these young adults are innovative in their use of mobiles, it's simplistic to assume that they're also all informed consumers who've carefully chosen options for the technologies and apps they use. Furthermore, just because today's new college graduates have grown up with mobile technologies, it doesn't mean that they know how to use them productively in the workplace. But most importantly, as my student internship data has shown, personal mobile use and work mobile use are often different.

Hopefully the data I've shared will help people working in IT and human resources to consider the needs of new college graduates and new employees when they construct BYOD-related policies for them. I believe it's a mistake to think that every new employee has mobile devices or even the ability to find the tools most capable of helping them be successful and productive in their job. Ironically, providing training in using mobile tools might be even more important than ever for young adults entering work today because they now have such established practices in their personal lives—practices that may actually hold them back in their jobs.

CHAPTER 8

Mobile Workers in a Hospital

Challenges for Microcoordination and BYOD

Bring-your-own-device policies, or BYOD, run quite the gamut these days, ranging from banning personal devices entirely from the workplace, as seen with the janitors in Chapter 5, to openly *encouraging* workers to bring them and use them.

In this chapter, I share data that my team and I collected in 2015 and 2016 from a teaching hospital. The workers there seem constantly on the go, seeing different patients, coordinating care with one another, and rarely sitting behind a desk. This innovative group of mobile workers, given the green light by their hospital, is experimenting with using their personal devices to connect their dispersed, diverse patient-care teams. Their organization's communication technology policies treat personal devices just like an extension of hospital-provided technologies. For example, one of their nine-page policy documents, active at the time of our study, mentioned BYOD once and focused exclusively on rules concerning how to use any device to access their organizational data and information.

At the time of our study, policies were evolving here as well as in many other hospitals; these hospital employees were moving technology use forward at a pace faster than formal written policy. Few people knew which hospital-wide policies were actually active, and supervisors often reinterpreted the rules. But that didn't stop the interprofessional team we worked with from actively encouraging people to use a text-messaging app to coordinate patient care. The story that follows provides a multifaceted example of how control is negotiated in an ever-changing work environment. Using a personal mobile device at work is simply different from using that same device in our private lives.

HOSPITALS AND COORDINATING CARE

First, a word about the hospital ecosystem and how its complex teams learn to coordinate patient care.

Have you ever been to a hospital? Most of us have, at least as a visitor, and even those who haven't tend to know that the typical big-city hospital employs a small army of care providers. Physicians play a key administrative role in determining specific treatments, making care decisions, and communicating with patients. Physicians have studied well beyond an undergraduate education by attending medical school, engaging in hospital residencies (a minimum of 3 years working as an active apprentice), and often then competing for equally long fellowships in specialty areas like surgery or radiology. Physicians who work exclusively in hospitals, rather than having a separate private-patient practice, are typically called "hospitalists"; many emergency physicians or trauma surgeons fall into this category.

Nurse practitioners are another type of provider playing a growing role in hospital care in the U.S. Much like physicians, they have the authority to make medical decisions such as prescribing certain types of medication. Nurse practitioners are registered nurses who have gained specialized graduate education but haven't attended medical school. These providers, like physicians, operate fairly independently in their care decisions,[18] but they also need to work closely with a team of other healthcare professionals such as physical therapists. They frequently join interdisciplinary patient-care teams that consist of members with different types of formal training ranging from nursing to social work. As you might imagine, these team members vary considerably in their expertise and authority, and getting them all on the same page to coordinate patient care can be challenging indeed.

Floor nurses—who provide primary front-line care for inpatients staying at least overnight—are the most visible care providers. Many times, there are floor nurses assigned to anywhere between four and eight patients each, and they're typically stationed close to their patients because regular contact is important for quality care. Ultimately, they're the liaison between the patient and the physician because physicians typically visit patients' rooms only once or twice a day. There are other types of nurses, some with limited patient contact, but from a communication and coordination perspective, floor nurses are the first line of contact.

Pharmacists are also key professionals in the hospital ecosystem. Just as in our neighborhood pharmacies, they're responsible for filling prescriptions, but they're often more invisible to patients and their visitors. Behind the scenes, they're constantly handling patient information, making dosing decisions, and performing medication safety checks.[8] Every time a provider prescribes a medication, the pharmacist must confirm the dosage, check for prior allergic reactions, and verify that there are no negative interactions between all the different medications the patient might be taking. After thoroughly conducting what they often call a "safety check," they release the medication for delivery to the patient. Now you know why there's sometimes a delay between when a doctor prescribes a medication and when a patient actually receives it. Although pharmacists only occasionally visit patients, they communicate frequently with nurses and other providers.

Hospitals around the globe recognize that emotional, social, mental, and spiritual care can be critical for ensuring that patients have a successful hospital stay and recovery. The World Health Organization, recognizing that hospitals truly are complex ecosystems, has taken a leading role in encouraging interprofessional education and collaboration in healthcare contexts ranging from hospitals to primary care.[48,49] A more nuanced view of interprofessional communication includes what are often called "allied health professionals"—psychologists, social workers, clergy, nutritionists, medical admitting clerks, massage therapists, and physical therapists— who can be asked to consult with patients[53] and join integrated-care teams.[38] Sometimes hospitals have these professionals on staff in the same physical location as the patient; at other times the hospital has to find someone available for an in-house consult.

The final major players in a care team are the specialists—physicians with practices outside of the hospital who are called in to consult or perform specific procedures. Some of them (e.g., a pediatric cardiologist or a neurologist) have surgery privileges they've negotiated with one or more hospitals. But the formal affiliation between these physicians and a given hospital can vary.[5] Sometimes, hospitals have a contractual relationship with individual specialists, while other times the contract includes all the physicians in a given practice. Then, to make matters even more complicated, in the U.S., insurance coverage can also be linked to a single physician, an entire practice, or a hospital. Suffice it to say, what visitors to hospitals see as a healthcare team might be a loosely formed group of providers, some of whom aren't direct employees of the hospital.[5]

EDUCATING AND SOCIALIZING HEALTHCARE PROFESSIONALS

This group of loosely formed professionals often needs to work closely to provide exemplary patient care.[1,38,53] But teamwork's hard, especially when there are well-established power differentials between job roles, like those found in the medical professions. While individuals on almost any team have to informally negotiate leadership roles and the accomplishment of specific tasks, the medical professions have added challenges. Healthcare workers learn their job responsibilities in isolation from each other. There are medical schools for physicians, nursing schools for nurses, psychology PhD programs for clinical psychologists, and schools of social work for social workers. While some medical education programs, like the one at the new Dell Medical School on the UT-Austin campus, are trying to integrate disparate but allied professions, the vast majority of healthcare workers are educated with their own groups.[40] Yes, they spend some time learning how to work on a healthcare team; but they're most often socialized separately, and they learn their job expectations within fairly narrow boundaries. Most of these professionals are licensed; they know what they can and cannot do. If they practice outside their license, they can be removed not only from their job but from their profession as well.

MOBILE DEVICES ENTER THE HOSPITAL

Given how hospitals work and how members of the different professions are educated and socialized, it shouldn't surprise us that creating successful interprofessional teams has been hard.[10,30] The current buzzword used to describe how these teams should function is "patient-centered." This concept has deep roots in respecting patients as unique individuals; thus, when working together, providers should coordinate care around the patient.[12] These coordination goals are where mobile devices have entered the picture. Let's see how they have influenced hospital communication.

PAGERS FOR MOBILE WORKERS AND PRIVACY

Hospitals hire many—perhaps mostly—mobile workers, making their environment very different from a typical office workplace where employees have desks and computers to "do" their work. Healthcare workers move between patients, enter data into healthcare-record systems, and trade medical shoptalk with others. Imagine this scenario: a floor nurse finds one of her patients suddenly in considerable pain. She needs to reach that patient's doctor to report the condition and ask about changing the medication or dosage. How can she find the doctor quickly? She can't leave the patient and run around the hospital until she locates that specific doctor.

This need to locate others is one of the main reasons pagers were implemented in hospitals starting in the 1950s. In addition to being relatively small and inexpensive, pagers are worn on the body; hence, their buzzing can be felt regardless of what the person's doing (Figure 8.1).[37] When all the staff providing front-line patient care have pagers, they can be reached no matter where they are, in the hospital or not. Messages sent through pagers contain only a return phone number, as mentioned in Chapter 1, because pagers are typically restricted to numeric characters. This means that people can be reached fairly quickly as long as they're able to respond when the call needs to be returned.

Sometimes staff have a list of pager numbers so that they can contact one another directly, but it's impossible to know all the numbers in a large hospital system, so often they go through an operator who can look up numbers by name, title, role, and even patient. The challenge with pagers is that they are only a *notification device*; people still need access to a phone to converse about the content of the page. In the example above, the nurse needed the physician to authorize the patient's medication change. If she didn't have his direct pager number, these are the steps she would use to contact him:

1) The nurse goes to a nearby landline phone, typically at the nursing station, calls a paging operator, and gives that person both the doctor's name and the phone number where she can be reached.

Figure 8.1. An image of a hospital pager

2) The operator looks up the doctor's pager number and sends a numeric page that contains only the nurse's call-back number.
3) The physician, now paged, finds a phone and calls the number back.

The elegance of the paging system is twofold: it allows individuals to reach mobile workers, as the example illustrates, and it also provides a gatekeeper who connects large numbers of people playing diverse, often changing roles.

In the hospital, these connections are often between different care providers, but the same gatekeeping system also is used outside the hospital to allow a patient to reach a physician after hours. Have you ever called your doctor's office and chosen the option to leave a call-back number? That's an automated paging system. It sends your doctor the phone number you leave, and sometimes she gets a voicemail message as well. Even though my focus in this chapter is on hospital communication, examining the patient–provider paging system sheds some light on why physicians like having these gatekeeping practices.

Before working on this research project, I had a conversation with an experienced pediatrician about the patient–provider relationship. She commented that some parents go absolutely nuts when their kids get sick. They'll call the office constantly and panic over what she has learned is likely more of a wait-and-see-situation. For example, when she determines that a child has a cold, likely caused by a virus, she tells a parent to love their child, give them fluids, keep them comfortable, and let them rest. Some parents don't want to hear that; they want the quick fix that often involves medication. Those are the same parents who, if she ever gave them her personal phone number, would call her at all times of the night, even if she were not the provider on duty.

This is why physicians like these paging gatekeepers. The gatekeepers help them maintain an appropriate relationship with their patients and automatically route them to the physician on duty or to an emergency room. Imagine experiencing a life-threatening emergency, and instead of reaching one of these gatekeepers, you left a message on your personal physician's voicemail. Your physician was off-duty at that time, attending her daughter's dance recital that lasted 3 hours. By the time she realizes she has a message, you could be in bad shape. A gatekeeper would've instructed you to go to an emergency room and would've sent a message to the provider-on-call at the time.

When the provider-on-duty returns the patient's call, he could be anywhere. It's not uncommon for a provider-on-call to leave dinner at a restaurant to handle an urgent situation. He returns the patient's call, and all the patient sees on her phone is "ID Blocked." Why is this? Because the medical providers are trying to streamline care by sharing responsibility for handling urgent requests. They need all calls to come into a centralized location so that patients don't get confused. If that same patient calls 6 hours later, there could be another provider on duty. If the caller ID had included a phone number, the patient might think she should call that number back instead of going through the centralized system.

In addition to safety, gatekeepers help providers maintain a professional distance from their patients. They want, and often need, privacy protection, especially when they're outside their work hours. Remember what the pediatrician told me? Parents don't always act rationally when they have a sick child. Most physicians work hard to put mechanisms in place to help them live a life outside of medicine when they're not on call. Pagers often serve this exact function.

A layer of privacy protection, along with a sense of routing to appropriate medical professionals, seems to diffuse into working relationships as well. This is especially relevant when specialists are called into hospitals. These are providers who don't necessarily work in a given hospital and are called in to consult or provide care for a specific case. Healthcare workers may not know the best phone numbers to reach a specialist, but there are external paging services that can reach any specialist registered in their system. The paging/phone operator might have four or five numbers to try when reaching a specialist. That's an advantage in some ways, but it can also slow down replies.

PORTABLE PHONES FOR MOBILE WORKERS

Efficiency is sacrificed with pagers, but that extra phone call to an external system maintains privacy while also helping with the logistical practice of locating a mobile worker.

So what happens when the nurse sends a page and then is called away to tend to an urgent need with another patient when the physician returns his call? That's an all-too-common frustration of most nurses.[4] It's the inevitable coordination nightmare called "phone tag"—when two parties try (often repeatedly) to reach one another by telephone but are unsuccessful. While phone tag is simply an annoyance to many people, it can be a huge problem in healthcare. If a nurse is waiting on approval to change a course of action, phone tag can delay treatment and potentially harm the patient.

This concern for timely patient treatment has led hospitals to create policies limiting how long people may take to return pages. Yet fundamentally it's very difficult to know what the person on the other side of the page is doing when the beeper goes off. Furthermore, when a return page is missed, there can be added frustration that might lead to blame and degrade trust between the two professionals.

In the late 1990s, many hospitals purchased portable phones, in addition to pagers, for their mobile-care providers. They thought that if mobile health-care workers always had a phone with them, they wouldn't miss as many return phone calls. Some of these phones contained features that allowed them to initiate calls; others were more of a call-receiving device. Actually, these phones are still fairly common around the globe. Take Manila, capital of the Philippines. In 2016, John Robert Bautista and Trisha Lin conducted in-depth interviews with nurses scattered among 11 hospitals in that bustling city.[4] All of those hospitals provide their nurses with portable phones. But even with these hospital-issued phones, the nurses reported using their personal phones as well. Why? Nurses wanted more functionality than what they found in the hospital phones. For example, they used their personal device to search for clinical information. But there was doubtless another reason: hospital-owned phones are almost comically bulky (see Figure 8.2).

Yes, they do help speed return calls in some situations, but I've watched nurses set their hospital phones down and not keep them on their bodies at all times. Because the phones don't fit in most pockets, they often have to be hand-carried. Naturally, when people need to use their hands, they'll

Figure 8.2. An image of a portable phone

set their phone down. And some nurses also find the phone's vibration distracting when talking with patients.

Let's see an example of how these hospital phones work in the data my team collected.

SHIFT WORK, I'M A NUMBER AND THAT'S FINE

Nurses often work shifts. In his book *The Patterns of Time in Hospital Life: A Sociological Perspective*, Eviatar Zerubavel provides a detailed account of patterns in hospital work and how they relate to time.[52] He showcases the importance of shift work by calling one of his chapters "Continuous Coverage: The Temporal Structure of Responsibility." Nurses' shifts are often 12 hours long (occasionally even 24 hours long), and then after 3–4 days, they're off for several days. These are well-established norms in the nursing profession because shifts can reduce the number of handoffs needed to provide patient care. Physicians, on the other hand, often work 8 official hours per day, though they're on call during occasional evenings and weekends.

The teaching hospital where my team collected the data shared here followed these shift norms. Furthermore, since this was a teaching hospital, it had additional physicians who were medical residents. Medical residents are licensed physicians (MDs or DOs) who've completed medical school but who are spending additional years in a hospital setting, under the supervision of an attending physician, to further their experience. After their residency, they graduate and are now themselves attending physicians, they move to private practice, or they enter a specialty requiring still further training. Residents often work long hours, and they're at the hospital on a fairly regular basis, with rotating on-site shifts for weekends and evenings.

Shift work is, in part, what justifies the story that follows. While about 40% of the nurses in this hospital used their personal mobile phones to communicate at least occasionally at work, all nurses were assigned a hospital phone upon arriving each day on their shift. As I said earlier, hospital-issued phones are daunting, being approximately twice the size and weight of a typical mobile phone. Moreover, these "bricks," as they're often called, contain no Internet access or texting capabilities. They're simply a real-time—synchronous—communication device that all nurses were expected to carry on their persons. But oh, the inconvenience! One look at these phones says it all. "It doesn't fit in my pants pocket and it sticks out when I put it in the pocket of my scrubs," complained Samantha, a petite floor nurse in this hospital. "I often set it down in the nursing station, but I can get in trouble if my charge nurse sees it left unattended."

When I began my observations at the hospital, I wondered how the brick phones worked. Did each nurse have the same phone number every time she came to work? If so, did the phone sit idle when she was not on her shift? It didn't take long for me to learn the process.

In each hospital unit, or "pod," you'd find a 10' x 10' whiteboard on the wall. The one I took to monitoring was typically quite dirty, the effect of nurses too rushed to carefully erase previous messages. It was partitioned into four columns. One day this is what I found written:

Number Notes	Nurse Name	Room Numbers
686-4123	Imelda Gonzalez	6B, 6C, 6H, 6I, 6M
686-4265	Elise Alexander	6A, 6D, 6E, 6F, 6J, 6K

I noticed that when one shift ended and another began, all the nurses met briefly to pass down written and verbal notes. At the same time, the charge nurses for the two shifts also swapped information. They'd sit at the edge of a long table with a log book in front of them and spend several minutes discussing all the patients in this particular unit. These charge nurses knew one another well, and after they finished their "shift handoff," they began laughing and discussing things in their personal lives. But as they departed the break room, their tone changed; clearly, the handoffs were complete, and it was time to start the next shift.

The incoming charge nurse was now all-business as she gathered the hospital phones and set them down right under the large whiteboard. She quickly erased the board and re-wrote the seven-digit phone numbers along with a nurse's name next to each one. I later learned that the phone numbers were assigned at random, and it was rare for a nurse to have the same number two shifts in a row. Because this is shift work and nurses often change shifts with one another, there's no guarantee who will be working on any given day.

As I took field notes during my observations of this hospital, I asked several nurses informal questions about the numbers and the phones. One young, bubbly nurse, Elise, explained that she loved the system. She grabbed her hospital phone, visited all her patients, and wrote her portable-phone number for the day on the small communication board located in each patient's room. When Elise finished her shift, the new nurse erased the old information and replaced it with his or her number for the following shift. Elise also explained that when physicians needed her, they called into the unit and asked to be connected to the nurse for patient John Doe or room 36. In this way, the physicians could always reach the nurse providing care for John Doe. However, Elise admitted she was always happy to leave that large, cumbersome phone behind when she got off her shift.

Physicians also found this process fairly efficient, except when there were missed calls. When nurses didn't answer their hospital phones, physicians would often call the nursing unit's landline phone—there was one phone for each nursing station. But this particular hospital recently had reduced its staff, and during my visits I often heard the unit phones ring and ring when the nurses hadn't yet returned to their centralized stations. When the physicians caught someone answering the landline phone, they could leave a message. For example, one time I heard a physician, Dr. Fisher, leave a message requesting that the nurse handling the patient in room 36 return his call, and he left a specific phone number.

As a researcher, I immediately noted that Dr. Fisher was identified by his name and always had the same return pager number, whereas the nurses were known only by the patients' rooms they covered for the day. "I only know a few of the names of the nurses," confessed one physician in our focus group who had worked at the hospital for some 10 years. Then he laughingly added, "I especially know the names of the nurses who are difficult." The other physicians in the group also chuckled and even made jokes about knowing the difficult nurses he was referencing.

The nurses who weren't part-time and those who had worked at the hospital for over a year knew the names of the physicians very well. They even knew most of the 50 residents' names despite the fact that a third of them were new to the program every July. Medical residencies were 3-year programs at this teaching hospital.

During my observations, I realized that there was something different about having a fixed number—even if it was just a pager number— associated with an individual's name. I even wrote in my field notes the following statement: "My colleagues and students know my name, and they can look up direct ways to contact me like my office phone number or email. No one ever says, 'I want to speak with the person who teaches Organizational Communication and Technology.'" I also cautioned myself not to jump to conclusions and assume that just because I found this practice odd, it might not be desirable in this particular hospital.

The physicians were known by their names. Further, they were invariably associated with the same number—traditionally a pager number. The nurses, meanwhile, were largely *anonymous*, known only by the rooms of the patients they cared for and by a random phone number that varied every shift. When I mentioned these observations to the nurses I later interviewed, they didn't find this difference problematic at all. It was just a part of the job, and it signaled their role in care; patients needed 24-hour attention, so naturally their patient-facing work would have to be shared with the nurse working the next shift. It made sense to them that the patient's room was the easiest way to identify them. Several of the nurses mentioned that they really enjoyed being able to leave that hospital phone at work and live their lives outside of their job. Many of these nurses drew clear lines between their work and life outside of work.[44]

In focus groups with the physicians and residents, they revealed that they'd never thought about this name/number difference before. When I mentioned it, they looked at me with a why-does-this-matter look. Several of them shrugged off my comments, saw this as part of their work practice, and explained that it wasn't a deliberate slight of nurses.

However, my data suggests that this *nursing anonymity* might be a key contributor to communication problems that developed as this particular hospital tried to implement a text-message application that lived on individual's mobile phones. With text messaging, you need to know the other person's name and phone number to send the message. How do you text the nurse who is caring for the patient in room 36? I share more examples and develop this further later in the chapter. But first, let's look at how this hospital came to experiment with text messaging and patient care.

THE PROMISE OF A PERMISSIVE BYOD POLICY

While I just discussed the growing popularity of BYOD policies in the last two chapters, they have been a bit slower to diffuse into the U.S. health-care industry because of patient privacy laws and regulations. The Health Insurance Portability and Accountability Act (HIPAA) of 1996 states that patient health information, of all types, must remain confidential.[25] Over two decades later, there's still considerable debate concerning how health-care organizations should keep patient information private, and personal mobile-device use at work is one of those contested issues.

Like many organizations in the early 2000s, this hospital had long banned workers from using their personal mobiles at work. Supervisors would see employees on Facebook and create policies to reduce what they viewed as "cyberslacking," or avoiding work by doing non-work-related activities.[45] Then, around 2012, several companies found ways to create mobile apps that can live on a personal mobile device and still be what's called in the U.S. "HIPAA-compliant." This hospital decided to change its policy and begin allowing workers to use this HIPAA-compliant mobile app. But the rollout of this policy was staggered, and like many organizations, their official hospital-wide policies changed several times. During one of my visits a manager tried to find the latest version of the policies for me, and he couldn't confidently say that what he printed for me was most current.

Not only did these policy changes confuse workers, but it was hard to implement them across the board. In some units, like critical care, mobiles were allowed, yet in others, if supervisors saw a mobile phone, they would reprimand the user.

The main reason this hospital shifted the BYOD policy to allow text messaging between professionals was management's commitment to improving interprofessional communication. Considering that so many different types of healthcare professionals need to communicate effectively to coordinate patient care, this is an important goal. The constant back and forth of having to page one another with a phone number and wait for a reply was inefficient and reduced the timeliness of their responses. One nurse explained, "I wish that we could just text them [physicians] rather than call the operator, then the operator calls them, and then they call us [nurses] back." Our focus-group participants mentioned that there were many times their returned calls were missed and that not only did this delay care but it frustrated the individuals involved in the phone tag. The hospital's interprofessional communication team saw the encouragement of a BYOD policy, even one that was in constant flux, as a way to improve response times and improve patient care.

In 2014, the hospital began implementing the HIPAA-compliant text-messaging system. This was an app that lived on people's mobile devices and contained a special password that let it function in a highly regulated environment like a hospital. As in many change implementations, this hospital included a small group of physicians as their initial product testers, and it purchased only a limited number of licenses. These physicians found the system easy to use, so the HIPAA-compliant text-messaging app was rolled out to all staff the following year. Then, the hospital administration began promoting this new mobile-communication app.

Encouraging team members to use HIPAA-compliant text messaging to coordinate care was certainly well-meaning, yet implementing it proved far more difficult than anyone had imagined. After a year with the permissive policy, 70% of the physicians were using their own devices to access the HIPAA-compliant text-messaging app, but only 40% of the nurses were. The hospital team offered several workshops to educate the healthcare professionals about the program, and they even added a name look-up system so that no one needed to exchange personal mobile numbers to participate in the text-messaging system. But these efforts didn't significantly increase use.

On the surface, it appears that a BYOD permissive policy would be liberating to workers and help them achieve their care-coordination goals. After all, most of these workers owned some form of personal mobile device, so instead of punishing employees for using theirs, the hospital began encouraging it. To explain the complications our team observed, I'll link the findings to several theories. Most of these realizations reveal the pivotal differences found between personal and workplace use of mobiles. The findings also demonstrate, and intricately link, social and political organizational factors with material and resource ones. Let's examine those next.

Introducing mobile devices into care-coordination practices seems to highlight the power differentials inherent in the medical professions. In the particular hospital that we studied, the attending physicians and residents often use mobile phones—typically iPhones—for much of their personal and work-related communication. In the focus groups my team conducted, the physicians frankly discussed how they'd decide to add a colleague—or not—into their personal mobile directory. Adding someone meant that they could easily communicate, often using normal text messaging or direct phone calls. But if the person was obnoxious or disrespectful of their time, they probably wouldn't add him or her. This meant that the next time that person needed to reach the physician, it would take some work. Some physicians were more selective than others because they wanted to protect their time and erect solid communication boundaries.

ONE-TO-ONE COMMUNICATION PROBLEMATIC WITH SO MANY PEOPLE

Think about your own mobile device(s) as I summarize what we saw in the hospital. With personal mobile use, individuals choose how and with whom they share their mobile numbers. While the number of contacts people have in their personal mobile devices obviously varies, it's reasonable to conclude that when calls or texts arrive, the receiver often has that person in his or her contact list. And when a text message arrives from someone who's not in their contact list, people find it odd because they have no context for the brief message. For example, recently I received a phone call at 10:45 p.m. from an unrecognized number. I ignored the call. Four minutes later I saw that I had a voicemail message and a text. The text said, "I didn't mean to call you, sorry." I was curious, so I listened to the voicemail as well; it was obvious that the call was accidental because all I heard was background music. Yet emails arriving on a mobile device are different. In a work context they come with many more details, including signature blocks and longer messages. Historically, emails are sent and received to a wider number of strong, weak, and relatively unknown ties (or people) in social networks than text messages.

When an employer asks us to use our personal mobile for work, that also means that more people, including unknown individuals, will be able to reach us directly. This is because we often have our personal contacts on the same device as our work ones. Therefore, using our personal mobile at work also means getting more calls and texts, along with being expected to be available to receive those additional messages.

People at this hospital, like most of the general population in 2017, had the industry-standard text-messaging app that comes with most smartphones. Newly arriving messages would announce themselves with a ding or a buzz, and with a quick glance people could read their message. The HIPAA-compliant texting app was different. This app sat on the same mobile device as people's personal conversations, and accessing the HIPAA-compliant app required employees to log in and out with every conversation. The log-in process made using this app much more cumbersome than simply sending a personal text message.

As mentioned earlier, when the administration of this hospital implemented the mobile app, they tested the system on a small number of physicians, who found it worked very well. Keep in mind that this group of physicians knew one another, and many of them were already connected through a physicians' registry as well as a mobile app–based expertise database. This new texting system meshed well with the mobile-device practices of physicians. Further, it allowed them to contact one another directly instead of having to call the operator and have their trusted colleagues paged or sent a message. Because it streamlined the communication, it seemed reasonable that this could positively impact coordinated patient care.

So in step two of the implementation, the hospital purchased enough licenses to allow all members of their interprofessional care teams to operate the HIPAA-compliant texting app. As mentioned before, after a year of implementation, 70% of their physicians reported actively using the system but only 40% of the nurses used it. What was the problem there? The data from our focus groups suggests four primary barriers to adoption:

1) The test population contained only physicians
2) Coordinating full-scale care involved the entire organization
3) Hierarchical differences
4) Personal preferences

I'll address each issue next by demonstrating the findings and using prior research to interpret and explain the meaning.

Diffusion of this new practice wasn't easy because it represented a change from an existing, albeit imperfect, system. Rogers has found that the innovations most easily diffused are (1) compatible with existing systems, (2) clearly more advantageous than the previous system, (3) easy to understand, (4) triable, and (5) able to make success observable.[39] This doesn't mean that every new practice, idea, or product needs to meet all these criteria, but the easiest changes happen when most of them are met.

The traditional communication system at this hospital (and most U.S. hospitals) was asynchronous, a paging system. Healthcare professionals often moved throughout the hospital, covered patients in different units, and worked on different floors. Most nurses, on the other hand, while mobile because they rarely sat behind a desk, were confined to patients in a single unit and cared for a limited number of patients. One way to think about the roles of the different professionals is that the nurses are in pretty much constant patient contact, while the providers—including specialists from outside the hospital's own physician system—are with the patients intermittently.

The nurses had used the large, hospital-assigned brick phones for many years, and while cumbersome and good only for synchronous communication, they were a fairly useful way to reach nurses. In addition to the brick phones, before cutbacks, there were clerks assigned to answer unit phones and notify nurses when they were needed. Finally, nurses were often available face to face. Since they were assigned to a given unit, other professionals knew their general location and could readily find them.

The paging system was certainly not ideal; but it had a long history, and all the players knew the rules surrounding the use of hospital-issued phones and page-and-wait systems. In many ways this was a shared understanding between the professions. But there were clearly problems with the system. Any nurses having urgent requests wanted answers immediately. And physicians, for their part, might slip in a quick call to a nurse between patient visits only to find that nurse unavailable. Additionally, both nurses and physicians needed to communicate with other hospital professionals like radiologists, pharmacists, and behavioral health providers. Despite prescribed time limits for when pages had to be returned, there were often extenuating circumstances, and the delayed nature of their system meant rounds of phone tag before these healthcare professionals connected and had their conversation.

So from a diffusion-of-innovations perspective, the page-and-wait system had its horse-and-buggy aspects, and everyone acknowledged them.

While acknowledging a problem is a key first step in any change process, the process used to implement the HIPAA-compliant text-messaging app was partially to blame for the slow uptake beyond physicians. Specifically, this hospital used an initial test group that contained only physicians. Granted, this app was a physician-driven initiative, so it seemed reasonable that when choosing a test group, the hospital chose physicians. The problem is that people representing different levels in the organization weren't included in the adoption decision or early testing.

It's actually quite common for healthcare organizations to implement new rules and technologies using a top-down hierarchical approach that involves formal leaders making the key decisions.[13,34] Yet Laurie Lewis, an organizational change scholar, argues that the implementation of change is a highly communicative process[20] and that a top-down approach often misses important operational process details that help organizations self-correct.[19,20] One main reason for this is that leaders are often isolated from critical employee voices that can mold the implementation and help make the best decisions for the entire organization.[20] For many decades scholars have shown that front-line workers can be effective organizational innovators if given the chance; when they're involved, they can embrace the change that occurs.[14]

Employees other than physicians shared their major concerns with our research team. Those concerns included (a) not wanting to pay for a mobile used for work purposes; (b) being punished for using a mobile at the wrong time, the wrong way, or in the wrong place; and (c) not wanting to be interrupted during important patient care. Some of these concerns were major financial barriers for certain professional groups; for example, paying for a mobile-phone plan was viewed as impractical, if not impossible, by employees in lower-paying jobs. By not including different professions in the mobile-app test population, the administrative team remained ignorant of these barriers to adoption.

FULL-SCALE CARE COORDINATION CHALLENGES

Coordination is an organizational activity that has been actively studied ever since Henri Fayol developed his administrative theory in the early 1900s. "Coordination" involves how we successfully manage interdependencies between people and tasks to accomplish our goals.[26] And one way we do that is by using managers and team leaders in organizational hierarchies. But coordination requires more than just formal structures. Social relationships prove no less important. Social scientist Robert Putnam, author of *Bowling Alone*, has persuasively argued that three key components of social life—networks, norms, and trust—are necessary for people to mutually benefit from coordination and cooperation.[35] Thanks to Putnam, our concept of coordination expanded to include both rational tasks and relational components.

Then mobiles entered the picture, allowing for an even more nuanced understanding of coordination to emerge. Rich Ling and his colleagues noticed that people were using their mobile devices for in-the-moment coordination of instrumental tasks, such as deciding on where to meet for lunch or telling a loved one you're on the way home. He called these practices "microcoordination and/or hyper-coordination" because these messages were often interpersonal and dyadic; both people needed to have direct contact with the other.[21,22,23] Note that microcoordination allows people to coordinate directly without the need for a manager to help them accomplish their goals.

In our hospital study of mobile communication, we directly observed professionals coordinating care and microcoordinating among smaller teams. But we also learned more about why the implementation of HIPAA-Text was less successful than management had hoped: *microcoordinating in our personal lives is different from doing this at work.* There are three themes that emerged in our data that support this claim: information technology consumerization differences, network size, and hierarchical barriers. I'll explore each of those themes next.

Using text messaging with colleagues is different from texting a close friend. You already know and trust your friends, so providing less context in your message is normally no problem: you're just winging them a quick text, not an email, and a lot can be assumed. Colleagues are another matter. While it's often valuable to receive a message from a team member that you can skim while not having to stop what you're doing, this bare-bones form of communication typically contains minimal context and thus can leave you with puzzlements. For example, a nurse could send this text: "Patient in room 30 needs new medicine now. See chart." Does that mean that the patient needs to get a different (new) type of medicine, or has the doctor changed to a new medicine that is listed in the patient's chart?

Joe Walther's interpersonal communication work on social information–processing theory has guided a considerable number of studies of asynchronous (i.e., not real-time) communication over the past two decades. He's found that using asynchronous communication takes people longer to develop trusting social relationships but that, given enough time, it can be as effective as synchronous communication.[46] This suggests that once you know a co-worker well, swapping text messages just might be effective.

But having stable teams and getting to know your colleagues well is not necessarily the norm in a hospital. The coordination and microcoordination deck is stacked against these co-workers because their patient-care teams are fluid, not fixed. In her work on healthcare teams, Bleakley explains, "Contemporary clinical teamwork then inhabits a place between established routines and improvisation under conditions of increasing uncertainty or ambiguity" (p. 19).[6] The teams vary in size, membership composition, and situational diversity. While it's possible for teams in urgent situations to develop what Sirkka Jarvenpaa and Dorothy Leidner have called "swift trust" that allows them to work effectively asynchronously, this form of trust is fragile and often short-lived.[16]

Most of the technology-in-teams research examines fairly small teams that work together over time and has found that many team-interaction variables play a role in coordination and performance.[28] Yet in their study of the implementation of instant messaging (IM)—another form of asynchronous communication that shares many features with text messaging—in an entire workplace, Ann-Frances Cameron and Jane Webster[7] found that critical mass[27] was necessary so that enough people were using the system to make it truly useful. They also found that IM was often used to supplement, not replace, other communication approaches.

Look in your phone and see how many contacts you have. Now consider how many of those contacts are people you know well. Chances are, you regularly converse with just a fairly small group of people. See Figure 8.3 for a representation of a typical personal mobile network at work. This is also the type of network that many of the physicians in our study had between themselves. The circles represent trusted colleagues—some, true buddies—who could be called up for advice or

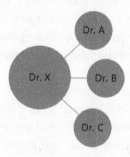

Figure 8.3. Personal mobile network of a physician

met over coffee for small talk. When Dr. X got a text message from Dr. A, he knew Dr. A and had some ongoing conversations that he could remember.

Now imagine that you are Dr. A. You've been using the HIPAA-Text system for a while, but now the hospital has added more licenses, and the number of contacts in your phone has expanded 10-fold. There are people texting you who you've never met and a few who you remember having talked to once but can't remember the specific situation. Then, you get a text from Alex Frohm, a nurse who bugs you because he always makes a big deal out of everything. Now he can reach you immediately through your mobile. A bit later, you start getting messages from Imelda Gonzalez while you're engaged in crucial patient-care situations, and you find yourself wondering, "Is Imelda Gonzalez the nurse working with the patient in 6B, or is she the social worker helping a different patient?" You don't know everyone's name.

Now imagine being Imelda Gonzalez, the nurse for 6B. You know Dr. A by name very well. You also know that Dr. A demands information quickly and gets nettled if you don't prioritize his patients. But Dr. A isn't texting back a response. You feel frustrated and send the same text again. Yet Dr. A has 20 active patients to see, and that means that he's coordinating care with 20 different nurses and different specialists for several of his patients.

When members of those teams go into the texting system to figure out how to reach a colleague, they might have to search through 750 people to find the person's name. It's difficult to remember that many names and keep people straight. For example, you might remember someone

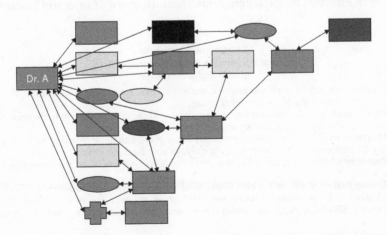

Figure 8.4. Fluid membership teams where Dr. A is actively involved

as Stephen but not know his last name, and there are 16 people with the first name Stephen; more confusing yet, they're spelled different ways. Figure 8.4 provides a glimpse into the complexity involved in this fluid membership team coordination. The different shapes represent people from different healthcare professions who all need to communicate to coordinate care. The 750+ people connected to this HIPAA-compliant text-messaging system don't necessarily know one another. Currently they're sending text messages without enough context to people they don't know or trust. In most cases, their personal mobile number remains private, but they still need to know a person's name to choose their message recipient.

COMMUNICATING IN THE HIERARCHY

Even before implementing text messaging, the patient-care teams at this hospital regularly stressed the importance of using a consistent communication process, aka "SBAR" (situation, background, assessment, recommendation), to share patient information. Kaiser Permanente developed this tool in 2002 by adapting a U.S. Navy concept to healthcare teams. The approach provides a communication framework that empowers nurses to convey relevant information quickly to a physician. Figure 8.5 shows the training tool, used by the American Association of Critical-Care Nurses (www.aacn.org) when they teach the SBAR process.[2]

Even people who have never seen this SBAR tool before can tell that it's designed to be used in a face-to-face environment. Notice that at the bottom of this process, redundancy and verification also play key roles in effective hospital communication. In much of my early research,

SBAR Communication Tool
Critical information needs to be transmitted
quickly and action taken.

S-Situation: Identify yourself and position, patient's name and the current situation. Give a clear, concise overview of the pertinent issues.
B-Background: State the relevant history and physical assessment pertinent to the problem, treatment/clinical course summary and any pertinent changes.
A-Assessment: Offer your conclusion about the present situation. Summarize facts and give your best assessment. What is going on? Use your best judgment.
R-Recommendations: Explain what you think needs to be done, what the patient needs and when.
Follow-up Action: What are the next steps? Who is responsible for follow-up?
Verify any critical information received, seek clarification, ask questions, and read back critical test results. SBAR does not replace verbal communication whether over the phone or in person.

Figure 8.5. SBAR Communication Tool

I examined how people used discrete and multiple media to communicate effectively. In our study of over 60 knowledge workers, we found that people often followed up an initial message using a different communication medium.[43] Specifically, people considered the degree of connection they needed with the other person and the extent of synchrony needed to convey their message. When people had more difficult communication tasks and needed a fast response, they often chose media that were high in synchrony (e.g., face to face or telephone). We claimed that using sequences of media for communication provided "error-reducing redundancy for equivocal and uncertain tasks" (p. 197).[43] Even though we didn't have any healthcare professionals in our study, these findings support the underlying mechanisms of the SBAR communication tool. Taken together, it's hard to see how text messaging can ever be a stand-alone communication tool in the hospital environment. A brief text might allow healthcare workers the flexibility to reach one another quickly, but the comprehensiveness needed to clearly communicate important patient information will likely occur synchronously in person or on the phone.

Collectively, it isn't surprising that mobile devices aren't fully integrated in this hospital and used by care teams. When this hospital scaled up from the small network of physicians to include all potential members of a care team, it became a large network of possible communicators using an asynchronous communication channel, all trying to communicate important information. These teams are fluid, the members don't know or trust one another well, and they're embarrassed that they don't know their colleagues' names well enough to find them in a text-messaging directory. While this embarrassment might persuade some employees to learn their colleagues' names, the cast of characters is always changing and there could be too many people to remember.

PROFESSIONAL HIERARCHY CULTURE

Even though the interprofessional team at this hospital included a mix of professionals who were nurses, social workers, pharmacists, and physicians, they still find it hard to overcome the natural hierarchy found in the culture of medicine.[15] Most physicians are trained to make decisions, while nurses are trained to provide the bulk of patient care.[30,40] These hierarchical relationships are often reinforced in the arrangement of hospital spaces,[10] and my team's research suggests that mobile technology also reinforces these differences.[44]

Healthcare professionals can be reached directly only if both parties have individual-based phone numbers in their mobiles or they know one another's names and can look them up in a directory. Physicians who are working with specialists—often not in the hospital text-message directory—tend to exchange their personal mobile information. One physician explained, "In the middle of the night, it's very difficult getting a hold of the appropriate subspecialists without [having their] cell numbers."

Newer employees are harder to reach because the only way for you to add a new contact to your mobile is to interact with that person and agree to exchange information. One male hospitalist working at this institution for a year explained, "When I started working here, the crucial communications between subspecialists didn't happen because people just didn't know my cell phone number." In addition, workers with less expertise in this organization, like medical residents, explained that no one gives them mobile numbers for the attending physicians. "Physicians will find us [residents], but generally we can't reach out to the attending until they've reached out to us," explained one medical resident.

The social forces at play have undertones of control and power driving some of this mobile phone number–sharing behavior. The irony is that this is a staff committed to improving coordination and communication, yet many of their behaviors suggest they're erecting barriers, consciously or unconsciously, that keep people out. There are also some employees whose prior bad behaviors (e.g., treating all situations as urgent or being uncooperative) make their colleagues reluctant to add them to their contact lists. And some of these colleagues are at the same hierarchical level! One physician used the term "buffer" to describe why his colleagues "don't give their cell numbers to just anyone, including physicians." Forcing others to make an effort to reach a specific individual makes those others think before they ask frivolous questions. Some physicians admit that this can be an advantage since it reduces the communication overload they experience. If a healthcare worker has to go through multiple steps to reach another person, it increases the likelihood that the worker will pursue the path of least resistance and not even try to reach the distant colleague.

USING A PERSONAL DEVICE "WRONG AT WORK" FOR SOME PROFESSIONS

One of the more obvious implications of hierarchy in this hospital concerns who is "allowed" to use mobiles. I put "allowed" in quotes because the employees had to deal not just with formal rules that were constantly changing but also with informal perceptions of mobile-use acceptability. The data illustrates how organizational members higher in the hierarchy express little to no concern about pulling their mobile out at work and using the device, even if the use might ignore the informal rules. This was the same type of behavior seen from the knowledge workers in the janitorial-supply company found in Chapter 5. They, too, were not concerned about breaking a few rules here and there.

But the nurses were more cautious in their decisions to use personal mobiles at work. They had a long history of being either formally or informally banned by their managers from using them. Because they had a designated work phone—the hospital-issued brick phone—even after the policy became permissive, some managers still saw any mobile use either as cyberslacking or as non-work use. One focus-group participant said she often used her mobile to play music while she worked the night shift. She didn't view this as a problem, but she also hid that use from her manager. Other nurses quickly said that using mobiles was fine in some units and banned in others. One nurse said she stopped using her mobile completely at work because her working environment changed all the time and she couldn't remember who approved or disapproved of mobile use. The messiness of policies is normal in organizations because managers will have different interpretations and opinions. That finding isn't surprising, but the fact that people lower in the hierarchy feel like they're sometimes punished for using their mobiles while higher-ups are not supports my claim that using mobiles is another way to reinforce existing organizational hierarchies.

Comments made in the focus groups concerning keeping patient data confidential could be unique to highly regulated industries. I've raised the issue before, but it's worth exploring again because some healthcare workers were concerned about having a HIPAA-compliant texting app on the same device they used to text close friends. Hospitals are busy environments where fast responses are valued. Several nurses expressed concerns that they might accidently send protected data through a non-HIPAA-compliant tool, especially if they're responding to someone's request. Like all medical professionals, nurses are trained to be careful, and most experienced nurses use some system, like SBAR, to help them communicate clearly and accurately. These nurses knew they could lose their jobs if they used their mobile in an unapproved manner. Their comments reminded me of the janitors' comments from Chapter 5. While it's possible that this was also a concern of the physicians, they never openly expressed a fear of losing their job if they made a mistake by using their mobiles at a time others might view as inappropriate.

Nurses also expressed considerable concern about using their personal mobiles in patients' rooms. Would their patients think it inappropriate? While several physicians mentioned being discreet with patients, nurses spend considerably more time in the physical presence of patients. One nurse explained that she often used her mobile as a calculator when she was in a patient's room, but she always told them what she was doing before she pulled the device out of her pocket. Since this hospital was a pediatric hospital, nurses often had more than one person to communicate with in a room. Not only was the child their patient, but nurses regularly communicated with the child's parents and families who stayed in the room with the child. Nurses didn't want the families to think they didn't care about their children. One nurse said, "I usually try and hide the phone from parents." When asked if that perception was different between nurses and physicians, a nurse explained that parents think the physician is doing important work on their mobile if they pull it out in front of them, but it's different for nurses.

It's important to realize that the comments made by healthcare workers are simply their perceptions. Yet in organizations, perceptions of hierarchy affect behavior. I'm not saying that these are correct perceptions or that they're inherently prejudicial. (See Appendix A for complete study details.) But these were interview, focus-group, and observational data that are subject to social-desirability biases. They reflect organizational life, and I've found many of the same behaviors emerging around mobile-device use that have been seen for decades.

Now I'll shift gears and share the final core theme that discusses personal preferences.

USEFUL MOBILE FEATURES AND PERSONAL PREFERENCES

The healthcare workers who used their personal mobiles in this hospital believed that it made their communication more efficient. This finding is supported by existing research that demonstrates how mobiles help healthcare workers reach the right people directly on the first try[31,32] and provide them access to resources and helpful information.[3] One charge nurse explained, "I'd say, functionally, I couldn't do my job as a charge nurse when I need to text a different unit if I couldn't bring my phone out." Yet the utility of using this portable device with a small screen was debated among the healthcare workers. One female physician in her 50s explained, "It isn't convenient for me to look up patient-related data on the phone because it's too small and it takes too many steps [to find what I'm looking for]." This physician, like most workers in this hospital, also has access to desktop and laptop computers that have much larger displays than most mobile phones. She used her desktop computer in her office for all data entry and for searching.

But a growing body of research is finding that hospital workers might not be able to accurately predict the negative effects of using mobile devices at work.[17,29,41] In their survey of 950 U.S. nurses, McBride and colleagues found that nurses believed their own mobile use rarely affected their performance but they also claimed that it did affect others' work. Furthermore, 69.5% of the nurses in their study said mobile-phone use at work negatively affected patient care.[29] It appears that some nurses are really struggling with how and when to use their mobile devices, and they're the loudest group raising patient-care concerns.

Listening to the workers in our study debate the pros and cons of using their mobiles revealed several things. They found mobiles most useful for microcoordination in small groups and reaching one another with simple questions and responses. Having to log into the HIPAA-compliant system with a complex password added considerable time to this process. One nurse practitioner lives with her mobile attached to her at all times, and it has become the only way she communicates and accesses data. Other healthcare workers compartmentalize their work tasks and use different technology tools for their diverse tasks. It's hard to say why they did this, but it appeared to be a combination of (a) finding a small screen inefficient for detailed work, (b) eyesight issues, and (c) a desire to do detailed work in a fixed—as opposed to mobile—work environment.

Another personal preference turned on people's varying toler-ance for mobile interruptions. Prior research has found that using mobile-communication devices in healthcare settings can increase interruptions.[36,42,47] Regardless of profession, some people have no problem glancing quickly to see what the text message says, but others report being *stressed out* by the interruption. Nurses explained that their job was to be present with their patients, and they couldn't afford to be interrupted as it could affect their quality of care, not to mention the patient and the family's perception of them. Yet several nurses and physicians were com-fortable letting their pocket buzz while with a patient; they checked their messages when they shut the door behind them as they left the patient's room. This varied so much between people that I listed it as a personal pref-erence when I analyzed the data.

The prevalence of different perceptions found in this data set probably helps explain why in their review of 18 studies that evaluated mobile-communication tools, Wu and colleagues called for more research on mobile technology in healthcare.[51] Most of the research conducted thus far that examined how hospitals coordinate care through devices has compared mobile phones to pagers.[9,11,32,33,36,42,50,51] But, as of today, it's still difficult to say if the early use of these mobiles helps, harms, or has no effect on interprofessional communication and important care-coordination outcomes.[24,33] We still have little understanding about how to improve the communication effectiveness of healthcare workers.

NEXT STEPS IN THIS HOSPITAL

Many organizational communication studies serve dual purposes: they provide the organization ideas to solve practical problems and they advance scholarly understanding. The practical question in this study focused on helping this hospital improve interprofessional communication between members of their patient-care teams. And already my team has shared several key insights with them. Specifically, we've identified a host of over 30 different information and communication technologies (ICTs) used at this hospital in their care-coordination attempts, something surprising to the hospital. Essentially, members of different professional groups (e.g., nurses and pharmacists) have a grasp on the ICTs used by co-workers in their same profession, but they have little knowledge of the communication practices within other professional groups. We have also found that some caregivers have no desire to integrate their work and personal lives on their mobile devices.[44] This affects their willingness to participate in coordinating patient care through their personal mobiles.

While my team was observing here, we realized that the implementation of this HIPAA-compliant text-messaging system had both practical and scholarly implications for interprofessional communication. On the surface, it seemed perfectly logical for this hospital to tap into the mobile devices that most of their staff were already carrying around with them. And, as we saw in Chapter 6's explanations for why BYOD policies are often implemented, some of their employees had been using their mobile tools under the radar, and flouting at least some of the formal policies, for a couple of years. But what we found revealed the intricate differences between using a personal mobile device at work and using it in our private lives. These are the key findings that justify my claim:

1) People don't necessarily know or trust their co-workers, especially in fluid, ever-changing patient-care teams. Mobile devices might be portable and provide more opportunities for timely communication

exchanges, but they cannot overcome what researchers have spent decades learning about effective coordination. Trust matters.

2) Mobile-device use at work can serve to reinforce existing job-role status and hierarchy differences. Even in a work environment where people are openly trying to create more egalitarian practices, hierarchy still permeates and influences the outcomes of innovative technology use.

3) Some people simply don't want to combine their personal and work conversations on the same mobile device. They don't want to be interrupted, make mistakes by sharing inappropriate information, or pay the bill for what they view as their employer's expense.

I'm left wondering if full implementation of the HIPAA-compliant texting app is ever achievable. What will likely happen is that specific pockets of care teams will implement that app and find that it significantly improves their work. These might be specialty teams, like neonatal intensive-care units, where members are well defined and have the time to develop close working relationships to facilitate successful asynchronous communication. There'll also be groups of caregivers who trust one another well enough to use this texting tool to microcoordinate and enhance patient care. There may also be new teams created between caregivers and patients where future versions of text-messaging apps might improve communication and quality of care.

CONTROL IN THE HOSPITAL

Hierarchical control has reared its head once again in this chapter, but here it's more informal than formal. Managers exercised some control over the specific mobile-communication practices in their units, but the hierarchy we saw here was embedded in the actual hospital professions. Physicians were trained to take control, while nurses were taught how to provide constant patient care. This is a part of medical culture, and it appears to infiltrate the use of mobile communication as well as face-to-face conversations.

The organization, as a whole, lifted a fair bit of its control by implementing a permissive BYOD policy. The interprofessional team we studied was virtually evangelical in encouraging all hospital staff to bring their personal devices to work. This dedicated team was committed to finding ways to break down these disciplinary barriers and level the playing field with the goal of providing high-quality patient care. Unfortunately, using HIPAA-Text was not the organizational answer. In trying to apply microcoordination concepts to their entire group, we learned that a lack of knowledge and trust in team members, hierarchical power differences, and personal preferences kept their teams from achieving critical mass with their use.

In the next chapter, I build on ideas of customer service and teamwork by exploring how people in a host of occupations use mobile devices to communicate. You'll meet a manager who's found creative ways to get her young employees out of bed and into her fast-food shop. Several young adults can't handle jobs where their friends and loved ones have to wait until they're on a break to talk or text. You'll get to see their struggles, often with themselves, as they try to negotiate control over their mobile communication.

CHAPTER 9

Negotiating Mobile Communication in Customer-Facing Work

NO USING YOUR PHONE OR YOU WILL BE SENT HOME!
Sign posted in the kitchen of Buffalo Wild Wings

I guess this is a lie—this sign is a lie!
—Emma, Waitress at Buffalo Wild Wings

But she also said:

If I'm texting around the tables and [customers] see me, I'm sure they would be like, "My wait-ress is texting when she could get me a refill!" And there goes my tip for the day, and that's my income, so I can't do that.

People notice when customer-service providers are using their personal mobile devices, and those same workers know full well they are apt to be judged harshly. The nurses in the last chapter carefully articulated concerns about dividing their attention between mobile technologies and patients, and given the choice, they choose building strong relationships without letting mobiles get in the way. Patients can be considered a type of customer, and with the shift to a customer focus in the healthcare industry, this is likely to continue.

This chapter expands mobile communication squarely into the realm of customer-facing employees. Here I ask the question: *What does mobile communication look like in customer-facing work?* I could have easily chosen the term "service provider" instead of "customer" because human service work is a broad category that reflects fundamental job roles of people who provide direct care to individuals in need.[31] But the data I collected is more easily understood as "customer-facing" because customers are sometimes located inside an organization; mobile-device use appears different when employees work with customers who are not also members of their same organization.

Related research has explored expected behaviors in front of customers including topics like "emotion labor"—the strategies that workers find themselves using to regulate and display their emotions—that are often present in employees whose jobs consistently involve wearing a smile no matter how they feel inside.[9,10,16] This is often an integral part of customer-facing and service-provider work. Kathy Miller and her colleagues studied a variety of employees working in several organizational environments— homeless shelters,[31] hospitals,[32,33] nursing homes,[34] and schools.[38] They found that communication plays an integral role in how these workers experience and cope with stress and emotion labor. Furthermore, the primary organizational concern with these workers is burnout—when employees become worn out from work pressures[29,30]—because this often leads to high turnover rates.[6]

While there is little research linking customer-facing work, mobile-device use, and burnout, recent studies have provided some insight into how these topics might entwine. In their research on burnout and communication-technology use, Claartje Ter Hoeven and her colleagues studied Dutch workers representing a variety of job roles. They found that technology both increases and decreases well-being and burnout because while people are more accessible and efficient, they are also interrupted more and can be hit with unpredictable situations.[40] Kumi Ishii and Kris Markman studied online customer-service workers and found that when they felt a high degree of emotional presence on the phone (i.e., they felt engaged with the customer on an emotional level) they also reported less burnout and were more satisfied with their job.[17] These studies begin the conversation linking customer-facing employees, technology use, and important individual and organizational outcomes, but we must have more data to truly understand what is happening.

In this chapter, I deliberately take a broad view in defining "customers," and I'm also interested in seeing how these workers do their jobs now that mobile technologies are an integral part of most people's lives. Emotion labor is just one of the anticipated demands in customer-facing jobs, so here I let the mobile-specific issues emerge from the data. In this process, I also include managers' perspectives; they tend to have strong opinions and make rules to keep their employees working productively while smiling in the faces of their customers. I've also included several people who provide contrast for these customer-facing employees. It appears that some individuals are simply not cut out to be fully present with customers because they don't want to give up their freedom to communicate on a whim.

CUSTOMER SERVICE MEANS EYE CONTACT AND NO MOBILE DEVICE IN SIGHT

It was only a decade ago when many businesses forbade company landline-phone use for any purposes other than work. Using a mobile phone, in particular, sends a different symbolic meaning than using a landline phone. It is also important to note that most often it is individuals who own mobile phones, while organizations own landline phones. While working in restaurants, several interviewees explained that when their colleagues and managers are on landline phones, everyone *knows* they are conducting official business. Ironically, two people mentioned giving out their restaurant's number to family and friends because their manager said it was acceptable for them to have personal conversations on the restaurant's landline, whereas conversing on a mobile wasn't.

While this was only mentioned by two interviewees and it's difficult to say if this is a trend, there are several reasons this might be happening. Managers agreed with the workers that landline conversations look more official and therefore are less annoying to customers. There's also a chance that as landline-phone use has declined, these company resources are underutilized, so allowing employees to use landlines doesn't tax company resources. What seems to be universal throughout the interviews and focus groups is that different types of phones—landline versus mobile—send diverse symbolic messages; mobiles typically signal inappropriate use at work.

NO MOBILES IN FRONT OF THE CHILDREN

Two people who worked closely with children shared the struggles they have in making sure the children don't see them when they want to have a personal conversation on their mobile. They felt it sent the wrong message when they picked up their personal mobiles because their job was to pay careful attention to the children. Let's meet both of them now.

Rose is the principal of a private school that's experimenting with ways to contact teachers in their classrooms. As a principal, she spends a fair bit of her day behind a desk and in meetings, but when she's roaming around campus or is off-campus, she explains, "I carry my cell phone with me in case they need to get a hold of me." This works for her because she isn't in front of kids when she uses it, but that isn't the case for her teachers. She says, "When I need to reach a teacher, I call them on their cell phone, which is crazy." She knows that the current system makes her teachers uncomfortable because they don't want to set the wrong example for their students. The school tried walkie-talkies, but "because we have our gym and the music room, we kept the walkie-talkies on, but they couldn't hear because [the kids] were running around." Rose also explained that "teachers don't want to wear them" because they're bulky. So now, they're trying to raise money for an intercom system because Rose hates to see her teachers on their mobiles in front of the middle-school students.

MICROCOORDINATING AROUND BREAKS

Caroline, a senior in college, works part-time at a child-development center. She might be young, but she's also held other jobs, one being in a shoe store that had a fussy older clientele who demanded exceptional customer service. For a 22-year-old, she has really thought out logistical concerns of using her mobile phone, but she's also human. Like many other people, when her phone's not re-charged, she feels out of touch. "Okay, so obviously I use my cell phone all the time," she says. "Right now it's dead and I feel like I'm lost in the world. Can't communicate. Can't communicate with anyone." But she's also conservative in how she uses the data plan on her phone because she doesn't get free data. She reminds us that "we take for granted having iPhones or smart phones, but a lot of people might not have them."

Using her mobile at work is a challenge because she's "interacting with [the children] and playing on the playground and stuff, so I don't keep my phone on me. I wouldn't want my boss to see me with it in my pocket." She also tends to wear shorts and T-shirt to work, so "there's nowhere to put it." Caroline does have a classroom while she's working, and typically she keeps her phone under the teacher's desk in that room; but she's cognizant that being in charge of children means giving them her undivided attention.

During her 4-hour shift, she gets one 15-minute break. She typically works 2–6 p.m. and takes her break around 4:30 p.m. This makes communicating with friends and family challenging because so many of her conversations are asynchronous—she isn't communicating in real time through a synchronous conversation. This creates delays that necessitate finding creative ways to coordinate around her limited availability to others. She says:

> I guess it's kind of frustrating for them, and it's frustrating for me [too] because if I send a text message 5 minutes into my break, they don't respond within 20 minutes. If we're trying to plan something for 7 o'clock and I don't get off until 6, [it's as if] I don't get to hear back from them until 6 o'clock.

Listening to Caroline articulate the logistics of microcoordinating around a job that only allows her brief windows of reachability sheds light on a different type of work. There are many jobs, especially hourly and non-exempt jobs, which have formalized breaks that occur at regular intervals. Assembly-line work, fast-food jobs, and even teaching a 90-minute class means there are times people simply can't be reached immediately at work.

But Caroline has a grounded approach to setting others' expectations, and she might also be selecting people to be in her life who understand her work–break, work–life pattern:

> No one that's in my life, that's really important, is super urgent about time. Yeah, like my boyfriend, who I communicate with probably the most, responds every 3 hours, so both of us are very independent. I have friends that if their boyfriend doesn't respond within 5 minutes they freak out and they think something's wrong. And I'm okay, yeah it's normal that they wouldn't have their phone on them all the time. My parents are the same way. If they need to get a hold of me they know I'll call them back.

I'LL QUIT OR GO TO THE BATHROOM

"I quit my job because I couldn't handle being forced to wait until breaks to check my messages," said Tammy, a 23-year-old sandwich-shop employee. Tammy felt like she could do her job just as well if she quickly glanced at her text messages in between serving her customers, but her boss didn't agree. "I have to talk to my boyfriend three or four times every hour. We need that connection, even when I'm at work," explains Tammy. After two warnings in less than a week, Tammy decided she had to get out from under these restrictive policies because she couldn't change her habits enough to avoid being fired.

"The bathroom . . . it's my texting refuge," Alexa, a cook in a burger restaurant, embarrassingly admitted. "Customers don't like to see people who provide them services [talking on their personal] phones. It's not polite and sends the wrong message." But Alexa goes on to explain that even though she knows it's not polite to text in front of other people, she can't work for hours without a connection. She hopes her co-workers don't think she's weird for needing to go to the bathroom so much, but she says that if it's a problem, she'll claim she has a medical condition.

Almost every worker interviewed in these two different studies who worked in a customer-facing industry vehemently insisted that it's inappropriate to be on a mobile device when customers can see you. But it's a different story when they're asked how they *actually use* their mobile devices. Some of them can't control the urge to catch a quick glance when a new message arrives, while others have developed ingenious strategies that let their loved ones know when they are available for contact and when they're giving their full attention to work.

"WHAT, YOU'RE NOT AVAILABLE?"

Caroline has a realistic understanding of being reached and reaching others, but her experiences aren't typical. In the focus groups where various full- and part-time workers shared their experiences, one of the dominant themes was dealing with the availability expectations of others. When they weren't available, people responded negatively.

Emma is an attractive, petite young woman who works at one of the busiest sports bars in Austin, Texas. When at work, she often puts her phone on airplane mode to save its battery. Many of her shifts end after midnight, so she typically calls her parents upon leaving the bar. Her parents don't live in Austin, Texas but just letting them know where she is makes her feel a bit safer.

Being a waitress is "very strange; you don't have an exact break ever," explains Emma. She describes the culture of this sports bar and the importance of keeping her customers happy:

> So when it's slow, you can kind of stand around or you can get something to eat. If it's a football game, obviously you can't. It's a sports bar, so typically I'm never supposed to use my phone because if I'm using it—if I'm texting around the tables and [customers] see me, I'm sure that they would be like, "My waitress is texting when she could be getting me a refill!" And there goes my tip for the day, and that's my income, so I can't do that.

While working her 7-hour shift, she can't use her phone for about 6.5 hours, and then she only uses it "for a small period of time because, for the most part, our managers like us to be outside; they don't want us in the kitchen standing around." Now, in the kitchen, there's a big sign posted that says, "No Using Your Phone or You Will Be Sent Home!" So Emma explains the meaning of that posted rule:

> *The managers don't care anymore, or I don't know when that sign was put up. It was there when I got hired and I know I saw it and I was like, "Okay, well, I guess I'm never using my phone [at work] because I can't use it outside and I can't use it in the kitchen." But then I saw everybody else using it in the kitchen and the managers were there, and sometimes [co-workers] would even be like, "Hey, look at this," and show something to the manager. So I was like, "Okay, I guess this is a lie—this sign is a lie."*

But there was one time, shortly after she was hired, when she was sneaking to use her phone. "We have to wear these aprons around us, so my phone, I kept it in my pocket and the one time that I tried to sneak to check my phone, one of my co-workers said, 'Oh my God, I thought you were grabbing your crotch!' And I was like, 'My phone is there!' And I was like, 'Okay, I'm never sneaking, trying to look at my phone again!'"

Being unreachable for large parts of her day can create some challenges. She had a "boyfriend for a while that was constantly texting me at work and I just wouldn't reply for about 3 hours and he'd be like, 'What's wrong?' I'm like, 'Nothing's wrong. I'm just working.'" She doesn't have that boyfriend anymore. But even her parents get impatient:

> *If they text me in the morning, but I'm already at work, I'll get a missed call and then I try and call back, hidden in the kitchen [and I say], "What's wrong?" Because calls are usually more important than text, so when I get a call from somebody I feel like there's an emergency or something happened. So then my parents call me and I'm like, "What happened?" "Nothing. Just wanted to see how you are." And I'm like, "I'm at work. Can I call you later?"*

One time Emma lost her phone, and it took her a couple of days to get back to her mom. This was when she worked at her former job at a grocery store. Managers had offices there, and they were separated from the clerks and checkers who handled groceries. She described her interesting workday this way:

> *I go into work at HEB and in the middle of working and they're like, "Hey, they need to see you in the manager's office," which is never a good thing. So I'm like, "Oh, great, what did I do now?" So they take me in and they're like, "Someone was calling, said it was your mom. She said she couldn't get a hold of you and she said if she doesn't*

hear from you in the next day, she's going to call the cops." [My mom] asked if I was working and they said, "We can't tell you," so she was like, "I'm her mother, what's your problem?" And they were like, "We just can't, but we'll relay the message onto her." My mom was so pissed off about that. So they got me right away, and were like, "Hey, your mom called. You should probably call her back." When I finally called her and I was like, "My phone's broken, it's not a big deal," she was so mad! I guess if my phone breaks, I should let her know.

Even her friends give her grief when she turns her phone off for her 90-minute yoga class. Emma explains:

I went to yoga last week and I posted a Facebook status before yoga saying, "Phone off, time for some me time." That's exactly what I said, and then I immediately turned my phone off because I really wanted to get into [class]. Then I get out, turn on my phone—mainly because I needed to use GPS to go back home—and the first thing I notice when I get back on Facebook is somebody comments, "What? You have your phone off?" And I'm like, "Just wanted some me time." That's exactly what I said and this person's like, "You turned your phone off? I always have my music on when I work out." And I was like, "This is yoga. It's not working out, but anyway, I wanted some alone time." It's just weird!

Some people are impatient, and Emma is fully aware that while others might want her to be always available, she has to set some boundaries. But her former boyfriend was a different story. He seemed to be unable to ever put his phone down, so people could always reach him.

My ex had this really weird thing where he would always take his phone in the bathroom and he would post on Facebook from the bathroom. He would spend forever in the bathroom and then I would find out that he's Googling things or playing a game on his phone. He wouldn't go to the bathroom without his phone ever! And it wasn't just around me. His friends would joke around about it with him and be like, "Oh, you have to go to the bathroom? Take your phone." So even his guy friends knew that was just something that he always did.

MORGAN, THE FINANCE AND ECONOMICS MAJOR

A quiet guy, sitting slouched in his chair, it's hard to imagine that Morgan is in business school prepping for the financial industry. He's never had even a part-time job, and he's very serious about his studies. He's one of those students, mentioned in the bring-your-own-device-to-work (BYOD) chapter, who doesn't have the latest technology. "My phone is sort of out-dated at this point," he says. "It's still the old iPhone 4, so I'm trying to upgrade. The thing about the Internet is, as phones get better, they require more of your phone, so when you have an old phone, it just gets worse as time goes on." But this doesn't stop his father from expecting quick responses. Morgan explains:

> My dad does this thing where he'll text and if I don't respond immediately, he'll call right after and it's annoying as hell. I'll be in class and it's like obviously I'm doing something right now and he'll call and I'll be just like, "Dude, no!" I think I can tell my dad, "Dude, I'm really busy at those times. If I don't respond, it's like I'll get back to you at some point." I just don't care to [be that direct with him].

So far, I've shared examples of young people who are in close contact with their parents and friends, even when they're at work. While it makes sense that parents might be worried about their youngsters discovering the world without them, the expectations of availability don't seem to be age-specific. Once a parent, always a parent. And when expectations are set, they might be cemented for life.

LOUISE AND HER 74-YEAR-OLD MOM

Louise is a retail manager in her 50s who openly admits she's not the most computer-savvy, or even mobile device–savvy, person, but she still has to use multiple devices constantly when at work. She finds it frustrating when her younger workers are relentlessly on their phones and their attention is sucked away from work tasks. She clarifies:

> You have to be careful, because one of my younger employees will turn onto whatever it is he's typing in there and kind of tune off to everything else. And I have to remind him two or three times, "Oh, I asked you to do such and such," and, you know, he'll go do it, but then five minutes later, he's back to type, type, type, type.

But Louise says she likes to "ignore the computer when I'm at home." She's an artist and loves to spend hours painting in peace. Even though she's been married and living on her own for over 35 years, her mother still expects her to be responsive to her emails. She explains:

> So the next time I hear from my mother—my 74-year-old mother in Florida—the next time I hear from her, she lets me have it for ignoring her emails. [She says] "Why

didn't you email me back? I didn't see it." And she lets me have it. I actually kind of think about it later. It's really funny.

FROM CONSTANT CONNECTION TO SURVEILLED DISCONNECTION

Expectations of availability can also be mutual. Rene is a 23-year-old law clerk who's tied at the hip to her boyfriend. When at work, she's essentially unsupervised, and filing legal documents can get quite tedious. Rene explains: "I'm in a room pretty much by myself and so I have my headphones in with my iPod. I can connect to Wi-Fi and I can also have my phone, cause the trainers don't, like, really watch us and it's a casual job for us, so me and the other file clerk, like, we can have our phone out."

Over the past few months, she and her boyfriend have started playing an online card game, and this happens while she's at work. "Yeah, it's a card game online and we can be talking on Facebook and then like switch to the game and then switch to texting," explains Rene. She was somewhat embarrassed to admit that this is how she spends her time at work, but as she described her interactions with her boyfriend, it became obvious that she epitomized the definition of a cyberslacker—doing non-work on company time.[42]

Rene was in a focus group with Kim, a call-center employee who had to last an entire shift without checking her mobile. As soon as Kim mentioned her regimented work environment, Rene loudly interrupted:

> I don't think I could go 9 hours without my phone! Well, just because, like, I don't know, it just feels like I, like, just because of, like, communication with my boyfriend, like I— I mean, it's not always constant, but it's just like we check up on each other throughout the day, and if we go 2 or 3 hours without talking, it's just like, "Hey, how's it going?" And so like 9 hours; I'd be worried if I didn't hear from him. I mean, I'm sure he's just sitting at home doing nothing, but still, just for peace of mind.

Kim, in stark contrast, spends her workday with a headset on and a computer connected to an automatic dialing system. She just celebrated her 6-month anniversary calling prospective donors to see if they are willing to support the university's education and sports programs. Her working environment is one of extreme surveillance as she describes:

> Since we're calling—we're fundraising for the university—people will give out their credit card information a lot. [Because] you can obviously write that down or record it or store it, it's in our contract that you're not supposed to have your cell phone out.

[Also] there's a webcam that's attached to the calling system, so alumni can watch and see that we're actually connected to the university, which is nice. If they see on the webcam that we have our cell phones out, it doesn't look very professional and it's a breach of contract. We also have the bosses looking at the camera every so often.

Fundraising shifts run a minimum of 4 hours, but Kim's normal shift is 9 hours. Her ability to manage the separation between her work and personal life had recently earned her a promotion to a training manager, and now she helps new employees understand they have to disconnect or quit.

She and her co-workers do get breaks during their long shifts, and on breaks, she explains, "You can use [a personal cell phone] as long as you're not in the center, so you have to go outside and use it." While they're working, they're required to keep their mobile devices in bags underneath a table; pockets are unacceptable. Even though she has adapted to this environment, she admits, "It's not the most ideal because sometimes you'll go to the bathroom so you can check it. I know the boss is like 'No, just don't take it, don't use it at all,' but we kind of need to check it sometimes because 9 hours is a long time to go without anything."

This 9-hour comment is what Rene, the law clerk in the same focus group, couldn't believe. Kim even turned to her and said, "To your point with you wanting to text your boyfriend all the time, a lot of people quit because they can't deal with the fact that they can't have their phones. Yeah, there's really high turnover. People stay for like 2 weeks and if they decide they can't deal with it, then they just go."

Yet wanting to use a personal cell phone while working in fundraising seems to be more than simply keeping in contact with friends and family; it also serves a vital supportive role when all you hear is no, no, and no! In her role as training manager, Kim explains:

I get to talk to the new hires about what's going on, what they're struggling with, what they like or what they're really good at. So you get to talk to them and see how they really feel about the job. A lot of them are just like "I don't like the rejection. I want to be able to talk to my friends. It'd be so much better if I was just able to get on Facebook while I'm waiting for somebody to answer the phone."

In addition to craving social support when handling all this rejection, employees have to adjust to being out of contact and unavailable to others for that long. But Kim reminds us of the reality that having a job, any job, requires some personal sacrifices: "So you have to deal with putting off your friends and your other commitments. But that's what a job is anyway, so you wouldn't have been in contact with them [anyway]. You would still have to say 'No, I can't do lunch with you.'" After working here for 6 months, she has most of her friends trained. "They know that I'm working here now, so they just ask, 'Are you at work?' And if I don't respond, they're like, 'She's at work,' which is good. The only people who really have trouble with it are my parents who are like, 'I called you, why do you not answer?'" Regardless of age, parents seem to be the hardest to train.

GROW UP! OR PERHAPS THEY CAN'T HELP IT

The stories shared so far suggest that some people simply can't handle jobs where they can't, or shouldn't, use their mobile devices when they want. Is this a lack of self-discipline? Or is there something else going on that pressures people into feeling this constant need for connection? Actually, it's probably some of both.

Joseph Bayer and his colleagues have been studying the norms and habits of mobile-technology use.[2,3,5] Their work is pushing beyond the psychological, predominantly personality trait–based research, by considering cognitive and even societal processes.[2,5] But even their work is showing that people who are more impulsive and mindless—two psychological self-regulatory traits—are more likely to engage in texting by habit.[3] However, now that people rely on the affordances of mobile technologies,[37] specifically the link to others, this can foster a dependency on mobile devices.[9,27] While most information and communication technology (ICT) use depends on the context where the ICT is used, mobile media, in particular, "blurs the lines between situation and disposition due to its constant companionship" (p. 91).[3] Mobile phones are with people always, whether at home, work, play, or somewhere in between.

Kathleen Cumiskey and Rich Ling acknowledge that work contacts, in addition to more intimate relationships, can make people feel a responsibility to keep their mobiles with them at all times, but their research doesn't dive deeply into availability issues of mobiles at work.[9] The data in this chapter does precisely that by revealing the struggles people feel when they need to be present with customers yet know that friends and family may also want 24/7 access. Jeffrey Hall and Nancy Baym, who've studied these interpersonal dynamics, found that while having mobile devices can lead people to feel more connected, they can also lead to overdependence and feelings of entrapment. Their study of friendships and what they call "mobile maintenance expectations" found that as people feel entrapped, they also become less satisfied with their friendships.[15] Too much connection can harm personal relationships, just like being too disconnected.

In addition to the impact on personal relationships, people can feel anxious when they aren't connected. Nancy Cheever and colleagues conducted an experiment with college students where they either took away their phones for the 75-minute experiment or asked them to power down and put them away. They also measured whether people were heavy, moderate, or light users of their mobile devices. Heavy and moderate users of mobiles became increasingly anxious over a 75-minute time period when they were restricted from use, but it was the heavy users who were considerably more anxious when their phone was physically taken away.[7]

These complex feelings of needing and wanting to be on mobile phones constantly have led some people to call this an addiction. But mobile scholars caution that we need more research to understand what is actually happening. After all, as people are throwing around the term "media addiction," this predominantly clinical term might be inaccurate.[20,21,22] Moving forward, we need to understand why people behave in these automatic ways and how they become so immersed in the events occurring through their mobile devices that they appear unable to disengage.[1,4]

Several of the people you've met in this chapter might be able to provide insight into mobile-device habits and immersive behaviors because they've managed to disengage for several hours at a time while working a customer-facing shift. I don't know how each of my study participants would score on a psychological-trait survey, but that would be useful data to combine with the type of qualitative study found in this chapter.

Let's turn now to how managers handle their employees' reluctance to disconnect.

BEING THE BOSS WHO CREATES THE POLICIES

Bridget is a 37-year-old manager of four different leasing companies who oversees a physical office but is also on the go and works remotely 1 day a week. She offers several perspectives on mobile-phone use at work because she sets the policies, enforces them, and then feels obligated—most of the time—to follow those rules herself. She's been working with this company for a couple of years now and manages 15 employees. But before this job, she worked in banking for 10 years, and she also has experience, through her husband, with mobile use in industrial manufacturing organizations.

I get to set the rules, so I made it a rule that there's no cell-phone use in the office, which is usually an 8-hour workday. I've noticed that I get more productivity out of the employees when I do that. I had to have that conversation with my employees. I don't want to come across harsh or mean, but by the time you spend time on your Twitter, your Facebook, your email, your texts, I've lost about 2 to 3 hours of your attention, so put it off and handle it on your breaks. I do make sure that they get two 15-minute breaks and a 30-minute lunch, so that way they have ample time to check messages. I use my phone a lot, but when I am in the office, I do the same thing out of pure respect for the rule. I've noticed I'm a lot more productive when I follow the rule myself.

Bridget certainly wants to keep her employees on task, but she also used her past experiences to help her decide that setting this rule was important for professionalism. She worked for "the number two corporate bank in the U.S. and they had tested [cell-phone use at work]." They found that when customers walked in the door and saw banking associates on their personal mobiles, they viewed this as unprofessional. At her husband's company, a major plastics and industrial chemical manufacturer, employees were banned from using smartphones at work because there "was a fear [of people] with smartphones taking pictures of trade secrets and sharing it with competitors." She also said that "safety is the backbone to a lot of those types of industries. They have corporate protocols and then they have social protocols. If you were to get hurt outside of the job, you might as well be on the job." So their mobile-use policies are quite strict and include forbidding driving when operating any type of mobile device.

But Bridget also knows that never using a cell phone at work can be hard, and because she often works remotely out of her home, she admits, "I kind of feel hypocritical" because at home she has freedom from that rule. She's also had jobs where she herself couldn't use her mobile phone. She admits the struggles and explains how she and her employees work around this rule:

I've been in positions at work where I sneaked, and I know this is terrible, but I'll be honest. I'm in the office. I've got to set the example. I can't have my employees watching me on a phone when I was like, "Don't you do it!" And so there's been times when [my cell phone] will go off and my instinct is to look at it and I have to—"oh, that's my boss"—kind of step out. Unfortunately, sometimes it's kind of a fib or white lie for me to step out and handle something that needs to be handled.

She also sees her employees and other people in her building sneaking out to respond to messages. "In hallways," she says, "they'll kind of veer into a wall and they do their texting [while walking]." She's also "seen ladies in the restroom, in the corner, and it's like, okay, so you have to go to a restroom to have privacy to text or post or whatever you're doing. So it's like there's no privacy. I guess the restroom is the closest you can get."

On days when she works in the office and abides by the rule she has set, her mother can sometimes be a problem, even though Bridget is 37 years old. "Oh, God love her, my mother has learned to text and she texts books! So if I don't respond very quickly, that leads to my mother worrying, and with me being 5 hours from home, it's not a good thing." Bridget tries to proactively let people know her availability, but this is cumbersome:

> I'm going to be working, I'm going to be unavailable, but my gosh, by the time you let your husband know, your mom know, your dad know, your brother. . . . Then someone is going to be upset because they didn't know you were unavailable. I have yet to learn the social protocol [helping people not] be offended if I don't answer or respond in some form, fashion, or way. I'm not dead. If you don't hear from me in 24 hours, then call the police.

But sometimes emergencies will arise. Back when she was working at the bank, Bridget was also taking courses at a junior college. Thankfully it was a small campus, but even so, it took school officials a while to notify her about an urgent situation:

> We were facing college exams and all cell phones had to be turned off. Mine was turned off. Unfortunately, I had a family member get in a very bad auto accident and pass away. My husband, of course, calls my cell phone, obviously knows it's off because it goes straight to voicemail, contacts the school to have the school come and find me at whatever class I was in. It was a night class and it took them 35 minutes to find me and we only have six buildings on the campus.

Bridget might be a manager, but her vast life experiences help her empathize with her employees. She knows that rules will help productivity, but she's also aware that emergencies can crop up and that her employees will work around the rules when necessary. She didn't say this, but during her interview I kept thinking that on her days out of the office, her rules probably don't apply. After all, how can she be the enforcer when she's not physically present?

MANAGING (E.G., MOTHERING) TO GET YOUNG EMPLOYEES TO WORK

In one focus group, I had three managers, all with similar experiences using their mobiles to manage their young, 20-something workforces. I'll introduce you to these managers because even though they had never met prior to the focus group, they bonded through their experiences adapting to what had become their reliance on using mobiles to microcoordinate.[17]

Jane is a 50-year-old owner of a mom-and-pop-sized copy center. She handles all the personnel issues, while her husband, the other owner, handles the finances and operations. She's been hiring 18–25-year-old young adults to work in her business for over 15 years, and she typically likes having the energy of these young people in her store.

Cindy, a 40-year-old mother of two teenage girls who barely stands 5 feet tall, manages a fast-food restaurant that's open 20 hours a day. She's a spitfire, always moving faster than everyone around her, including her employees. Unapologetic and willing to do whatever it takes to get the job done, Cindy has made her location one of the highest-performing branches of this growing bagel-food chain.

Sitting in between Jane and Cindy is calm, cool, and collected Jake. Barely 30 years old, he manages two locations for a dine-in restaurant chain. He's worked his way up in this organization, and he's constantly shifting between the two locations, as well as shifting between managing people and running behind-the-scenes operations.

These three managers built on one another's conversations to chain out a perspective that resembled what I've termed "extended mothering." They all had trouble getting their employees to come to work on time, so they were often having to locate them and prod them into work. Mobile phones were essential for chasing down their slackers. But once at work, employees could only use their mobiles during breaks. That rule made sense, given that almost all of their work time was spent directly in front of customers.

When Jane communicates with her employees, she "knows who's going to check their text, who's going to pick up the phone, and who's sleeping and needs to have multiple alarms. So we try to cater to the individuals." Jane only has five to eight employees, so this personalized approach works fine for her. Cindy, on the other hand, manages 14 to 15 employees. When she needs to reach all the employees, she sends out a mass text. "I have all their phone numbers in my phone. It's funny because we have 726 different stores around the country, but no web thing for our schedule. I type it up, [then] post it out on a clipboard. If it needs to changed, I have to let people know."

Cindy, Jane, and Jake use their personal mobiles to get their employees to come to work. Here's how they discussed this issue:

CINDY: What happens is I've got three of my kids who live in the same apartment. So I text one of them and I'm like, "Wake your buddy up."

JAKE: That's happened a lot at my store, too, where a lot of people end up being roommates, or they get a job because, you know, "My roommate needs a job. Do we need a busboy?"

CINDY: Yeah, and sometimes it's like, "If you can't wake up Kevin, then you have to come in and cover his shift." "Kevin will be up," they tell me. Guess what, Kevin will be there at 2 a.m. for his shift because Karen doesn't want to have to come in.

JANE: But I tell you what, they show up 5 minutes later, and they don't look good.

CINDY: They look really, really rough, but I don't care.

Jane and Cindy also found that their employees' mobile numbers weren't always activated, and that created problems in reaching them for work. But certain mobile carriers, like Cricket discussed below, still allowed people to receive text messages even if they didn't pay their mobile bills. This was the managers' perspectives on dealing with this issue:

JANE: Yeah, because they don't pay their bill, and their landline phones are almost a thing of the past. And sometimes you're just SOL [shit out of luck]. Because you can't get a hold of them, you've got to go to plan B.

CINDY: I love it when my kids have Cricket, because with Cricket, if their phone's cut off and you can't call them, they can still get text messages. So it's like, cool, just send them text messages.

JANE: Work around, work around, work around.

CINDY: Oh, and I've learned to ask, "Who's your carrier?" "Cricket." "Fantastic." A little asterisk. "Good, so I know if your phone says you're out of service, I can text you still, and you can't tell me that you didn't get my message, because I know you did."

[laughter broke out in the focus group]

CINDY: I have a kid right now who sent out a mass text [saying] "My phone's going to be shut off for a couple of days, so Facebook me or leave a message at work." And then you have their mommas calling going, "Hey, is . . ." "Yeah, she's here." But that's fine.

JANE: Well, that brings up another point. I have—and I'm sure that everybody who has employees has the same thing—we do have emergency contact information.

CINDY: Absolutely.

JANE: And I had one go AWOL, and he's from out of state, and I called the mother. And it ended up he was up in Dallas and lost his ride and stuff like that, and we got him back into town.

Cindy and Jane have also called police stations and hospitals to find employees. It's hard to know if their management style is effective, but they know their employees quite well and don't hesitate to use every means possible to get them to work.

Cindy's employer provides her with a landline phone, but it's not very useful. During her workday she's always on the go: "I have to hit the ground running. I throw my purse in the office and come right out front. If somebody needs to get in touch with me, they have my cell phone, they have my text." This is her personal cell phone, and she freely gives that number to people who need to reach her. But there's one thing she never forgets. Who gets her personal number is 100% directly under her control.

MANAGERS NEED EMPLOYEES TO HAVE MOBILES TO MICROCOORDINATE SHIFTS

This work-related example in my data closely resembles what Rich Ling and Birgitte Yttri found when they examined mobile-phone control issues between parents and their teens.[27,28] They explain that mobile devices provide parents a direct channel to reach their children at any time, regardless of location.[28] They further explain that having a mobile "allows the adolescent to be in touch with peers during traditional 'family times.'" They position this as a challenge with respect to power and control, and their data shows that the adolescent, in many ways, is emancipated from strict parental control.[28] I've seen these same trends in the data I've shared here; but these were not adolescents, and one mother was actually 74 years old.

While I've read many papers on the personal use of mobiles, Ling and Yttri's example was especially helpful during my analyses of this particular data set. I found myself substituting the term "work hours" for "family time" and realized that many of the work-related narratives I've shared here reflect the same negotiation for control seen in families. Furthermore, when I interviewed Cindy, the manager of the fast-food restaurant, she acted like she was a parent to the group of young adults who worked for her. She referred to them as "kids," called them at home to remind them to come to work, and was even willing to bug their friends and pressure them into finding her missing employees and send them back to her, safe and sound at work. Cindy's behavior provides an example of what Erica Kirby referred to as organizations appropriating family roles, a practice that can be helpful but can also be an unwanted form of control.[18]

ORGANIZATIONS FORCING WORKERS TO USE PERSONAL MOBILE DEVICES

Despite this mixed bag of when and where customer-focused employees and managers use their mobile phones, some workplaces are practically requiring employees to use their mobile devices in front of customers. Take Emily, in her late 20s, who works in a clothing retail store. It's a large department-store chain that's experiencing increased pressure to increase sales. Emily expressed frustration with a recent organizational policy that requires her to use her own personal mobile device to interact with customers. She explains this pressure:

> It's so awkward to pull out my mobile phone and show customers photos of the clothes they are trying on in different colors. We are in the dressing room and my boss wants me on my phone pulling up accessories to increase our sales.

Sometimes Emily slips into one of the unused dressing rooms to pull up the examples to show the customer because she thinks it's rude to stand in front of the customer and use her phone. She's also a bit worried that customers might think she's trying to take photos of them in the changing room. This store is trying a new "upsell" strategy to increase sales, and managers require their employees to engage in these business-development techniques.

There are two issues with the upselling strategy mobile-use policy. First, as Emily mentions, using a mobile device around the customers' dressing rooms and even on the sales floor can be misinterpreted. The customer might think the salesperson isn't being attentive because, as we've seen in other examples, many people equate mobile-device use with slacking off and diverted attention. Another issue is more subtle, but it relates to an increasing practice of having employees use their personal mobile devices for their employers' benefit. While I've discussed BYOD policies earlier in this book, these acceptable-use policies are often created to regulate the devices people bring to work. Organizations often forget that personal mobile devices, and their usage plans, can be costly in some countries like the United States. Asking employees to use their own mobile devices for work purposes can be a financial burden.

Forcing mobile use at work can also be a way to reinforce existing power structures, but it's different from a ban. Mandating mobile use is a type of overt control that a manager can exert over a subordinate. You might recall that in the beginning of this book, I introduced Delilah, the police dispatcher. She too was forced to use her personal device to text her manager. While managerial control is a normal occurrence in many workplaces, the fact that a mobile device is often something purchased by an individual introduces a different dynamic. In this case, the manager is essentially forcing a subordinate to spend money to keep his or her job. Most managers aren't in the same financial situation as their subordinates, and they may be quite unaware that their simple request is economically burdensome on their subordinates.

Now for a counterexample. In 2001, when retail was declining and online purchasing was soaring, Apple Computers expanded its retail operations by creating the Apple Store.[12] Then, as mobile phones became more affordable and the sale of iPhones and other mobile devices exploded, Apple continued to expand its retail operations. With every new device released in the early 2000s, people camped outside the Apple Store to be among the first customers to put their hands on the latest iPhone, iPad, or wearable computing device. Once in the store, there were mobile devices everywhere! Visitors could play with computers that were carefully positioned on desks or try out the latest iPad. They signed into the store through an Apple device and once their name was called, they were greeted by an Apple Store employee who used his or her mobile phone throughout the customer sales and service experience. When writing up an order, the salesperson simply typed the customer's email and credit card information into his or her mobile device and handed the customer a shiny new gadget. At Apple, the paper receipt had become ancient history.

So Apple integrated mobile devices into its retail operations, and its salespeople were on them constantly. What was different from Emily's experience working in the retail clothing store? Until she shared her experience in one of my 2014 focus groups, I'd never considered the differences between retail contexts—clothing retail versus computer retail—and how device ownership and use could influence a customer-facing job role. Apple was essentially using its products to sell its products. People working in its stores were provided with Apple devices, and quite often they could use them outside of work as well.

Around that same time, UPS and FedEx expanded their use of handheld computers to streamline the delivery of packages. Their drivers would scurry up to a customer's home or office, set the package by the door, and record its delivery on the spot, in their mobile device. Yet the average customer didn't wonder if the driver was cyberslacking. We also didn't question what the Apple representative was doing when he or she was on his or her device in the store.

While there is limited research on perceptions of who "should" and who "shouldn't" use a mobile device at work, this is clearly an opportunity for future research. The symbolic perceptions of mobile use seem to vary, but in my data, customer-facing employees believed they shouldn't be regularly on their mobile devices in the presence of customers. However, many of the people in my data sets were actively serving or interacting with customers, not trying to sell technology or use a mobile device as an integral part of their job. This could change over time, but undoubtedly Emily did not appreciate being "forced" to use her personal device in hopes of increasing retail sales.

EMOTIONAL LABOR AND AVAILABILITY FOR MOBILE COMMUNICATION

We now return to the concept I used to frame this chapter, the emotional labor involved in forcing a smile and how that might interact with the work demands of avoiding mobile communication in customer-facing jobs. In his research on mobile use for socioeconomic development, Jonathan Donner uses the phrase "blurring livelihoods and lives" to describe the work–life boundary-expansion potential of mobiles.[11] While the idea of managing these boundaries is not new, and scholars from a host of disciplines are considering how workers navigate these spheres,[13,14,16,19,35,36] the focus on workers who aren't traditional knowledge workers is rare. There is growing research, such as Donner's work[11] along with that of scholars like Arun Chib,[8] Margaret Williams,[43] and Richard Ling and Heather Horst[26] trying to better understand how technologies are woven between and among the lives of workers outside of high-tech companies and those engaged with traditional knowledge work. But very little of this existing research speaks to the customer-facing data I've presented in this chapter.

As I examine this growing body of research focused beyond knowledge work and compare it to the data I collected from these customer-facing workers, several differences emerge. I group these into two categories: reachability is segmented into windows and rules and resource limitations are adapted. The first category is visualized in Figure 9.1.

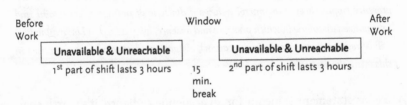

Figure 9.1. Example of reachability windows in shift work

Reachability is segmented into windows:

1) Customer-facing workers have extended time periods where they can't or shouldn't use their personal mobile devices. Breaks are the designated time for handling what are often considered personal activities.
2) Family and friends don't often understand the limited windows of availability for customer-facing employees. They pressure them to be more responsive.
3) People in customer-facing jobs vary in how they cope with their limited mobile reachability that comes with the nature of their work.

There's a new type of emotional labor emerging in this customer-facing work environment, and it stems from a mismatch between communicators' windows of reachability. It's not necessarily being driven by what is happening in the work environment but occurs through negotiations of availability with people outside of work. Coordinating communication with friends and family around breaks represents a violation of the availability-expectation norm that we see with the proliferation of mobile devices and communication in people's personal lives.[2,11,24,25,41] In my team's recent research, we found that these external pressures to respond are a contributor to communication overload.[39] So it's highly likely that when people know others are trying to reach them but they cannot respond, this creates an added emotional burden on customer-facing employees.

This incongruity in availability patterns means that some workers, like Kim, the call-center training manager, have developed strategies to cope, while others experience stress or quit their jobs. As I coded Kim's data, I called her behavior "training her loved ones." And it was painfully obvious that most of the other people in my data sets were struggling in handling the mismatch in communicative availability. Christian Licoppe, a communication and media sociologist, elaborated this availability negotiation in 2004, and it is precisely what this chapter's data illustrates.[23] He said:

> It becomes necessary to be available for interaction, or necessary to justify and re-negotiate one's unavailability. The very possibility of the expectation of connected presence tipping over into control induces a dialectic of normative constraint and internalized discipline in which presence and absence, availability and unavailability, will be regulated in a game of expectations, obligations, and constraints practiced in this microphysics of the link. (p. 153)[23]

While his statement is meant for an academic audience, it's worth sharing because it pulls together several bodies of literature in a few sentences.

His idea of a "dialectic of normative constraint and internalized discipline" means that people are pulled between norms and their own ability to exercise discipline by negotiating with others and establishing boundaries. There's a norm of connectedness in the broader society,[2,23,41] and being in a job without this capability can be difficult. Some people can't handle being unavailable, or they haven't learned how to negotiate their availability windows, conditions that lead to workarounds and turnover. The prominent example in this chapter of a workaround is the use of a bathroom as a refuge, a place to escape from view and still be responsive.

MOBILE RULES AND RESOURCES IN CUSTOMER-FACING WORK

The next set of key differences found in customer-facing workers concerns how rules and resource limitations are adapted. Here are those findings:

1) Managers of customer-facing employees often implement rules to establish what they view as a professional environment—one without the presence of mobile devices unless they are used as part of the customer-engagement process.
2) The socioeconomic status of some customer-facing workers decreases the stability and reliability of using mobile devices for coordination.
3) Managers of customer-facing employees can reach outside the work-hour boundary to nudge workers to make their shifts.

The managers in this data unearth the reality that their hourly workers often have mobile-resource limitations and that one of the duties of managers is to establish rules that enhance the professionalism of their workplace. It's easy to forget that owning a mobile device and having a data plan can be too expensive for many people. In other chapters I've shared examples of employees who only have text-messaging plans, but here we see workers who are having their service disconnected because they can't afford, or simply forget, to pay their bills. But mama-manager comes to the rescue in this data. The managers are coping with this reality by capturing the brand of phone their employees own and by being willing to reach out to anyone who might be capable of finding and pressuring their young workers to make their shift.

The managers' behavior is an elaborate example of microcoordinating that extends beyond standard work hours. When considering some of the issues raised in Chapter 6, BYOD and exempt—or hourly—workers, nudging hourly workers to get to work could be problematic if those messages are exchanged during a time when their employees are off the clock.

A LOOK AHEAD

As this chapter on customer-facing work ends, I'll invite you to consider the range of work and workers that I've introduced throughout this book. Some people can use mobiles at work, while others are banned. Managers range from those who set firm rules to those who feel guilty about being overly controlling. Organizations struggle to create policies that protect their data but allow workers flexibility in making mobile choices. And boundaries between work and home might not be blurred in all cases; personal preferences and types of jobs can help establish more rigid barriers.

The next chapter pulls together all this data and compares mobile communication between these diverse workers. Walking away from that summary chapter, you'll better understand the key characteristics of working environments that influence availability and acceptability of mobile use. The final chapters in this book tie together threads of control, negotiation, and the practical findings from this longitudinal study.

CHAPTER 10

Mobile Communication Comparisons Between Diverse Workers

In this book, I've shared data representing over 150 different people across 35 diverse occupations. My first chapters focused on employees who were early users of cellular phones—people tagged "knowledge workers." Then, as the cost of mobile devices came down, workers in a variety of jobs began bringing their devices to work, whether or not it was against the rules. I've shared stories of organizations banning mobiles and those implementing mobile apps to actively encouraging work use. Finally, in Chapter 9, I shared a mix of stories from people in more customer-facing job roles.

It's easy to say that either being a knowledge worker or being customer-facing is what's influencing how people use mobiles at work, but my analysis paints a more nuanced picture. Table 10.1 provides a sorted list of the major people represented in this book. As I coded the pieces of data and compared the themes that emerged,[6,7] I found four overarching categories that informed the question: *What are the characteristics of specific jobs that interact with mobile communication happening in organizational life?* Those categories are:

- **Autonomy:** To what degree does this worker enjoy autonomy in his or her work tasks?
- **Mobility:** What's the degree of mobility with respect to where work is accomplished?
- **Task variability:** How much do work tasks vary during a given day?
- **Communication focus:** Who or what gets this worker's primary communication attention?

Table 10.1 JOB CHARACTERISTICS AND MOBILE COMMUNICATION PATTERNS

Pseudonym	Job Type	Degree of Autonomy	Degree of Mobility	Variation in Job Tasks	Primary Communication Attention	Chapter where Discussed
Samantha	Online learning employee	High	High	High	Customers (ex)	1
Keri (actual name)	Sales engineer	High	High	High	Customers (ex)	1
Ted	Police officer	High	High	High	Customers (ex)	1
Bill	Semiconductor engineer	High	High	High	Labor tasks	1
Evan	Digital learning mgr.	High	High	High	Subordinates	1
Stephanie (actual name)	Graduate student	High	High	High	Admin. tasks	2
Kjell	Owner, start-up in Norway	High	High	High	Subordinates	2
Matt	Sales mgr.	High	High	High	Subordinates	2
Amanda	Crisis comm. mgr.	High	High	High	Customers (ex)	4
Cedric	Advertising mgr.	High	High	High	Customers (ex & i)	4
Tommy	Exec. fundraiser	High	High	High	Customers (ex)	4
Cathy	Team leader software	High	High	High	Subordinates	4
Sally	Executive VP operations	High	High	High	Subordinates	4
David	President & COO advertising co.	High	High	High	Subordinates & customers	4
Varied	Physicians	High	High	High	Customers (patients & i)	8
Jake	Coffee shop mgr.	High	High	High	Subordinates	9
Gabrielle	Banker	High	Medium	High	Admin. tasks	1
Andy	HR worker	High	Medium	High	Customers (i)	4
Olivia	HR mgr.	High	Medium	High	Customers (i)	4
Bridget	Leasing mgr.	High	Medium	High	Subordinates	9

Cindy	Fast-food mgr.	High	Medium	High	Subordinates	9
Rose	School principal	High	Medium	High	Subordinates & customers/parents	9
Ann Marie	CTO advertising co.	High	Medium	Medium	Customers (i)	4
Jane	Copy store owner	High	Low	Medium	Subordinates	9
Rene	Law clerk	High	Low	Low	Admin. tasks	9
Louise	Retail mgr.	Medium	Medium	Medium	Subordinates	9
Allison	Marketing mgr.	Medium	Low	Medium	Admin. tasks	4
Varied	Hospital pharmacist	Medium	Low	Low	Admin. tasks	8
Varied	Janitors (over 30 in study)	Low	Medium	Low	Labor tasks	5
Varied	Nurses (over 15 in study)	Low	Medium	Low	Customers (ex)	8
Caroline	Child-care worker	Low	Medium	Low	Customers/children	9
Delilah	Police dispatcher	Low	Low	Low	Customers (ex)	Introduction
Emily	Retail sales	Low	Low	Low	Customers (ex)	9
Emma	Waitress	Low	Low	Low	Customers (ex)	9
Tammy	Sandwich shop	Low	Low	Low	Customers (ex)	9
Kim	Call center	Low	Low	Low	Customers (ex)	9
Alexa	Restaurant cook	Low	Low	Low	Labor tasks	9
Cordelia	Admin asst.	Low	Low	Low	Admin. tasks	4 & 5

Note: i = internal customer, ex = external customer

AUTONOMY

Here I define "autonomy" as *a condition when workers can do their work without direct managerial involvement.* Whereas researchers who've studied knowledge workers have found that their skilled and self-directed work tends to afford them rights to autonomy,[1,5,12,17,20] I see evidence in this data that autonomy can be independent from the type of work. For example, Rene, the law clerk discussed in Chapter 9, enjoys so much autonomy that she's often playing mobile games with her boyfriend while at work. Even with no manager around, she seems to accomplish her tasks and still have time to play around on mobile devices. In my coding definition, autonomy relates both to direct managerial oversight, which varies a lot regardless of job role, and to tasks common in highly skilled, cerebral, knowledge-generating work.

Besides defining autonomy narrowly with respect to the type of worker, scholars like Manuel Castells and Rich Ling claim that technologies in general, and mobile in particular, provide increased communication flexibility, freedom, and autonomy.[3,13,14] The law clerk, Rene, could never have played mobile games had she not owned her own device and if it weren't small enough to be used fairly unobtrusively. But realize that autonomy isn't always desirable. Several scholars, including Melissa Mazmanian and Sirkaa Jarvenpaa, have studied knowledge workers and found that autonomy doesn't come without strings.[11,15] People feel both liberated and controlled by having autonomy in their work because powerful norms can leave them feeling like they actually have no autonomy at all.

Based on the comments made by my interviewees and focus-group participants, I found that I could characterize their autonomy as being high, medium, or low. Those with high autonomy either had almost complete control over their workplace decisions or had virtually no managerial oversight. Sally, the senior vice president from Chapter 4 with the rule of "no thumbs under her table," illustrates just such a person. People in the medium category had some independence in their work, but they were also limited at times by their manager, their customers, or the nature of their work. Oliva, the human resources (HR) representative from Chapter 4, illustrates that kind of person. She had autonomy, but she also attended many meetings that restricted her use of mobile devices. My interviewees in the low autonomy category, meanwhile, had direct managerial oversight during virtually all their work hours. Kim, the call center representative, is a good example of this complete oversight; she even had camera surveillance during her work hours.

MOBILITY

The meaning of "mobility" in and around work has changed considerably now that information and communication technologies (ICTs) connect people across space and time. It's pretty easy to identify workers who are stationary at a fixed workstation while doing most of their job. These can be office workers who come to a building to sit behind a computer every day or fast-food workers who stand behind a counter and simply take customer orders. At the other extreme are workers who are constantly on the go, rarely running their business out of a single location. These "road warriors," like sales or customer service representatives, historically have been the first employees to get mobile tools because they work out of their cars.

But there are gradations of mobility in work. Jakob Bardram and Claus Bossen refer to the middle ground as "local mobility."[2] They studied a hospital, and, much as I myself showed in Chapter 8, they found that many of these employees were constantly on the go. These workers aren't easy to catch in a face-to-face environment, but they still do their job at a single location.

As I examined the job descriptions and type of work performed by people in my studies, I found they fell into a three-category system of mobility. Highly mobile workers were those who were actively on the move from place to place and customer to customer. Ted, the police officer, and Matt, the sales manager, are good examples. The workers I identified with medium mobility fell into Bardram and Bossen's view of local mobility.[2] The nurses from Chapter 8 illustrate this form of local mobility. I also placed people in this category when they worked primarily in a home office and telecommuted several days a week. Bridget, the manager of the leasing company, is such a one. The low-mobility workers had a single location where they did their work. Often, they were customer-facing workers, but several of the more traditional office workers fell into the low-mobility category as well. Delilah, the police department dispatcher who worked in an office, was coded into this category.

TASK VARIETY

This category emerged because some people switch between diverse tasks at work, whereas others do more routine, often repetitive job tasks. This category is informed by past research suggesting that task variety can be related to how people use mobiles to cope with boring or stressful work. For example, in her research on migrant workers in Beijing, Ke Yang studied security guards who'd use their mobiles to text their friends and play games in an effort to reduce work-related boredom.[21] These workers were on call constantly but had few formal tasks.

Most people in my data had high, or at least medium, levels of task variability. This was especially the case with managers who often worked with a variety of subordinates and had administrative duties along with supervisory ones. People coded into the "medium" category were those who said explicitly that their jobs were limited or defined in a manner to contain their task variability. Finally, many of the customer-facing study participants who worked in a single location also engaged in a limited number of tasks, so they were categorized as low on this category. For example, Emily, the retail sales clerk who was pressured to use her mobile phone with customers, was required to be on the floor selling and answering customers' questions.

COMMUNICATION FOCUS

To code the final category, which covers who or what gets a worker's primary communicative attention (i.e., communication focus), I reviewed the literature for some definitional guidance. Gert Hofstede, the scholar who did the foundational research on international cultures, published research on organizational subcultures in the late 1990s.[10] While he focused on a single insurance agency, in his quantitative grouping of subcultures, the notion of a "customer-interface subculture" resonated with the observations in my findings. Identifying a coherent coding scheme for this category that emerged from my own data was challenging because my study covers so many industries and types of jobs. "Customers," in my data, can be defined as internal or external to the organization. Salespeople have external customers, while Ann Marie, the chief technology officer of the advertising company whom you met in Chapter 4, had internal customers pushing her to stay on the bleeding edge of her organizational technology decisions. Furthermore, customers can be groups of people like children at a childcare center or patients at a hospital. So you'll notice I coded these types of workers as having an external customer focus.

Besides people whose job roles had them directly engaged with customers, there were people who focused more on tasks like administration and manual labor. The janitors discussed in Chapter 5 were coded into the manual-labor category, and Cordelia, the outspoken meeting notetaker from Chapters 4 and 5, was coded as focusing on administrative tasks. Finally, people who supervised others had a distinct focus, so they appear in the last category: subordinates are their communication focus.

OVERVIEW OF TABLE 10.1

For each person whose story I shared in the book, I provided the name, job title, and chapter where the story appeared, and then I identified where that person fit in each of the four major categories. I created a three-level system for the first three categories: high, medium, and low. For example, I coded Bridget, the leasing manager in Chapter 9, as high on autonomy because she managed her own leasing organization. But because she did most of her work from that single office location, with occasional days when she worked from home, I coded her mobility as medium. As the manager of an entire office, she did a wide variety of tasks, so I coded her as high on variability of work tasks.

Now that I've described the coding process, I invite you to examine Table 10.1. The order in which I present the four categories there isn't random. It represents the influence each category has in answering the research question. To determine the influence order, after creating the table I systematically conducted four separate sorts in Excel; each one assumed a single category as being the primary driver. After comparing each of these possible tables against my data as a whole, it was clear that autonomy was the primary driver. After all, if someone's mobile behavior is extensively controlled by a manager's rules, it often supersedes the other categories. I repeated this sorting-and-comparing process and found that mobility was secondary, task variability was tertiary, and the primary communication focus was last.

Table 10.1 reveals the importance of including these four variables and not oversimplifying explanations of how people use mobiles at work. It's easy to conclude that people who are customer-facing use mobiles a certain way, but that's not quite correct. Actually, you'll see that workers with external customers can be at the top of the table, with high autonomy, high mobility, and high task variability, and they can be also located at the bottom of the table. Being in outside sales, which is a highly mobile job, means that you have intermittent, not constant, contact with customers. But being a child-care worker involves truly constant customer contact. The only time you're out of the presence of the children is during your break.

While engaging in the analysis, I also searched the literature for insights that could help explain my four core categories. I reviewed the literature on workplace flexibility,[4,8,9,16] a concept describing employees who have temporal flexibility to change the hours they work, place flexibility to adjust where they work, and task flexibility to manage the ebbs and flows of their work.[9] This description resonates with my first three categories I labeled "autonomy," "mobility," and "task variability." Many past studies have concerned themselves with knowledge workers, and Melissa Mazmanian and her colleagues have shown that autonomy and control are actually paradoxical.[15] This commonly cited autonomy–control paradox is also found in Sirkka Jarvenpaa and Karl Lang's work,[11] as well as in Linda Putnam, Karen Myers, and Bernadette Gailliard's critical review of the literature on workplace flexibility initiatives.[16] I also explored research linking professions and ICT use like Richard Susskind's work on the legal profession[19] and the work he's done with David Susskind that crosses many different professions.[18] Their work challenges inherent assumptions in professions and even suggests that prolific ICT use and availability make it possible for shifts in the types of tasks that some professions will perform in the future.

But because this data contains employees from many types of jobs, I'm able to paint a broad understanding of how my four core categories describe and interact with each other when people use mobile communication in and around work. Let's see those specific nuances next.

INSIGHTS FROM THESE COMPARISONS

Three main insights emerge from the data in this table form:

1) People aren't always *reachable* or able to use their mobile devices while at work. Workers with a high degree of autonomy tend to have more mobile access during the workday, but their access is not always predictable, varies day to day, and is woven in between work activities. For example, if Matt, the national sales director, received a voicemail from one of his managers, he could probably call him back the same day, but it might need to be after he finished a meeting.

Workers with low autonomy have predictable times when they have mobile access because they get scheduled breaks; however, they also spend the bulk of their workday without mobile access. Kim, the call-center worker and training manager, is a good example of this type of employee. She can't use her personal mobile phone at all while she's hooked up to a headset asking alums to make a donation. That phone shift lasts 3–4 hours; then she gets a break and has legitimate mobile access only if she leaves the building. But texting in the bathroom is the skirting-the-rules option.

2) It's not always *acceptable* to use, or be seen using, a mobile device at work. The data suggests that while people at the top of the table—high

autonomy, mobility, and task variability—experience more times at work when it's acceptable to use their mobile device, it's not unlimited and constant. The most prominent example in the data concerns meetings and how various people don't approve of multicommunicating and multitasking in the presence of others. Remember Sally, senior vice president of operations, who made it perfectly clear there would be "no thumbs under her tables"?

People on the lower end of Table 10.1 are often subjected to more rules—even bans—that restrict workplace use, except during breaks. Managers enact rules to curb cyberslacking and improve the professionalism of their work environment. This is what Bridget, the leasing manager, did with her employees. But this is where the communication focus has a direct impact on perceived acceptability of mobile use; customers want attention on them, not on a mobile device. Ignore these unspoken rules and workers find themselves without tips or marked down on satisfaction surveys. Emma, the waitress at Buffalo Wild Wings, said it bluntly, "If I'm texting around the tables and [customers] see me, I'm sure they would be like, 'My waitress is texting when she could get me a refill!' And there goes my tip for the day, and that's my income, so I can't do that."

3) Types of *control* surrounding mobile use vary. There's more managerial control when people have less autonomy, are less mobile, and have more repetitive work tasks. These people, located toward the bottom of Table 10.1, are typically co-located; managers can observe their behaviors and create rules that are actually enforceable. Next time you go into a fast-food restaurant, like a sandwich shop, you can see this type of work environment in action. Employees are lined up, often in assembly-line format, taking orders, and creating the final product, a custom-made sandwich.

People located at the top of Table 10.1 are also subject to control, but the mechanisms are often different. Controlling people who have autonomy, are mobile, and do a variety of work tasks means that control is less obvious and includes things like organizational norms and group-level concertive control. You might recall that it's these types of workers who often get "permission" to bring their own devices to work; they're allowed to participate in bring-your-own-device-to-work policies. But, as we saw in Chapter 6, those policies are themselves a control mechanism.

WHAT'S NEXT?

I've given you a lot to digest in this chapter, so it's deliberately brief. Look carefully at the table, and feel free to go back into the chapters where I tell these people's stories. See for yourself how details related to each individual contribute to the creation of these four main categories and three overarching insights. In the next chapter, I'll unpack these insights and elaborate on the four major theoretical contributions of this book. The final chapter is brief and focuses on practical insights and future research ideas.

CHAPTER 11

Understanding Mobile Negotiation

Contributions and Theory

In each chapter of this book, I compiled my data sources, analyzed them using a constant comparative method, and, in some cases, did detailed coding along with descriptive and/or thematic analysis. This approach allowed me to summarize the narrative data in each chapter and make claims concerning what it showed. Chapter 10 provided a more macro-level analysis where I combined all the data and compared mobile communication across job types. This chapter continues the macro-level analysis and elaborates the four major contributions:

1) Over the arc of time, organizations play an integral role in controlling mobile communication in and around work environments.
2) Negotiations for control include the temporal communication affordance of reachability, which comprises both work and personal conversations.
3) Mobile communication acceptability at work is entwined with perceived power and the attention desired by others in that particular moment.
4) An overarching framework explains a dialectic of control involved in mobile communication at work.

As mentioned earlier, I didn't begin this project intending to develop a theory of control negotiation. I proposed to use more of a descriptive diffusion-of-innovations framework, and while that structure clearly guides the contributions, themes relating to control kept emerging. The findings shared throughout this book are grounded fully in the data, the real value of using a constant comparative method as a qualitative data-analysis approach. I'll illustrate each of these contributions next.

VALUE OF A LONGITUDINAL PERSPECTIVE ON ORGANIZATIONS' CONTROL AND MOBILE COMMUNICATION

Being able to provide a two and a half–decade longitudinal perspective on how mobile devices have diffused into organizations allows me to develop a big-picture understanding of communication practices. So much of the research on information and communication technologies (ICTs) has been snapshots in time, focused on a single organization. Before I compiled all this data and strung the pieces together to craft this narrative, most of my published work also had been snapshots of cross-sectional data. But my book is unique; I've been fortunate to experience and study the rise of mobile communication at work. And being a scholar of organizational communication and technology, I'm in an ideal place to build this story into a theoretical contribution.

Let's begin with a picture, developed from the data, that provides a macro, cross-organizational perspective linking mobile diffusion with organizational control.

Figure 11.1 compiles the society-level phenomena that occurred as mobile devices became affordable, along with organizational and individual swings in how control has shifted over time. I characterized those broad changes through the phenomenon of enterprise consumerization[25,33,34,75] and the resulting norms of connectedness.[4,44,46] It's vital that these be included in the backdrop of organizational considerations because they seep into individuals' lives. Mobile-device users as well as organizations are experiencing these changes and adapting their communication and information practices.

The second tier of Figure 11.1 illustrates how organizations and individuals have danced, and sometimes struggled, with one another as mobile technologies have advanced. There was a time when organizations provided mobile-communication tools, and while managers typically set some rules, individuals had little direct control over these resources (e.g., cellular phones) because they viewed them as company-provided technology. The slight blips and curls in the graph of organizational control are deliberate, and they represent times when some individuals brought their

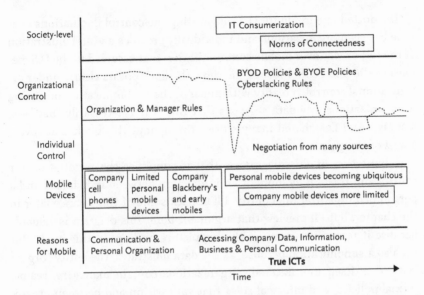

Figure 11.1. Mobile-device diffusion and negotiations for organizational and individual control. BYOD = bring-your-own-device-to-work; BYOE = bring-your-own-everything; IT = information technology.

devices to work before it was a trend; but that had little impact on organizational control. My data suggests that these early adopters[67] of mobile devices were sometimes noticed; but they weren't asking to access organizational computer networks, and there was no Wi-Fi, so they stayed under the radar.

BlackBerrys and early mobile tools provided employees opportunities to check email, thus prompting a new conversation about control. For the first time, hordes of predominantly knowledge workers could access and carry company proprietary information and records of communications on their handheld devices. These handy devices were considered expensive, so managers made tough choices about who "needed" or "deserved" them. There were other mobile devices around the globe, but in the U.S., BlackBerrys were the dominant portable communication tool.

Then, a virtual army of personal mobile devices invaded U.S. organizations, and it didn't take long for information technology (IT) teams to respond. These departments scrambled to decide how to handle mobile devices because their employees insisted they get to choose their own and they also wanted access to company Wi-Fi. Now it was not just knowledge workers who were using mobile tools and company networks, but people in every level of organizations began pressuring IT to let them at least access Wi-Fi.

The dotted line in Figure 11.1, illustrating the control fluctuations over time between organizations and individuals, provides a visual illustration of the tug-of-war over mobile communication that occurred in the U.S. between 1990 and 2018. Most of the time, the line appears clearly under organizational control, a reality with much of the communication occurring in organizations. My data suggests that this is not necessarily "bad"—it just "is." And I've shared many stories throughout this book that reveal places of struggle.

A limitation of this diagram is that it simplifies the negotiation for control and treats it as more of an interaction between individuals and a personified organizational entity. I'll unpack some of this nuance later in the chapter, but I'll preview that argument here. This diagram is valuable because it represents many of the big-picture findings in this book. But it's also a simplification because, as the data illustrates, the entity "organization" is itself multifaceted. Organizations contain managers, teams, formal policies, and informal rules that vary within and between organizations. Furthermore, there's evidence in this book of organizing practices entwined with mobile ICTs, not simply organizational entities involved in the negotiation. For example, the struggles in the hospital, Chapter 8, are centered on coordination and using mobile tools to microcoordinate between different professions, clearly a set of organizing practices. Before I elaborate on the particulars, I'll briefly link this longitudinal perspective to theory in organizational change and diffusion.

DIFFUSION AND A NEW WAY OF THINKING ABOUT ORGANIZATIONAL CHANGES

Organizations are accustomed to driving changes, especially when major purchases are involved. Technologies such as new employee-benefit systems or enterprise-wide email are often expensive and involve logistics like training, installation, and maintenance. There are vast bodies of literature in fields like organizational and communication studies on change.[39,40,41,42,43,51,59] In a project I did in 2003 with Laurie Lewis, we examined the popular-press books on organizational change, and we found scant research focused on communicating or meaningfully involving individuals in the change process, especially those without formal power.[43] One exception was Debra Meyerson's book *Tempered Radicals*. But even her book, based on over 15 years of research on organizational behavior, talks about individuals walking a fine line between conforming and rebelling with the goal of influencing larger organizational change initiatives.[51]

But there's something different about organizational change when it's initiated by the individual members at all hierarchical levels simultaneously. This is what happened as mobile devices entered workplaces, and Figure 11.1 illustrates the struggles involved as organizations tried, with new rules and policies, to rein in employees using resources under their control. IT departments and human resource (HR) departments found themselves in a quandary. They needed to protect proprietary organizational information and their image—some employees were using personal mobiles to post information on social media—and they had to do that using technology that individuals were bringing into the workplace.

Diffusion of Innovations, Everett Rogers' landmark book originally published in 1962 and revised four times by 2003,[67,68] is an excellent explanatory framework that helps us understand how personal mobile devices have diffused into organizations. While much of the organizational-change literature assumes that the initiator of the change is the organization, diffusion of innovations can account for a bottom-up or grass-roots type of technology adoption. Diffusion of innovations is especially helpful in understanding what matters most when adopting interactive communication practices and products. Rogers claims that there must be a critical mass of users, the use must be regular and frequent, and there must be a way for individual users to reinvent and modify the innovation.[68] Whereas change theories can be considered more as macro-level theories because they focus on organization- or institution-level changes, diffusion of innovations focuses on micro-level processes where individuals adopt an innovation.

The reason bring-your-own-device-to-work (BYOD) matters for organizational scholars, and individuals interested in understanding these trends, is that there is now a middle ground between organization-driven change and micro-level technology diffusion into organizations. *My data suggests that organizations have coped with these changes by co-opting individuals' devices for organizational communication.* This is why the negotiation for control exists and why this conversation will continue, at least for a while. And if current IT industry publications are correct, over time, carrier fees will drop, employer subsidies reimbursing mobile plans will decrease, and eventually the norm will be for employees to provide and pay for their own devices.[82] But there are also predictions that split-billing—allowing personal use to be billed separately from company use from the same device—will be offered by 30% of large organizations in the near future.[50] At this time in 2018, some mobile devices, like Android devices, already offer separate partitions in the same device; but the future with wearables and the expansion of IT consumerization invite us all to consider how control will continue to be negotiated.

Let's move beyond this macro-level diagram and interrogate what's happening between societal norms, organizations, and individuals. I'll also ask you to be open to the fact that people use their mobiles differently, have diverse jobs, work for separate managers, and might be members of multiple teams. Furthermore, much of the use of mobile communication supports prior claims that use can be paradoxical in nature.[1] One consequence of these differences can be understood through the temporal affordance of reachability; the norms of connectivity leak into expectations and assumptions that people are always reachable.

ELABORATING THE NUANCES OF THE AFFORDANCE OF REACHABILITY

Cordelia, the meeting note-taker from Chapter 4, may have had it right. She didn't want the police department to give her a laptop or any type of mobile device. Without one, she was free when she was away from work. The nurses in Chapter 8 experienced a similar detachment between being on- and off-shift. The organizational and professional mechanisms of shift work have helped them be free from work responsibilities when they're no longer on the clock. But the managers in Chapter 9 report calling their hourly workers' personal mobile phones to remind them to get out of bed and make their shifts on time. And the janitors in Chapter 5 struggled with deciding if they should give their personal numbers to their managers. It appears that even with shift work, employees can be contacted outside of work hours if their employer has access to their personal number.

Contrast these examples with the more traditional knowledge workers and managers who seem to have little concern about reaching out, often after work hours, if they need tasks accomplished. These workers have flexibility to leave their workplace and run personal errands, like Andy did in Chapter 4; he got physical therapy during work hours. These workers are provided lots of autonomy, but that doesn't come without strings attached. Most of the prior organizational-technology research on work–life concerns has focused on knowledge workers who feel handcuffed to their devices because that flexibility also means they feel compelled to do work on their personal time.[22,23,27,28,48,54,64]

My research here agrees with the bulk of this prior research on knowledge workers. What I add is the broader occupational perspective on mobile communication, not only on what happens outside of work but also on what happens during work hours. In Chapter 10, I compiled all the varied workers into a single table that was sorted based on the four categories that emerged from my macro-level qualitative analysis: autonomy, mobility, task variability, and communication focus. As I worked in that data and used existing research to guide me in my constant comparative method,[20,21] one affordance of mobile communication rose from those four categories: reachability. It wasn't that people who ranked high or low in those four categories could draw on the affordance of reachability more, but instead there were nuances within and between these categories that spoke to how the affordance of reachability had to be negotiated between work boundaries. This mobile-communication affordance existed as a relational bridge between individuals and their perception of both their work and personal environments. It's not a feature of mobile devices or a direct outcome of using a mobile device; it exists as what affordance scholars call "a possibility for action."[16] Reachability makes it possible for people to be "found" or contacted and to reach others for outcomes like coordination and relationship development.

Before I share the conceptual development of the communication affordance of reachability, I'd like to review the research literature that helps justify a deep dive into understanding this temporal affordance.

EXISTING RESEARCH ON COMMUNICATION AFFORDANCES AND REACHABILITY

Just because different types of mobile devices are being used in and around organizations, they haven't predictably caused users and organizations to behave in specific ways. It's how users interact, communicate, and relate that shape how mobile devices are used in organizational life. This explanation of what I see in the data follows an affordance approach, originally articulated by James Gibson, an American psychologist.[16] His work wasn't technology- or organization-specific, but it provides a type of framing that scholars have used to move beyond deterministic assumptions of technology use in organizations.[13,15,36,37,38,47,57,65,70,73,79]

What makes this perspective especially useful for communication research is that we can emphasize the relational components in affordances. The impact that others have on how technology can be used for communication is seen throughout my data and has strong support in existing research. One organizational-technology branch of this research has focused on social media. Jeff Treem and Paul Leonardi (2012) identified four core affordances of enterprise social media that set them apart from other communication tools: visibility, persistence, editability, and association.[79] Note that none of these four affordances is unique to social media but that all four of them tend to be present in social media. In his research on organizational social media, Leonardi demonstrated that affordances are not just an individual-level perception; they can be collective or shared as well as individualized.[37] Several scholars have built on this early work and have shown that these affordances also help explain how organizational members navigate the tensions associated with being open and sharing information yet also managing others' impressions of them.[15] Additionally, Leonardi elaborated on the affordance of visibility and connected it to organizational knowledge and innovation in his development of a grounded theory of visibility.[38]

In an attempt to move beyond much of the early work linking affordances to a specific technology, Ron Rice and his team developed the concept of "organizational media affordances."[65] These are viewed as organizational resources that exist independently of a given technology and acknowledge that a single medium, like texting, is associated with several different organizational affordances such as pervasiveness and editability. His team also developed some of the first scales used to measure them. Drawing on this organizational communication work, Sandra Evans led a team of communication scholars who reviewed the literature and determined three criteria for identifying a communication affordance: (1) it's not a feature of an object (e.g., a specific technology), (2) it isn't an outcome of use of the object, and (3) it must have variability.[13]

Andrew Schrock expanded the affordances perspective to mobile media by identifying four communication affordances suggested by the literature.[70] He notes that mobile researchers have either directly or indirectly indicated an interest in affordances in much of their work.[26,30,31,45,75] The four affordances he identified are portability, locatability, multimediality, and availability. Portability, locatability, and multimediality, as Schrock suggests, are more closely aligned with perceptions of the physical characteristics of mobiles.[70] His final affordance, availability, is a concept similar to Katz and Aakhus' potential for perpetual contact.[31] Schrock describes availability as complex, negotiable, and capable of strategic use, all important factors when elaborating a relational affordance.[70]

Schrock's work on affordances of mobile media is described as exploratory, and it's not necessarily set in an organizational context; but that might be exactly what's needed to reveal the pervasiveness of a reachability affordance. I debated whether to adopt Schrock's claim that the affordance is one of availability or if my data suggested that reachability was more accurate. I settled on reachability because, following Leonardi's view of communication affordances,[37] being reachable is more dialogic than being available for communication and lends itself well to a shared perspective.

As I further develop and conceptualize this affordance, you'll see that reachability isn't something that exists exclusively within either a work or a personal context; it's always with us, it's multifaceted, and it can be drawn upon from individuals, groups, or organizations.

CONCEPTUALIZING REACHABILITY AS A MOBILE COMMUNICATION AFFORDANCE

When Sandra Evans and her team combed the literature on technology affordances, one of their main criticisms was that researchers often identify lists but rarely spend the time to conceptually explain specific affordances.[13] Here I remedy that situation. Reachability, made possible by mobile devices, helps us reach others and be reached by them, through two mechanisms: reach frequency and reach predictability.

While reachability is a communicative affordance that crosses the work–personal life boundary, it's important to realize that not everyone can be reached during work hours; therefore, there are limits for when people can draw upon the affordance of reachability. This is not something people realize because most people in my studies gauge the reachability of others based on their own experiences. In contrast, my data suggests that reachability is often a function of organizational and job constraints that are related to temporal availability. As we saw in Chapter 10, when people work shifts, they might only be accessible during breaks, a temporal concept I termed "windows of reachability." In their extensive integration of literature relating organizational contradictions, dialectics, paradoxes, and tensions, Linda Putnam and her colleagues prod researchers to consider the role of temporal features instead of assuming that processes follow routines and patterns.[61,63] The analysis I conducted here on windows of reachability followed this advice. I had process data, and by bracketing my observations I identified this temporal pattern.

This realization makes it possible to classify people's type of work using two overarching temporal variables: frequency and predictability. These variables form the axes of a 2 × 2 matrix depicted in Figure 11.2. This matrix identifies four types of workers according to how they can be reached while at work.

The first category, with low reachability and low predictability, is called the "sequestered worker." I don't have people in the data that exemplify this, but I've heard stories of people who work for governmental agencies and organizations handling classified documents where they're required to hand over their mobile devices when they go to work. It can be days

	Frequency of Reach	
Predictability of Reach	**Low Frequency**	**High Frequency**
Low Predictability	1. Sequestered workers (no instances in my data)	2. Mobile workers *Reached between their work commitments*
High Predictability	3. Shift workers *Reached during scheduled breaks*	4. Always-on workers (by job or choice) *Reached any time*

Figure 11.2. Worker reachability and temporal considerations

before their work is finished and they return to being reachable. The second worker category is the mobile worker. These workers are on the go, and while the nature of their work may have them actively involved for 45 minutes on one task and 30 on another, throughout their day they have many windows of time available for communication. But these are not set times, like we see in shift workers, the third category. These workers can be reached during scheduled breaks, which are often the same time every shift they work. But they may have only two or three breaks during an 8- or 10-hour shift, so they have limited times to be reached.

ALWAYS ON AS JOB REQUIREMENT OR CHOICE

The final category contains the "always-on workers," who, by job role or choice, can be reached almost always, and people working around them know this. The crisis communicator from Chapter 4 is a good example of an employee whose job dictates she be always on. She was quick to tell me that reporters need answers immediately, so if she misses a call, it's highly likely she'll hear on the evening news there was "no comment" from her organization.

But there are other people scattered throughout the data who say they're always on, like Cedric, the creative manager at the advertising agency in Chapter 4. At the beginning of his interview, he pointed to his BlackBerry and told the interviewer that if a call came in, he would have to answer it, even if they were in the middle of a question. When I consider the comments from others in his organization, it's obvious that he made this *choice* and that it's not formally required. He has chosen to be always on by setting the expectations of those around him that he's reachable anytime, anywhere.

The "always-on worker" is a phrase commonly used in research and the popular press to depict people who are connected to their work 24/7.[3,58] Naomi Baron even used the phase in the title of her book published in 2008.[3] I've used that term in the 2 × 2 matrix in Figure 11.2 because it accurately depicts the type of control people have over their time during work. But if I extend these explanations beyond work hours, I also see evidence of people in all categories who are reachable outside of work.

The differences between worker types in their reachability outside of work hours are primarily in the *reasons* people engage in this extra effort. For shift workers, the primary reason is to coordinate and modify shift times, not to do actual work. The nurses in Chapter 8, the janitors in Chapter 5, and the fast-food workers in Chapter 9 were all reachable—sometimes grudgingly—to change or be reminded about their shifts. Mobile and always-on workers, meanwhile, are reachable because they're accomplishing work tasks outside of normal work hours.

ELABORATING THE NUANCE OF THE MOBILE COMMUNICATION AFFORDANCE OF REACHABILITY

Many people treat the affordance of reachability as a given, something that shouldn't vary; after all, most people have mobile devices always with them. But, as I've just shown, during work hours people's reachability will vary. This is not unlike what my communication overload team found when we identified an "availability–expectation–pressure pattern" that people used to describe how they are communicatively overloaded.[77] For example, one young woman in that data said, "If I didn't have technology, when I went home I could sit in peace instead of always being available." She was a college student, working a part-time job, yet she felt pressure to be always on. She believed that others expected her to be always available and that pressure—justified or not—led her to feel the negative outcomes of being overloaded.

The limited research on why people feel responsible to be responsive is ripe for development. For example, Perlow's explanation of what she calls a "cycle of responsiveness" is related to reachability.[58] When employees started using ICTs almost constantly at work, their colleagues and clients began expecting immediate responses, which in turn led employees to monitor their communication channels to avoid missing work conversations. This is very similar to what I shared about my graduate student, Stephanie, when she got her first iPhone. That little message, *Sent from my iPhone*, signaled her availability. My request back to her activated the cycle of responsiveness, and while we accomplished our task, she also worked all weekend to make that happen. The analysis I've shared here shows a much more nuanced understanding of the affordance of reachability and how it integrates considerations of work, as well as the communication wants and needs from others outside of work.

This research chains out how individuals draw upon the affordance of reachability in diverse ways, and it also illustrates the added layer of controls that occur when people are at work. Individuals still have agency in how they draw upon these affordances for communicative practices, but their agency is not unbridled. I'll expand and link this notion to organizational and individual control throughout the rest of this final chapter.

NEGOTIATING REACHABILITY AS WELL AS UNAVAILABILITY

In every chapter of this book, reachability is being negotiated. But it takes different forms depending on the relationships between the people involved. Always-on and mobile workers are negotiating many things: reachability while in meetings, coordinating with co-workers, responsiveness expectations during and outside of work, and reachability outside of work hours. Shift workers, on the other hand, report their biggest negotiations are with friends and family: people who have personal reasons for staying in touch with them but don't seem to understand there are large blocks of time when they're simply unavailable at work. Andrew Schrock reminds us that "affordances can make communication possible, but it is up to individuals to use these affordances in more or less strategic ways" (p. 1236).[70] Some people in my data seem to have the strategy of communicating reachability down pat. Kim, the call-center worker who was training newcomers starting their jobs in how to cope with their long stretches of unavailability, is one such person. Her friends and family know that if she doesn't respond, she's at work.

A growing body of research led by Jeremy Birnholtz and Jeff Hancock has focused on a concept their team uses called a "butler lie."[6,7] This concept has been mentioned in research before mobile technologies emerged, and it explains how people manage their *unavailability*. For households that have a butler to answer the door, one of the first things he or she does is announce the visitor's presence; if the employer doesn't want to see the visitor, the butler politely lies and says he or she is unavailable. Birnholtz and his team summarized their aggregated findings from several studies. They claim that approximately 10% of the unavailability messages that people give to others are deceptive.[6]

Birnholtz and his colleagues believe that research and technology design should move beyond a focus on co-presence and coordinating around when people are available.[6] They argue that focusing on availability, as well as unavailability, will help us acknowledge the ambiguity associated with coordinating while still maintaining relationships. While their research program focuses primarily on how people use deception to communicate unavailability,[6,7] the people in my studies might learn something by considering how they might negotiate unavailability, either deceptively—to save themselves time or give them a break—or under legitimate job constraints.

Let's return to a quote I shared in Chapter 9 from the sociologist Christian Licoppe. In 2004 he predicted that people will need to "justify and renegotiate [their] unavailability" (p. 153) in addition to their availability because of the growing norms for connectedness.[44] When people believe that everyone around them is always reachable, it will take new strategies to help others understand that there are limits, often out of their direct control, that can make them unavailable during work hours and their personal lives. I also wonder what will happen as locatability becomes an integral part of mobile devices. While locatability is sometimes challenged because of privacy concerns in shift-worker situations, this might be ideal in communicating unequivocally about unavailability. Family members can see that their loved ones are at work and not able to respond, so they don't worry.

Always-on and mobile workers may need to use different negotiation strategies for effectively communicating unavailability than they did when discussing reachability. These could be strategies for managing time and regaining some of the control they think they've lost because they've avoided these expectation-setting conversations. Alexandra Samuel, author of *Work Smarter with Social Media*, recommends that people "set an email budget" complete with scheduled times to glance and other times to meaningfully read and respond.[69] This is a timely recommendation because most knowledge workers, in my data, say they check email on a mobile device. She acknowledges that there are connectedness norms but says people can be transparent with their practices. "Make your plan explicit with colleagues and clients so they know when you'll respond, and how to reach you in between times," she recommends.[69] By doing this, people can negotiate reachability and unavailability and regain some control over their time.

MOBILE-COMMUNICATION ACCEPTABILITY AT WORK ISN'T ALWAYS NEGOTIABLE

Workers might feel like they need to be reachable for communication with co-workers, managers, and friends or family; but what will others think if they see someone grab his or her mobile at work? It depends. People in some roles seem to be given tremendous latitude, while others are judged quite harshly. The data shared in this book suggests that people's interpretations of acceptable mobile use at work are entwined with two things:

1) Perceived power in the form of occupational or job prestige
2) The attention desired by others in that particular moment

Why can the doctor glance at her mobile phone in front of a patient but the nurse can't? How does the waitress know that she'd better hide to use her mobile phone if she wants a decent tip? Why would an office worker complain about seeing a janitor texting in the hallway?

In my meeting-study interviews I asked, "How do you know if someone is on task or off task when using his personal-mobile device?" In every case people chuckled and then shared their thoughts. Here are representative ones: "They probably aren't [on task] but I don't care." "If they're laughing, they're not doing work." "I can tell if they're on email or texting, and texting isn't serious." "Most people are just goofing off." "I have no idea what they're doing, and that makes me suspicious." Not a single person suggested that seeing someone else on a mobile device meant that person was automatically on task. The very next question I asked was, "What about pen and paper? On task or off task?" Responses immediately shifted, and people said, "Oh, they're on task." I ended that series of questions by saying, "Don't you ever get a piece of paper out and write down your grocery list or your to-do items when you're bored in a meeting?" In almost every case people sat quietly and then admitted they've done exactly that. They doodle or make lists, simply trying to pass the time. But you can't interact on a sheet of paper, and that seems to make a difference when predicting what people are doing on their mobile devices.

Acceptability perceptions could be heightened when it appears that the people in front of them are interacting and communicating with others through their mobile devices. But some people seem to have permission to multicommunicate, while others, not so much. During the hospital-study focus groups, nurses repeatedly said that it was okay for the physicians to check a message in front of the patients but not them. The nurses developed a simple strategy for making their intentions known before they reached for their mobile: they verbalized—signposted—why they were using it in front of the children and their parents. To my knowledge there isn't a study that's tested these nurses' assumptions, but their claims seem based on a combination of communication focus and occupational prestige. Their assumptions have led them to adopt the practice of being transparent by using verbal communication. For example, nurses use non-communicative functions like a calculator on their mobile devices when they need to double-check medication dosing. They explicitly tell their patients what they're doing to avoid speculation. Nurses don't believe they have permission to multicommunicate—carry on more than one near-simultaneous conversation[66]—but, by being transparent, they do seem to be granted permission to multitask—doing two tasks at approximately the same time.

The conclusions I draw from this set of analyses aren't pretty, but they provide insight into how acceptability might be negotiable in many situations. For simplicity—realize there's variance here—I've identified four categories of acceptable use and how they interact with perceptions of acceptable mobile use.

1) Acceptable if "always on" is a job-role requirement (e.g., crisis communicator)
2) Acceptable if the person has occupational or job-role prestige (e.g., doctor, executive)
3) Unacceptable when people are in lower-prestige jobs that are customer-facing (e.g., waitress)
4) Unacceptable when people are in lower-prestige jobs and observers suspect they are goofing off while on the clock (e.g., janitor)

These acceptable-use categories are laden with power and control. People with lower-prestige jobs are judged harshly when they engage in mobile communication; more powerful workers are assumed to be on task. It's as if onlookers want to control and punish what they perceive as inappropriate mobile use. Managers tend to do the same thing, but, to some extent, that's their job.

This typology suggests that the nurses from Chapter 8 may have a useful strategy that could be adopted in other situations. When people's job roles don't provide them with *assumed permission* to use a mobile device, they may want to verbalize how they're using them. For example, no one would think twice if a waitress said, "Let me look that up online right quick to see if the brand of tomatoes we use contains gluten." As a professor I've also used this strategy while teaching a class. I've told the students that I'm expecting an urgent call from a physician, so I'll need to handle that during class if the call arrives. They know that I rarely bring my mobile to class, so when it shows up, and I announce the reason, they grant me latitude.

I've kept the description of this acceptability finding brief, but it actually reinforces what we know about power and control in organizations. It is real, and organizational members often adapt without fully understanding the adaptations they make. As I elaborate on the final major contribution of this book, I'll also integrate all these findings into a model that depicts how control is negotiated.

ORGANIZATIONAL MOBILE COMMUNICATION AS A DIALECTIC OF CONTROL

Throughout this book I've demonstrated the negotiations for control involved with mobile communication in and around organizations. Note that I'm deliberately including "around organizations" because, as I analyzed my data across organizations and job roles, I found that formal work environments are often interlaced with people's personal lives. The original model of organizational control that I proposed in Chapter 3 needs to be expanded to account for work boundaries that cannot be separated from people and activities happening outside of work. Furthermore, as James Beniger illustrated in his book *The Control Revolution: Technological and Economic Origins of the Information Society*, information and communication are entwined with control.[5] As communication has become mobile, and people are able to draw upon the affordance of reachability, boundaries are dissolved. The affordance of reachability exists regardless of context, and so do the pressures others place on us. This is not an organizational affordance or a work-specific affordance.

In most research on organizational control, the focus is "inside" the organization,[74] and when scholars include external stakeholders, they're typically considering collaborative relationships found between organizations.[24,55] I put the word "inside" in quotes because it reflects an older organizational argument that focuses on the notion of rigid boundaries. The simplistic explanation of an organizational boundary defines where an organization begins and the external environment ends. Organizational scholars have argued against using what is often called a container metaphor because it's difficult to tell what's actually "inside" and "outside" an organization.[9,49] In my team's work published in Michael Gordon and Vernon Miller's edited book *Meeting the Challenge of Human Resource Management: A Communication Perspective*, we argue there's been a "paradigm shift from a 'contained' organization to a translucent one" (p. 217).[78]

While our argument considers changes that have occurred with the proliferation of social media, it's based in the reality that now the public can see inside the inner workings of organizations. It doesn't matter if individuals are working for an organization or not; boundaries are fluid and often transparent, and as people pass back and forth across them, their mobile is in their hands, which means they're constantly crossing boundaries.

Organizations, as a whole, can be considered structures that pull people together because they "provide the setting for a wide variety of basic social processes, such as socialization, communication, ranking, the formation of norms, the exercise of power, and goal setting and attainment" (p. 7).[71] But my data shows that stakeholders—external customers and friends and family—located beyond the organizations where people work often have some pull on how people communicate, especially with personal mobile devices. As the fully developed model shows later in this chapter, this is more complex than I developed in Chapter 3, so I'll spend the rest of this chapter explaining each part of it.

STRUCTURATION TO FRAME THE MULTILEVEL MODEL

The fully developed model depicted at the end of this chapter, uses key components of structuration theory[17,18,19] and my longitudinal data to pull together the control processes at play with mobile communication in and around work. Anthony Giddens developed structuration theory to argue against prior thinking that privileged either action or social structures in trying to explain how social changes happen over time. When people interact, they rely on their past experiences, but that doesn't limit what they can accomplish in the future. His theory isn't predictive, but communication scholars have used it to explain phenomena like policies, membership, and technology use.[8,11,32,60,72] Structuration theory is useful for my purposes because I have data at multiple levels that impacts one another. For example, mobile-device use can be influenced by pervasive norms of connectedness that function at a macro-society level. But those same norms of connectedness emerged because of the everyday use of mobile devices, a micro-level phenomenon. This type of theoretical thinking provides a framework that will allow this model to change as mobiles continue diffusing and morphing around new communication practices and material devices.

I begin by defining relevant terms from structuration theory and linking those concepts to the data found in the prior chapters. I've defined some of these terms before, but it's important to clarify them as I present this overarching framework.

AGENCY, STRUCTURES, AND POWER

"Agency" is considered the capacity to act, and an "agent" is defined as who or what does the acting. Giddens defined "structures" as "rules and resources, organized as properties of social systems" (p. 66).[17] "Rules" are identified as behavioral guides, and they exist at different levels.[19] For example, rules typically constrain action, and they can be more superficial and unenforced or deeply understood between all social members and obeyed. *Resources* are a source of power in routine interactions because they make action possible.[19] There are two basic forms of resources: authoritative, which involve coordinating human activity, and allocative, those related to controlling others or material products.[19] This definition is similar to Etzioni's claim, discussed in Chapter 3, that there are three forms of power: coercive, normative, and utilitarian.[12] Giddens' authoritative resources can be coercive or normative, while his allocative resources are similar to utilitarian power. Power is closely related to control, and it is manifest in everyday communication practices that reveal particular interests of individuals and groups.[10,52]

Giddens also explains that social structures and human action cannot be analyzed independently because they exist as a duality; human actions create, maintain, and change structures, but without structures, humans can't engage in action. People's interactions over time allow them opportunities to change their goals and make new plans that fit emerging situations. This reflexivity practice means that individuals aren't acting alone in making ongoing changes.[14,51]

In the data, these definitions help us understand why mobile communication has changed over time. There are evolving formal and informal structures that both facilitate and hinder mobile communication. Let's turn now to see how these ongoing changes are linked with agency and notions of control.

DIALECTIC OF CONTROL

While the data in this book suggests that hierarchy and job role perform a part in people's mobile use in organizational life, individuals aren't without agency; they don't just sit down and play by these rules. People still have choices and strategies; sometimes their actions—either conscious or unconscious—are effective. Giddens' definition of *dialectic of control* speaks to the "two-way character of the distributive aspect of power (power as control); how the less powerful manage resources in such a way as to exert control over the more powerful in established power relationship" (p. 374).[19] Even people in occupations with little prestige still have some resources they can wield, personal mobile devices being one of them.

The term "dialectic" describes the dynamic interplay between two opposite extremes that are also interdependent.[53] Linda Putnam suggests that dialectics embrace "the 'both–and' of the poles as opposed to making an 'either–or' choice between them"[62] (p. 707), which describes the type of negotiation for control, seen in my data, quite well. Carsten Sørensen, in his book *Enterprise Mobility: Tiny Technology with Global Impact on Work*, also finds that paradoxes, contradictions, and tensions are an integral part of his model on work performance and affordances.[75]

Yet many of the participants in these studies aren't actively acknowledging that they have power and choices in how they approach mobile communication. Some people feel like the consequences of violating a policy are so severe they choose not to act. But numerous examples from the data speak to a dialectic of control. For example, when fast-food workers told their supervisors they needed to use the restroom repeatedly and they instead hid in there to check their text messages, they had essentially shifted power. The supervisors needed their labor, but they were reluctant to set limits on personal needs like bathroom breaks. Several of the unintended consequences resulting from the banning of mobiles with janitors speak to the importance of a dialectic of control. For example, after unsuccessfully running up and down the stairs looking for a colleague to help him move heavy equipment, one janitor was frustrated and simply sat down and waited for someone to find him. By banning mobiles and thus removing his ability to microcoordinate behavior, he had a legitimate excuse to take an early break.

In his review of Giddens' influence on managerial scholarship, Whittington explains how a distributed notion of power undergirds Giddens' view of agency and dialectic control.[81] Giddens acknowledges that structures can distribute resources asymmetrically, but Whittington interprets Giddens by saying, "so long as actors retain the capacity to refuse, even in suicide, they remain agents" (p. 696).[81] Furthermore, Whittington suggests that all actors in Western business organizations have at least the power of defiance.[81] The examples here, in this book, present a robust range of defiance. And as long as organizations and their managers need to rely on employees' personal mobile devices, there will also be a dialectic of control where power shifts and control are constantly negotiated. See Figure 11.3 for an example of this dialectic of control.

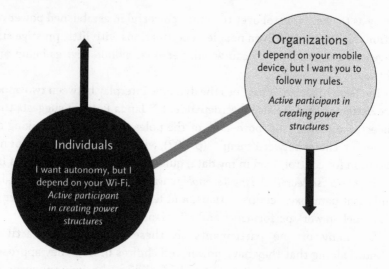

Figure 11.3. Example of the dialectic of control in mobile communication

ELABORATING A MULTILEVEL MODEL

In the full model I develop next in Figure 11.4, there are five agent groupings depicted: self, group, organization, customers, and interpersonal. Within each agent grouping, there are two key mobile-communication structures that are present in all the different agent groupings. The first structure is resources, both allocative and authoritative. These can vary depending on the specific agent, but they're always present. Think of parents paying for a mobile-phone plan to retain some control over their daughter, even when she's at work. Managers can also act this same way to either control or free their subordinates.

"Norms" are a structure present in all groupings where there are multiple members to create, reinforce, or change expected actions. It's a norm in customer service for the provider to pay careful attention to the consumer. Teams also agree on working hours and have norms for how they cover for one another when emergencies arise. Finally, "formal policies" are structures that tend to fall primarily in the organizational agent's purview. Within mobile communication, the only rules that become so formalized that they rise to a level of policy tend to be under organizational control. BYOD and banning mobile devices altogether are two such examples.

Now that I've defined some of the structuration-oriented terms used in the model, I'll elaborate on the various types of control found in the data. I've chosen to represent a dominant form of control in the overlapping spaces between the agent groupings. All forms of control are present at varying levels, at different times, but what's most helpful is to see what emerges as most influential from the data.

I'll begin with the most overlapping form of control that's seen in self, group, and organizations: hierarchical control. Hierarchies are a part of most organizations, and while they're often explicit through managerial control[29]—like Matt the national sales director—they can be implicit in job roles and perceptions of occupational prestige. Consider nurses and physicians; nursing managers typically supervise nurses, not physicians. Yet there are perceived hierarchical differences seen throughout the hospital data. This is why I called this type of control "hierarchical" instead of the more general term "managerial." Hierarchy works in both overt and covert ways to control workers and groups.

Free control,[35] discussed extensively in Chapter 6, emerged as a form of control that binds the individual to the organization in a powerful but almost completely hidden manner. Aurelie Leclercq-Vandelannoitte and her colleagues refer to this as a form of coercive autonomy because people who are being controlled are completely unaware of this.[35] The history and evolution of BYOD policies led me to realize the supremacy in this form of control. People who want flexibility to bring their own devices to work want this so badly that they're willing to click any button and agree to restrictions. They actively participate in creating this form of free control.

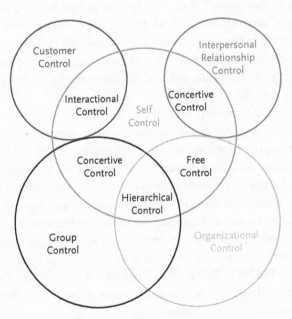

Figure 11.4. Multilevel model of mobile-communication control

Employees who don't have the freedom to participate in BYOD are typically controlled by formal policies, so that's another part of the control process that functions between organizations, individuals, and groups.

Concertive control, also known through the "iron cage" metaphor,[2] not only is dominant in the relationship between individuals and groups but also seems to explain the control present in interpersonal communication with those outside of work. This hidden form of control, where groups of people agree on core values and then hold one another accountable no matter what, is well established in work teams. But I see this present in interpersonal relationships outside of work organizations. Parents and their children of all ages agree that they love one another so much they always want to be there for each other. That core value means that when family members are unreachable, they've violated the bond and can be chastised until they find a way to manage their reachability and fulfill their relational dynamics.

Finally, I've called the key form of control found between customers and individuals "interactional control." There is a constant negotiation between individuals when they are interacting in pursuit of communicative goals. "Relational control" is a similar concept used in the book *Organizational Control*.[74] John Hagel, John Seeley Brown, and Mariann Jelinek describe the type of collaborative work seen at the interface between different organizations as a form of relational control, and that depiction is also reflected in the data in this book.[24] These scholars claim that this is a highly negotiable form of control because both parties are trying to work together.[24] Many times this is the same situation when individuals and customers are working toward a common goal. The customer (e.g., the children at a child-care center) needs attention, so the child-care worker puts her phone away to meet those needs.

The concept of relational control also provides insight into what might be different between multitasking and multicommunicating when people are negotiating their interactions.[66,76] Multitasking could be less irritating than multicommunicating because the interaction remains under the control of the present communicators, instead of including non-present others. For example, when a customer believes that an employee is inviting a third party into their conversation, he or she experiences reduced control in the relationship, and that can evoke many negative emotions. The customer wonders why the conversation is happening and what is being said behind his or her back. This analysis suggests that the transition between multitasking and multicommunicating is one of the break points likely to provoke a response from a customer.

While past research has shown that people's perceptions of a given technology's use can be different when that technology is used at work, as opposed to outside of work,[56,79,80] I see many similarities between work and personal contexts when mobile communication technologies are used. As I mentioned in the beginning of this book, mobile devices often allow us to use several different communication channels in just one device.[26] They are combinatorial ICTs, and this could expand the utility of this type of communication. Another explanation for why mobile communication seems to cross contexts is that regardless of where this form of communication is occurring, people have similar connection or information goals.

This chapter has grounded the historical perspective on mobile-communication control, elaborated the temporal affordance of reachability, shared the reality of perceived acceptability of mobile use at work, and created a model illustrating that mobile-communication control exists across boundaries and functions as a dialectic. While Figure 11.4 is drawn as a two-dimensional representation of the relationships between the different agents involved in mobile communication at work, please realize it's dynamic, not static. The sizes of the overlapping circles are in constant flux because control is dynamic and under constant negotiation.

The final chapter will be brief and focuses on two practical takeaways and tangible directions for future research. As I wrap up this book, I want to accomplish three things. I want individuals to critique their own behaviors and remember that they have agency; agentic control is only partially negotiated. I'd like to have HR and IT managers realize the work they have ahead of them to make policies and training opportunities available to all their workers, regardless of job title. And finally, I hope I've inspired scholars to tackle new research that will continue developing our understanding of the ongoing negotiation of mobile communication.

CHAPTER 12
You Can't Assume a Spherical Chicken

When my husband was an undergraduate physics major at Texas A&M University, I remember him explaining that theoretical physics problems often needed to be simplified to solve for a solution. On one assignment set, his professor began each problem by saying, "Assume a spherical chicken with a radius of. . . ." Then the students would calculate the velocity at impact if a chicken were thrown off a 20-story building, and then a 50-story building. I always found these problems a bit odd—in multiple ways—but I understood that the calculations would need to be much more complex if students had to include the chicken's head and feet.

It doesn't take a physics major to realize that if we really need to know the exact velocity of a given chicken at impact, the assumption that the poor chicken is spherical won't yield accurate results. This is simply a starting point, an estimate. I think this is what we're doing right now with mobile communication. We're assuming a spherical chicken. I've made a grand claim here, so let me give you an example. Control, as an organizational practice, is often explicitly and implicitly treated as a straightforward process. Organizations create policies and provide resources, while managers enforce them, and together, this directed control motivates desired employee behavior.

Ah, would that it were this simple!

I hope this book makes people stop and think about differences in mobile-communication practices. Yes, there are norms for connectedness,[1,7,14,18] and more and more people have mobile devices that include Internet connections; but there's also a lot of variability in use. Most people assume that everyone else engages in mobile communication just like they do, but not everyone can be reached immediately at work. Some people have overly controlling managers or policies, while others have jobs that legitimately require their full attention until they take a break. People in certain jobs are provided mobile devices and their service plans are reimbursed, while others can't pay their bills and their personal service gets turned off. And it appears that quite a few people have friends and family who won't leave them alone, even when they're working. To make sense of this difference, it helps to have some takeaways. I'll share those next.

TWO PRACTICAL TAKEAWAYS

1) Self-discipline and human-to-human conversation are key in mobile communication.
2) Bring-your-own-device-to-work (BYOD) still needs organizational attention.

I've read much of the research on mobile communication in interpersonal relationships, and I never expected it to play such an important role in organizational communication. It might be bold of me to say this, but I don't think we can understand workplace mobile use without considering employees' personal communication. Much of the academic research on knowledge workers bemoans work intruding on personal time, especially with the proliferation of mobile information and communication technologies (ICTs), but my data shows that bi-directional work–life boundaries are an issue for all types of workers. And, for the most part, none of us are navigating these boundaries very well.

Whiners, grow up! That's exactly what I had to fight back, in my mind, during more than one focus group I conducted with customer-facing workers. Some people had what seemed to be unhealthy co-dependent relationships because they had to talk with their significant other multiple times an hour. This data made me think of what my college students tell me about why they handle messages *during my class*: if they don't respond, they get punished. Punishment entails having a friend spam them with over 40 messages because they wanted a response right away. I was shocked that the data shared here reveals that people of all ages have trouble with their parents treating them the exact same way. This is concertive, and often overt, control over actions within personal relationships.

I also found myself frustrated with several people in my data who'd complain about always being reachable and working 24/7 because it seemed like they lacked the self-discipline to manage their own time. They knew there was a problem, they were stressed, and they couldn't see that they were largely responsible for their own situation. Why weren't they taking control of their own time?

Enter this pesky little thing called a norm of connectivity. Simply put, it's a violation of others' expectations for a person to be unreachable. But wait! Haven't time-management books always talked about trade-offs and priorities?[6,17] Yes, and several people in this data share strategies that might help with this situation, but I'll caution you that there won't be one correct answer in solving this growing concern. What I can say is that human-to-human conversations and actual negotiations about these challenges seem to matter. Just declaring one's temporal availability or un-availability, without conversation, can be a problem. Imagine being on a team, actively engaged in a project with a due date in a week, and without notice, one member sets an out-of-office email message saying he'll be un-available for 2 weeks. Or imagine being on that same team and having one member declare that she won't respond to email on Fridays. If you all agree to a no-email-on-Fridays rule, that can be fine, but when one team member makes a declaration without considering others' schedules, that can be a problem. In work and personal relationships we need to make the time to talk about time.

The second practical takeaway concerns BYOD practices. If the trend of requiring employees to bring their own communication and computing devices to work continues, human resource professionals should be pre-pared to enhance the training they provide to employees. While I presented this challenge specifically for new college graduates in Chapter 7, my observations inside of over 50 different organizations in the last 15 years suggest that many people aren't sure how to use the devices they own. From the college student who pulled out her mobile phone and couldn't understand how Excel could possibly be useful considering her screen was so small to the office worker who couldn't send files from her Mac to a PC, training is essential.

People who write and decide on BYOD policies should find the narratives in this book helpful. I've used the term "knowledge worker," sometimes cautiously, throughout the book because there isn't an easy way to differen-tiate types of workers. But my data suggests that workers with diverse job descriptions are using their mobile devices to access information and gen-erate "knowledge." For example, the janitor in Chapter 5 used his iPad to find out how to properly lift heavy equipment. If that information changed his practice or if he shared that with others, isn't that generating a certain type of knowledge? I'm not the first to suggest this. In their 2010 *Harvard Business Review* article, John Hagel, John Seely Brown, and Lang Davison presented an argument that all employees could be considered knowledge workers.[9] The problem is that many of the existing BYOD policies try to identify the type of worker who can use the policy.[11] My data suggests that everyone might need to use that policy for legitimate work needs. After all, as James Beniger stressed in 1989, information and communication are entwined with control.[2] But get ready, because my data also suggests that regardless of job role most people are going to goof off a little. And I'm not sure a BYOD or highly restrictive cyberslacking policy is going to restrict that behavior.

WHERE DO WE GO FROM HERE?

As a researcher, nothing is more encouraging than finishing a project and having it generate lots of new ideas. While the findings in this book are meaningful and helpful, they also reveal the work left to fully understand how we use mobile communication at work. There are four sets of questions I believe are worthy of addressing in the immediate future.

First, how do people manage their impression successfully and still negotiate boundaries for reachability? This question crosses all job roles and gets to the heart of the norms of connectedness. Studying this type of question will require gathering data, much like we do with 360-degree feedback—multiple perspectives are needed. People might think they're managing their impression splendidly, but their moms are furious. They might believe that their constant connection to their mom is a signal of their family values, but their team members at work wonder when their parents will stop helicoptering in.

A related question asks how people come to realize patterns in the availability and unavailability of others. I'm struck by the temporal affordance of reachability because so many people are stressed when they're made to feel that they missed an opportunity for communication. Are we aware that some people around us communicate differently when they're "at work"? What about weekends, and how's communication different when people's days off aren't traditional Saturdays and/or Sundays? These questions can't be answered by simply interviewing individuals or by surveying them. It'll take ethnographic fieldwork to make careful observations and have conversations to elaborate on what those observations mean. Furthermore, it'll be important to interview dyads or families and teams to see how an individual person's reachability is understood from multiple perspectives.

We need more theory-driven research on BYOD policies. There are few studies that have examined if and how people comprehend these policies, and if the goal is to get people to be responsible in their use, they need to know what they've agreed to when they click the button. We might examine research on medical informed consent from health-communication scholars like Erin Donovan to help us further explore how to make BYOD understandable.[8] There's also organizational-communication scholarship on policies that might guide an understanding of how to communicate the policy[4,5] as well as how to ensure that all workers have access to the policy.[12,13] This type of research could be very applied and practical, but guided by evidence-based theory and data.

While I included workers from many different professions, we need more focus on people who fall outside the traditional knowledge-worker category. In the U.S. 49% of all workers are considered blue collar (as contrasted with professional workers).[3] In a 2015 *Forbes* article, Scott Hartley argued that global job growth will be in local markets with lower-skilled work, and thus there'll be a rise in blue-collar high-tech workers.[10] But there's a real problem currently in the average person's perception of blue-collar work and mobile communication. In his book *Working Class: Challenging Myths About Blue-Collar Labor*, Jeff Torlina provides a provocative look into what he calls the circular reasoning that has created, and sustains, people's perceptions of blue- and white-collar differences.[16] He contends that academics and other white-collar workers have made claims that blue-collar workers aren't skilled, and this is why they get paid less. Then, when they're actually paid less, people assume they must be unskilled. He provides rich stories that show how many blue-collar workers have chosen their profession, enjoy their work, and are actually highly skilled. But the myth, as his title suggests, persists because maintaining the status quo is in the best interest of white-collar workers.

Looking through Torlina's book after I collected and analyzed most of my data really clarified what I saw; be they knowledge, manual-labor, clerical, or customer-service workers, ICTs are an integral part of their work. They might use mobile devices, software, and the Internet in different ways, but *access to people and information is important for all jobs*. Even though my studies contained quite a few people in this blue-collar category, there are still many occupations to further explore. For example, health and safety information increasingly is available on mobile devices, and with few exceptions,[15] we know very little about it. In industries like construction, industrial-chemical manufacturing, and biomedical manufacturing, employees in many job roles could find helpful information online, but how and when do they use it? On the flip side, studying workers, such as Apple salespeople, who use mobile devices constantly in front of customers might provide an additional perspective on customer expectations and mobile use.

You'll probably think of other useful next steps in things to study that can help us better understand mobile communication at work. I hope you'll leave thinking about differences: we can't assume a spherical chicken and understand the challenges and opportunities of mobile communication at work.

APPENDIX A

Data Sets and Analyses Used in This Book

The data shared here was collected through a series of institutional re-view board (IRB)–reviewed research studies. The two exceptions are my narrative in Chapter 1 and Stephanie's story of *Sent from my iPhone*, found in Chapter 2. In both cases, I had people involved with the story check the accuracy of my recollection. The reviewers recommended some major changes to clarify the details of the stories, and the versions that appear here are our agreed-upon representation. Most of the raw data in the re-maining studies were collected in the form of interview, observation, and/or focus-group data. These data were transcribed (and translated from Spanish to English in one case), and stored on UT-Austin-approved storage devices. See Table A1 and the description listed after the table, which elaborates the specific data-collection details by chapter.

I collected this data over a span of almost two decades, something es-sential for the goals of this project. But that also means that many of these studies weren't designed as qualitative-only studies. In most cases, I collected mixed-method data as part of the broader study goal, and I've published the quantitative portions of those studies. That doesn't mean I didn't rely on the qualitative data; it provided contextual framing that guided my quantitative study and helped me interpret the numerical data. However, I always planned on conducting a robust qualitative analysis of the data, so these studies were designed with that in mind.

In collecting the qualitative data, I always followed a semi-structured interview-question format that solicited opinions or attitudes and allowed flexibility for question probes.[1] My goals were to use probes to solicit details and to encourage elaboration with examples.[8] In each of these studies, as my teams collected the data, we compiled the interviews

Table A1. SUMMARY OF DATA, PARTICIPANTS, ANALYSES, AND MAJOR FINDINGS BY CHAPTER

Chapter	Guiding RQs	Type of Data	Number of Participants	Analysis Approach	Core Categories
Intro	Sets the stage, no RQ	Focus group	1 out of 18 (PD study)	Selected narrative	
1	How did early mobile-device use at work enable and constrain the resulting negotiation for control over mobile communication?	Semi-structured interviews & personal story	72 (KW study)	Constant comparison	1. Business tools for knowledge workers 2. Individual agency: experimenting with bringing devices to work
2	What did early negotiations for control look like?	Semi-structured interviews (1 from Norway)	72 (KW) & 42 (meetings study)	Constant comparison	1. Experimenting with availability and control 2. Work boundary negotiations
4	How does mobile communication happen in organizational meetings?	Semi-structured interviews	42 (meetings)	Constant comparison	1. Negotiating acceptable use: rules, norms, reachability, concertive control 2. Work boundary negotiations
5	How do manual-labor workers use mobile devices at work?	Focus groups	28 (janitor study)	Constant comparison	1. Banned, which is job role-specific 2. Just-in-time information matters 3. Managers sandwiched between types of use
7	How have BYOD concepts changed over time for college interns?	Survey & open coding of text	164 (college interns)	Descriptive statistics & constant comparison	1. Provide their own devices for their jobs 2. Specific ICT use has changed over time 3. Using ICTs at work is different from personal use

| 8 | What do hospitals' microcoordinating attempts reveal about work and personal mobile use differences? | Focus groups | 75 (healthcare workers) | Constant comparison | 1. Mobile communication requires trust
2. Mobile use reinforces hierarchies
3. Some people want boundaries |
| 9 | What does mobile communication look like in customer-facing work? | Focus groups | 35 (customer-facing workers & managers) | Constant comparison | 1. Reachability is in windows
2. Microcoordinating happens around shifts
3. Rules are driven by symbolic perceptions driven by job prestige |

Note. ICTs = information and communication technologies; KW = knowledge worker; PD = police department; RQ = research question.

and/or focus groups and made notes concerning which pieces of data might be most helpful for a future analysis. Sometimes the students involved in these projects used this data to write teaching case studies and final papers for their independent studies. That pre-work was quite helpful when I embarked on the current research.

For this bigger project, I compiled data and analyzed it at two levels. Even though I had research questions (RQs) pertaining to the corpus of data, I knew that a more nuanced analysis was essential before I could tackle those bigger questions. For example, I had to characterize mobile communication in manual-labor jobs (Chapter 5) as well as in customer-facing jobs (Chapter 9) before I could compare mobile communication across different types of work. So I created a guiding RQ for each data chapter and pulled together the specific qualitative and/or quantitative data that helped me answer it. In many cases, this meant I had to re-organize data and look back into the specific interview schedule for each of the studies included in that chapter. Not all of the original data I had collected were relevant for this study; approximately 30% of the collected data were used here. Table A1 provides the details of the chapter-level RQs, the type of data used, the sample size, the analysis approach, and the core categories that emerged from those analyses.

INTRODUCTION, CHAPTERS 2, 4, AND 5: POLICE OFFICE AND OFFICER DATA

The interview schedule for my police study contained 13 questions, and I conducted four focus groups to supplement the survey data. There were questions about communication in general, specific questions on media use for communication, and a section on information sources. I used the data from all four focus groups to help me select the narratives I shared in the book. The three different people whose data I shared in different chapters attended separate focus groups. Delilah's "Flicked Me a Nickel" story and Cordelia's "Meeting Note-Taker" story were both unique, but they supported what I found in the quantitative data. The police officer's story was representative of what I heard from other officers in their focus groups.

This police office had approximately 95 employees, and I had conducted a survey of their communication satisfaction prior to the focus groups. There were 80 participants in the quantitative study, of whom 40 were police officers. This was an office that was having trouble with its communication, and approximately a year after my study ended, several mid-level managers stepped down from the organization.

CHAPTERS 1 AND 2: KNOWLEDGE-WORKER ICT-USE DATA

The knowledge-worker data set consisted of 72 semi-structured interviews collected by Larry Browning, Jan Oddvar Sørnes, Alf Steinar Sætre, and me between 1999 and 2002. Approximately half of the interviewees were from Norway and half from the U.S. We also made a concentrated effort to include knowledge workers who were client-facing and those who worked primarily inside an organization. This study was funded by Hewlett-Packard, and the commitment we made to them was a series of reports.

This data set served as the base for my dissertation and was one of the papers in Jan Oddvar's dissertation. When I began writing this book, I looked back through all the interviews and identified 16 that focused heavily on mobile devices instead of general organizational technology use. It was those 16 interviews that I coded and selected narrative data from to illustrate concepts that emerged in these chapters. In addition to what appears in these chapters, the following publications were generated from this data set:

Browning, L. D., Sætre, A. S., Stephens, K. K., & Sørnes, J. O. (2008). *Information & communication technologies in action: Linking theory and narratives of practice.* New York, NY: Routledge.

Sætre, A. S., Sørnes, J. O., Browning, L. D., & Stephens, K. K. (2007). Enacting media use in organizations. *Journal of Information, Information Technologies and Organization, 2,* 133–158. Retrieved from http://jiito.informingscience.org/articles/JIITOv2p133-158Saetre100.pdf

Sætre, A. S., & Stephens, K. K. (2006). Tricking your customer without cheating them. In S. May (Ed.), *Case studies in organizational communication: Ethical perspectives and practices* (pp. 225–237). Thousand Oaks, CA: Sage.

Sørnes, J. O., Stephens, K. K., Browning, L. D., & Sætre, A. S. (2005). A reflexive model of ICT practices in organizations. *Informing Science, 8,* 123–142. Retrieved from http://inform.nu/Articles/Vol8/v8p123-142Sorn.pdf

Stephens, K. K., Sørnes, J. O., Rice, R. E., Browning, L. D., & Sætre, A. S. (2008). Discrete, sequential, and follow-up use of information and communication technology by managerial knowledge workers. *Management Communication Quarterly, 22,* 197–231. https://doi.org/10.1177/0893318908323149

Stephens, K. K. (2007). The successive use of information and communication technologies at work. *Communication Theory, 17,* 486–509. doi:10.1111/j.1468-2885.2007.00308.x

CHAPTER 4: ORGANIZATIONAL MEETINGS DATA

The data used in this chapter came from one-on-one semi-structured interviews with a total of 58 individuals representing 14 different organizations. This study has been amended four times to add more diverse samples and is still active with the UT-Austin IRB. The bulk of the interview details shared here came from a focused study of a single, large, governmental organization where we interviewed a total of 32 mid- to high-level managers between 2007 and 2008. Jenn Davis was my primary research partner on this study, and Frances Hamker also interviewed eight people. The remaining interviews represented a variety of organizations, and they were conducted between 2007 and 2016. The advertising study data shared in this chapter was collected by Abbey Grossman, an undergraduate research assistant with our team in 2007–2008.

The interview schedule for this study contained 16 primary questions, and we often used follow-up probes. Four questions were narrowly focused on multitasking in meetings: (1) How often do you use technology to communicate with others and multitask during your meetings? Probes: What tools do you use and for which activities? Are there ever situations when you don't multitask, turn devices off entirely, or not use them at all? (2) Who do you see communicatively multitasking in meetings? Probes: High-level managers or those at lower levels in the organization? (3) Describe to me the people who should not be seen multitasking in meetings. Probe: Who must multitask during meetings? What do you think of others who multitask during meetings? (4) What are the positive and negative business impacts of meeting multitasking? Probes: Access to information that resides outside the meeting? What about effectiveness, efficiency, usefulness, perceptions of being rude, making meetings longer or shorter? The responses from these questions constituted approximately 80% of the data I used for the analysis shared in this chapter. The remaining 20% of the data included context and examples that were more generally related to technology use at work.

I've never published any of the qualitative data from this study. My team also collected quantitative data, and that was cited in the chapter. These are those related publications:

Stephens, K. K. (2012). Multiple conversations during organizational meetings: Development of the multicommunicating scale. *Management Communication Quarterly, 26*, 195–223. doi:10.1177/0893318911431802

Stephens, K. K., & Davis, J. D. (2009). The social influences on electronic multitasking in organizational meetings. *Management Communication Quarterly, 23*, 63–83. doi: 10.1177/0893318909335417

CHAPTER 5: JANITORIAL-SUPPLY COMPANY DATA

The data used in this chapter came from five focus groups conducted in 2013 with a single cleaning company in the U.S. There were 39 individuals who participated, 14 of whom held supervisory positions, and one focus group was conducted in Spanish. The focus-group schedule contained 14 primary questions, and we followed up with additional probes to elaborate on our research questions. The restrictive mobile-use policy was only one of the RQs we addressed through this focus group because we were also interested in organizational identification and team-based communication in this type of organization.

When the data about the restrictive mobile-use policy emerged from the focus groups, we also interviewed managers and knowledge workers in this organization. We learned details about the strategically ambiguous policy from a vice president and two higher-level managers in the organization. We only interviewed two knowledge workers because I had experience collecting data from them for 2 years prior to this study. Jessica Ford was my primary research assistant on this study. These are the studies we've published from this data set, and the data presented in the chapter represent a different analysis:

Ford, J. L., Stephens, K. K., & Ford, J. (2015). Digital restrictions at work: Exploring how selectively exclusive policies affect crisis communication. *International Journal of Information Systems for Crisis Response and Management, 7*, 19–28. doi:10.4018/IJISCRAM.2014100102

Stephens, K. K., & Ford, J. L. (2014, May). *Banning mobile devices: Workplace policies that selectively exclude can shape crisis communication.* In S. R. Hiltz, M. S. Pfaff, L. Plotnick, & A. C. Robinson (Eds.), Proceedings of the 11th International ISCRAM Conference (pp. 284–288). Retrieved from http://idl.iscram.org/files/stephens/2014/975_Stephens+Ford2014.pdf

Stephens, K. K., & Ford, J. L. (2016). Unintended consequences of a strategically ambiguous organizational policy selectively restricting mobile device use at work. *Mobile Media &Communication*, 4, 186–204. Retrieved from https://doi.org/10.1177/2050157915619211

CHAPTER 7: COLLEGE INTERN DATA

The data in this chapter was different from that in any other chapter because it came from brief surveys conducted over a 6-year time span. I collected data from my internship classes almost every spring that I taught the class; then, at the end of the semester, I shared their data back with them. I explained in the chapter that this was not a study designed before I began collecting data, and the survey questions changed to fit the needs of the students. Despite these changes, their data provides a longitudinal perspective on how 164 college interns have been expected to provide their own devices, as well as how their information and communication technologies (ICT)–use patterns are different when comparing work and personal use. Additionally, there were open-ended questions on these instruments. Their responses were brief, but I still coded this data and conducted a fairly simple constant-comparison method to reveal the findings I share.

CHAPTER 8: HOSPITAL DATA

My team and I began this study in May of 2015 when I joined the interprofessional communication improvement committee at a pediatric teaching hospital. In August of 2015, I spent approximately one month collecting field notes from observations there. After this participant observation, my team created a focus-group schedule, and we specified different times for workers in various healthcare job roles to attend. For example, physicians were not in the same focus groups as nurses. Our observations and prior research literature suggested that there's a natural hierarchy between these job roles, and we could gather the most representative data by separating the groups. We conducted two nursing-specific focus groups, one pharmacy focus group, three physician focus groups, one team-member focus group, and five resident-physician focus groups. The resident focus groups were only used for context information in this chapter; data from the other focus groups was used for the analysis. My team members on the broader part of this study included Josh Barbour, Millie Harrison, Yaugang Zhu, Terrie Hairston, Meena Iyer, and John Luk.

While our IRB authorization is for up to 650 participants, in the qualitative portion of this study we've worked with a total of 96 subjects in focus groups so far. This study is a work-in-progress, and while the data and findings appearing in this chapter are original, we have published one paper in a conference proceeding so far:

Stephens, K. K., Zhu, Y., Harrison, M., Iyer, M., Hairston, T., & Luk, J. (2017). *Bring your own mobile device (BYOD) to the hospital: Layered boundary barriers and divergent boundary management strategies.* Proceedings of the 50th Annual Hawaii International Conference on System Sciences (HICSS) (pp. 3517–3526). Washington, DC: IEEE Computer Society.

CHAPTER 9: CUSTOMER-FACING WORK

My team member on this study was Jessica Ford; but I also collected some of the data on my own, and I did all the analyses for the chapter. There were a total of 39 participants in the 10 focus groups I analyzed for this chapter. This is one of the only sets of focus groups where open coding alone was insufficient. The managers, in particular, interacted with one another so much during this focus group that in addition to coding their responses, I copied the sequences of their conversations and reported those in the chapter. There was a range of diverse participants in these focus groups, as you can tell from the stories I shared in Chapter 9.

DATA ANALYSIS APPROACH

After compiling the appropriate data to address each chapter-level RQ, I engaged in constant-comparative analysis.[4,5] First, I read through all transcripts and coded every incident where a participant talked about concepts related to my chapter RQs. I open-coded my data with the goal of "moving beyond concrete statements in the data to making analytic interpretations" (p. 43).[1] I didn't pre-determine a unit of analysis to code—as in content analysis—but instead I created codes representing "chunks" of data in varying sizes (p. 71).[6] Starting at this first step, I wrote memos and noted particularly vivid examples so that I could reference them at the end of my analysis. My memos mostly contained ideas for connections between the codes,[3] but I also wrote memos when respondents' comments seemed contradictory or left me feeling conflicted as I tried to make sense of the data.[5] This form of memoing is especially helpful when the ultimate goal is to reach abstract, but connected, theoretical concepts.[1]

In most chapters, I found I needed to engage next in axial coding—looking for causal relationships between open codes and finding meaningful ways to begin seeing connections between them.[3,5] For example, in Chapter 1, my RQ focused on understanding how early mobile-device use set the stage for the resulting negotiation for control over mobile communication. Many of my open codes suggested that cell phones were business tools, so I needed to also ask how the work context and goal-oriented activities of these specific respondents led them to view their cell phones as work resources. This more extensive coding was followed in tandem with selective coding, where I combined and compared codes to create some overarching categories.[2] I grouped these categories and gave them conceptual phrases as the final step in my constant comparison method.[5] You'll see these final core categories in the last column of Table A1.

You might be wondering how I chose the stories and examples from the vast data I analyzed. Yes, these stories represent the most provocative data examples, and they also represent interviewees who were articulate and self-aware. But just because the stories I chose are more colorful, don't think they're outliers. These stories illustrate the core categories and findings from my analyses. The stories provide the context and bring these major findings to life. Delilah's story at the beginning of the book, while a bit shocking, represents the type of comments many subordinates made about the power their managers hold over them, the fear they feel about losing their jobs if they don't comply, and the socioeconomic concerns that lurk beneath the surface of mobile communication. You'll remember that story, and hopefully, it also brought the findings to life.

SECOND-LEVEL QUALITATIVE ANALYSIS

For this project, I did two levels of qualitative analysis. In addition to the chapter-specific analyses, there are two overarching RQs that led me to derive the theoretical and practical contributions as a whole. In Chapters 10 and 11, I pulled the data from every person or group represented in this book and did two different analyses. In Chapter 10, I asked this RQ:

RQ: What are the characteristics of specific jobs that interact with how mobile communication happening in organizational life?

After an additional round of open, axial, and selective coding, I identified four core categories: (1) workers' degree of autonomy, (2) mobility (as opposed to doing work in a stationary location), (3) task variety, and

(4) primary communication target. While I used a constant-comparative method to identify these findings, I found it hard, at first, to see if there was a priority to these categories. I wanted to know if one was more important than the others. I mentioned this in Chapter 10, but I used a spreadsheet to systematically display each of the four categories in a different prior order. Through this comparison, I found that autonomy was the primary driver and the next three influenced mobile communication in descending order.

In Chapter 11, I combined these four core categories concerning job differences and asked a broader RQ:

RQ: *What do we learn about mobile communication in organizational life by taking a longitudinal, multiple-industry, and diverse–job role approach?*

To address this question, I created a timeline of the chapter-specific findings and through another round of open, axial, and selective coding, I identified four major findings. During this step, I found the axial coding quite informative because I was looking specifically for how groups of people and organizations adjusted, reacted, and even changed their goals over time. This is a summary of what I elaborate in Chapter 11 as those key contributions:

1) Organizations have always needed to have a level of control over mobile communication. Whether they provide the mobile technology or create policies to control mobile communication, they seek a steady state. See Figure 11.1 for an illustration of this longitudinal finding.
2) The mobile communication affordance "reachability" is nuanced and involves negotiations with others at work and with friends and family outside of work. See Figure 11.2 for this finding.
3) Acceptability of mobile communication is situated, symbolic, and hierarchical.
4) There's a dialectic of control present in mobile communication at work, and it involves ongoing negotiations between and among individuals, groups, and organizations. See Figures 11.3 and 11.4 for illustrations of these findings.

QUALITY QUALITATIVE RESEARCH

Before I began these analyses, I examined the data as a whole and found that they meshed well with Sarah Tracy's eight markers of quality qualitative research.[7] These are: (1) worth, (2) rigor, (3) sincerity, (4) credibility, (5) significant contribution, (6) resonance, (7) ethics, and (8) meaningful coherence. Keep in mind that when I began collecting these data, Sarah Tracy hadn't written her qualitative methods text, so for the earlier studies, I relied on my training and prior research experiences, with Larry Browning in particular, in grounded theory, constant-comparative method, and thematic analysis. But as I looked over the data, I believe that every study represented these eight pillars of quality—not objectivity, and not necessarily generalizability, but consistently robust qualitative research.

MY QUEST TO INCLUDE MANUAL-LABOR WORKERS IN THIS PROJECT

One of the most meaningful contributions of this book is that it includes different types of organizations and diverse workers. An important turn in my research trajectory occurred when I was asked to conduct a quantitative employee-engagement survey with a janitorial-supply company. During that data collection, I got to know the janitors, and our informal conversations led me to understand more about their mobile policies. As I finished the quantitative report for that organization, I asked to do the focus groups that are reported in Chapter 5. But before I did that immersive interview and observational research, I knew there were reasons I was drawn to their plight and that my background could influence how I approached that data collection. In her qualitative research methods text, Sarah Tracy emphasizes the importance of being self-reflexive, especially when conducting interviews and interacting with participants in qualitative studies.[7] What appears next is the story linking my past work experiences with a desire to better understand these janitors. Unfortunately, there's rarely space in a journal article to share these self-reflections, but it's important for readers of this book to know that my personal experiences shaped my interest in these diverse workers and could have influenced my interpretations. One of the main reasons I documented these initial beliefs was to remind myself, during the analysis, that I have biases that need to be carefully considered to enhance the quality of my research. I'll share my reflexive writing next.

SELF-REFLEXIVITY IN STUDYING DIVERSE WORKERS

I began my working life in customer service while I was still in high school, and then, later, I worked in a manufacturing factory. I knew that I'd need to support myself through college, so in high school I landed a wonderful part-time job as a waitress for the country club in my hometown. I spent 3 years working weekends, spring breaks, and summers, and I met some splendid people along the way. There was an older couple who came in every week, and their only request was that I keep their coffee cups full. That was easy for me because my mom trained me well: she loved hot coffee. They ordered two steaks and coffee, and when I kept their cups full, I saw a $50 tip. That was more than the entire bill—even for two steaks—in the late 1980s. Being a waitress taught me a lot about paying attention to other people, learning what they want, and providing great service.

I also had diverse co-workers at the country club. I spent many evenings in the kitchen practicing my Spanish with several members of the staff. I remember a conversation one night where we talked about stars and astronomy. I grasped only about half of their meaning, and they were both patient and amused as I tried to follow along.

In my senior year of high school, I received a 4-year college scholarship from a company located in my hometown of slightly fewer than 10,000 people. The scholarship came with an opportunity for me to work in the plant, which manufactured computer tape. Eventually, once I had more chemistry classes under my belt, they told me I could work in the industrial-chemical laboratory, but the first year, I wasn't any use to the lab.

I started my position in June, right after graduation. They put me in Quality Assurance (QA), a small team of three women and a supervisor whom we occasionally saw. The other two women, both in their mid- to late 20s, were supposed to take me under their wing and show me the ropes. Our job was to go onto the manufacturing line, randomly pull a dozen round 10''-by-0.5'' spools of magnetic computer tape, and bring them to our machines to see if the operators were doing their jobs and removing contaminants on the tape. Their jobs combined manual labor with extreme concentration because they loaded their tape on a machine and hit a button, and when the machine stopped, it meant there was a glob of slurry (the material that coated the computer tape) that needed to be manually scraped off with an X-Acto knife. I occasionally filled in for these line operators, so I knew quite well what their jobs entailed. Contaminant removal was essential because the computer tape needed to be free from defects to be reliable for our customers' data storage.

My two colleagues were kind and helpful, but they made it clear to me on my first day that I was taking a job away from one of their friends who needed to support her family. I was seen as the "privileged college-bound kid," even though everyone knew that both of my parents were public-school teachers and we often lived paycheck to paycheck. This was a new experience for me, a life-changing experience. Even though my parents had little extra money, I was never hungry and I could get healthcare when I was sick. I came to learn that in this work environment, that's all it took to be considered privileged. And going to college? Not even considered an option by most people working on the production side of the company.

Less than a week after I started my summer job, I walked through the break room expecting to be alone. As a QA worker, I had much more autonomy than the actual assembly-line workers. In the middle of the room there was a long wooden bench with lockers on either side, and I heard a woman moaning as she wrapped her body around the wooden bench with her abdomen compressed tightly. I ran over to see if I could help. She was crying and told me she would be OK in a few minutes. She looked terrible, but it was obvious she wasn't going to tell me, a random 17-year-old stranger, any details. I took my time going to the restroom, and when I came out she was doubled over trying to walk out the door. I asked again if I could get her anything or take her to the nurse. She screamed, "NO! Just leave me alone!" and I watched her hobble back to her computer-testing station on the assembly-line floor.

I decided to avoid the break room if at all possible. Eighty percent of the assembly-line workers were women, and many were single mothers trying to support multiple kids with no help from a deadbeat father. Breaks were a time for these workers to cry, laugh, share stories, and self-medicate. The woman I'd seen writhing in pain in the break room had extreme endometriosis—a condition afflicting several other women working there as well. Over-the-counter painkillers were no longer strong enough, so she had turned to illegal drugs to knock her pain long enough for her to work her shifts. She swallowed the drugs during breaks, but it took them a while to make her pain tolerable. She was trying to support her three kids, all under 5 years old.

I naively asked one of my co-workers why this young woman didn't go to the doctor, and I still remember the look of disbelief on her face. She told me doctors were expensive and surgery wasn't an option for most of the workers. You see, the year before, the company had fired most of their workers and then re-hired them as "part-time" workers, a strategy common in the late 1980s to cut employers' health-insurance costs. There wasn't a union at this workplace, and in a small town, workers have limited options; so while they got to keep their higher hourly pay, they lost their health coverage. Several of the women had been diagnosed with illnesses, like endometriosis, while they still had health coverage, but after they were reclassified as part-time, even a doctor's visit had to be weighed against the competing need to provide basic necessities like food.

Over the next 3 years of college, I returned to work here every break and summer. I needed the money, and this was relatively high-paying work.

After I had 2 years of chemistry under my belt, the managers moved me to the chemistry lab where I ran tests on the computer tape and on the solvents we used to dissolve the tape coating—aka "slurry." In addition to running the chemistry tests, I had to go into the large, outdoor, storage-tank area to pull test samples by opening the valve on the drum and filling a bottle with liquid products. To pull these samples, I put on my lab coat, wore closed-toed shoes, and donned a hard hat in bright yellow. In the outdoor storage-tank area, the workers were almost all men; and they performed what we might call today "dirty work"—meaning they got filthy from moving products, cleaning out the large storage drums, and keeping the area clean. I didn't really need help to pull a sample, but there was always someone right beside me, talking with me—sometimes flirting—as I did my work. I remember thinking that I never got that much attention in high school; but in this part of my job, I was one of two women, and I always felt the eyes on me as I did my job.

I worked hard to develop professional relationships with the men who worked with the storage tanks, and I often stopped back in on the testing assembly line or the QA area to maintain my relationship with the single moms and young women, who eventually accepted me—somewhat. But I also remember going home at night and crying, partly because I didn't know how to help them and partly because their situations scared me. Most of these workers hadn't chosen their line of work, but they took any available job in an effort to support their families. I'm not sure career options were ever discussed as they were growing up. I even tried to help two of the young women, both childless, by bringing them information about the local community-college courses happening right in our town. I was taking these courses while working in the plant, and I knew they were smart and capable of joining me. I was never successful, but I think our conversations helped them realize they might have options in the future. At least I hope I had at least a small impact on them. They certainly impacted my life profoundly.

You can understand, then, my motivation to look beyond knowledge workers and include diverse samples and people in my research. Listening to these workers' stories all summer made me almost beg to start back to college. I knew that a college degree was the path to broaden my options. It was years later, after returning to graduate school and becoming a professor, that I found a small way to repay my prior colleagues for the incredible life education they provided me. Now I can give them voice through my research. I also actively seek students who have great potential but need someone to understand that not all college students come from privileged backgrounds.

APPENDIX B
Acknowledgments

Let me thank, first, the hundreds of research subjects who've allowed me to learn from their experiences and opinions. I feel honored to share their stories here. Through my analyses, I hope to give fresh voice to often-ignored workers and to inspire you readers to stop and think beyond your own mobile-communication practices.

This book wouldn't be possible if Rich Ling hadn't read one of my early papers on mobiles in organizations and told me that there's a real gap in this type of theoretically driven research. He encouraged me to pursue this project, and, as you have seen, his work on mobiles has informed many of my explanations. Jim Katz provided me feedback on my early mobiles-in-meetings research, and Janet Fulk's recommendation, after responding to one of my conference papers, sent me down the path of exploring the notion of control as an explanation for what my qualitative data unearthed. Conversations with my dissertation advisors, Larry Browning and Ron Rice, have shaped my thinking on this topic, as have conversations with the following colleagues: Jan Oddvar Sørnes, Alf Steinar Sætre, Dawna Ballard, Josh Barbour, Laurie Lewis, Craig Scott, Sharon Strover, Wenhong Chen, Kerk Kee, and Matt McGlone. Jeff Treem met with me several times to discuss my findings, and his feedback and literature suggestions proved invaluable. Barry Brummett and Talia Stroud provided me guidance in how to manage a book-length manuscript, while Rod Hart and Jay Bernhardt provided college support through undergraduate research grants and a faculty research grant.

Several people generously read drafts of my work and provided me valuable feedback. Two reviewers read my entire manuscript, and their feedback substantially improved the clarity of this work. Chapter 1 included recalled, personal data, and without the comments of Dahlia Riley,

I wouldn't be confident in the story I told. She remains the most influential mentor I've ever had. Her expectations for my work are so high, I have to jump to get there, but her direct approach has taught me how to mentor others and help them achieve beyond their goals. Niki Acosta, one of my undergraduate students from the early 2000s, read the first part of my book and offered her perspective as well as encouraged me to "rock on!" Stephanie Dailey read her story *Sent from my iPhone* and provided me precise feedback; she also permitted me to use her real name. I did so because she and I both use this story in our classes. It's a sobering reminder of how, even with good intentions, we can take advantage of others' willingness to help and be taken advantage of ourselves. Larry Browning reviewed all my theory chapters and provided me extensive feedback on my grounded theory and the literature on control and dialectics.

Jeannine Turner read my meetings chapter, shared it with her students at Georgetown University, and provided me helpful feedback. Heather Canary also spent hours discussing policy and structuration theory. She also hosted me when I gave a colloquium at the University of Utah, where I shared my early data analysis with their faculty and students. Hope Koch guided me to helpful MIS literature. Zach Steelman, Carsten Sorenson, and Sirkka Jarvenpaa met with me at HICSS 2017 to share their insight into this literature. Special thanks to the students in my fall 2016 graduate seminar on organizations and technology and my 2017 summer seminar at North Dakota State University. Their early feedback pushed me to create a book that weaves narrative and theory without losing sight of creating a readable, engaging piece of work.

John Trimble edited my book and taught me how much I have to learn about punctuation, narrative lines, and brightening my prose. You've also made my writing clearer and taught me how to think like an editor. These lessons will last me a lifetime. Afterward, JiHye Kim compiled my manuscript, carefully edited my APA references, and made the document consistent throughout.

I've also had the great pleasure of working with a number of students and collaborators in the data collection for these various projects. I thank Ashley Barrett, Ignacio Cruz, Minhao Dai, Jenn Deering Davis, Maureen Edobar, Jessica Ford, Elizabeth Glowacki, Elizabeth Goins, Abby Grossman, David Guzman, Fran Hamker, Millie Harrison, Abby Heller, JiHye Kim, Dron Mandhana, Melissa Murphy, Gabriel Pantoja, Meagan Quejada, Will Ragan, Sarah Rayburn, Devin Ruthstrom, Erin Scott, Caroline Sinclair, Nhi Tran, Cynthia Velasco, Eric Waters, and Yaguang Zhu. I also thank my collaborators at Dell Children's Healthcare Center—Terrie Hairston, Meena Iyer, and John Luk—and the team at UT-Austin that facilitated access to several of my meeting study participants. This includes Cindy Posey, Rhonda Weldon, and Pat Clubb.

I also need to thank random acquaintances, friends, and family. Yes, I'm that researcher who, while standing in line at the grocery store, leans over to the mom in front of me and asks questions about the scheduling app I see her open. One time, when I saw a campus police officer typing on his mobile laptop, mounted over the passenger seat of his patrol car, I tapped on the window to ask him if he was provided training on multitasking while driving. Surprisingly, I've never had anyone ignore me, even the host of random strangers I've quizzed while standing in an elevator and being the only person *not* on my mobile phone. Thank you all for indulging my insatiable appetite for learning more and more about people and how they use their technology to communicate.

Team Texas Climbing friends—Gennie, Randy, Leslie, Tammy, Natasia, and Kathy—have listened to me and patiently shared their ideas. My hairdresser, Karen, and my amazing convenience store clerk, Sarah, have helped me understand client-facing work from multiple angles. My MacTheatre friends, Maria and Dave, my Facebook friends, as well as my parents, Eddie and Leslie, have also supported my journey. Finally, my husband and kids have played both a grounding and a feedback role. Sarah Kay and Kyle have tolerated my inquiries about the latest social-media tools, and they've also asked insightful questions that only tweenagers and teenagers could. Tab was my comprehensive support: intellectual sounding board, cheerleader, and amazing father who took our kids places on the weekends so that I could bury my head and write.

REFERENCES

Introduction

1. Bayer, J. B., Campbell, S. W., & Ling, R. (2016). Connection cues: Activating the norms and habits of social connectedness. *Communication Theory, 26,* 128–149. doi:10.1111/comt.12090

2. Bittman, M., Brown, J. E., & Wajcman, J. (2009). The mobile phone, perpetual contact, and time pressure. *Work, Employment & Society, 23,* 673–691. https://doi.org/10.1177/0950017009344910

3. Browning, L. D., Sætre, A. S., Stephens, K. K., & Sørnes, J. O. (2008). *Information & communication technologies in action: Linking theory and narratives of practice.* New York, NY: Routledge.

4. Cameron, A., & Webster, J. (2010). Relational outcomes of multicommunicating: Integrating incivility and social exchange perspectives. *Organizational Science, 22,* 754–771. Retrieved from http://www.jstor.org/stable/20868891

5. Cameron, A. F., & Webster, J. (2013). Multicommunicating: Juggling multiple conversations in the workplace. *Information Systems Research, 24,* 352–371. http://dx.doi.org/10.1287/isre.1120.0446

6. Campbell, S. W., & Park, Y. J. (2008). Social implications of mobile telephony: The rise of personal communication society. *Sociology Compass, 2,* 321–387. doi:10.1111/j.1751-9020.2007.00080.x

7. Chib, A., Malik, S., Aricat, R. G., & Kadir, S. Z. (2014). Migrant mothering and mobile phones: Negotiations of transnational identity. *Mobile Media & Communication, 2,* 73–93. doi:10.1177/2050157913506007

8. Donner, J. (2009). Blurring livelihoods and lives: The social uses of mobile phones and socioeconomic development. *Innovations: Technology, Governance, & Globalization, 4,* 91–101. doi:10.1162/itgg.2009.4.1.91

9. Drucker, P. F. (1969). *The age of discontinuity: Guidelines to our changing society.* London, United Kingdom: William Heinemann.

10. Evans, S. K., Pearce, K. E., Vitak, J., & Treem, J. W. (2017). Explicating affordances: A conceptual framework for understanding affordances in communication research. *Journal of Computer-Mediated Communication, 22,* 35–52. doi:10.1111/jcc4.12180

11. Gibbs, J. L., Rozaidi, N. A., & Eisenberg, J. (2013). Overcoming the "ideology of openness": Probing the affordances of social media for organizational.

knowledge sharing. *Journal of Computer-Mediated Communication, 19,* 102–120. doi:10.1111/jcc4.12034

12. Gibson, J. J. (1986). *The ecological approach to visual perception.* Mahwah, NJ: Erlbaum.

13. Golden, A. G. (2012). The structuration of information and communication technologies and work–life interrelationships: Shared organizational and family rules and resources and implications for work in a high-technology organization. *Communication Monographs, 80,* 101–123. doi:10.1080/03637751.2012.739702

14. Golden, A. G., & Geisler, C. (2007). Work–life boundary management and the personal digital assistant. *Human Relations, 60,* 519–551. doi:10.1177/0018726707076698

15. Haddon, L. (2003). Domestication of mobile telephony. In J. Katz (Ed.), *Machines that become us: The social context of personal communication technology* (pp. 43–56). New Brunswick, NJ: Transaction.

16. Harris, J., Ives, B., & Junglas, I. (2012). IT consumerization: When gadgets turn into enterprise IT tools. *MIS Quarterly Executive, 11,* 99–112. http://misqe.org/ojs2/index.php/misqe/article/viewFile/416/313

17. Helles, R. (2013). Mobile communication and intermediality. *Mobile Media & Communication, 1,* 14–19. Retrieved from https://doi.org/10.1177/2050157912459496

18. Jarvenpaa, S. L., & Lang, K. R. (2005). Managing the paradoxes of mobile technology. *Information Systems Management, 22,* 7–23. doi:10.1201/1078.10580530/45520.22.4.20050901/90026.2

19. Jensen, K. B. (2008). Intermediality. In W. Donsbach (Ed.), *International encyclopedia of communication* (pp. 2385–2387). Malden, MA: Blackwell.

20. Jensen, K. B. (2010). *Media convergence: The three degrees of network, mass, and interpersonal communication.* London, United Kingdom: Routledge.

21. Katz, J. E. (2007). Mobile media and communication: Some important questions. *Communication Monographs, 74,* 389–394. http://dx.doi.org/10.1080/03637750701543519

22. Katz J. E., & Aakhus, M. (Eds.). (2002). *Perpetual contact: Mobile communication, private talk, public performance.* Cambridge, United Kingdom: Cambridge University Press.

23. Koch, H., Zhang, S., Giddens, L., Milic, N., Yan, J., & Curry, P. (2014, December). *Consumerization and IT department conflict.* Paper presented at the 35th International Conference on Information Systems, Auckland, New Zealand. Retrieved from https://pdfs.semanticscholar.org/9ffd/5c3d0511c8841f9bbe6b38b1e542dea13da7.pdf

24. Köffer, S., Ortbach, K., & Niehaves, B. (2014). Exploring the relationship between IT consumerization and job performance: A theoretical framework for future research. *Communications of the Association for Information Systems, 35,* 261–283. Retrieved from http://aisel.aisnet.org/cais/vol35/iss1/14/

25. Köffer, S., Ortbach, K., Junglas, I., Niehaves, B., & Harris, J. (2015). Innovation through BYOD? The influence of IT consumerization on individual IT innovation behavior. *Business Information System Engineering, 57,* 363–375. Retrieved from http://aisel.aisnet.org/bise/vol57/iss6/3/

26. Leonardi, P. M. (2011). When flexible routines meeting flexible technologies: Affordance, constraint, and the imbrication of human and material agencies. *MIS Quarterly, 35,* 147–167. Retrieved from http://web.

stanford.edu/group/WTO/cgi-bin/wp/wp-content/uploads/2014/pub_old/Leonardi%202011b.pdf

27. Leonardi, P. M. (2013). When does technology use enable network change in organizations? A comparative study of feature use and shared affordances. *MIS Quarterly, 37*, 749–775. https://pdfs.semanticscholar.org/75c7/4e15c88494118a72a94de4eb5a877a46a543.pdf

28. Leonardi, P. M. (2014). Social media, knowledge sharing, and innovation. Toward a theory of communication visibility. *Information Systems Research, 25,* 796–816. doi:10.1287/isre.2014.0536

29. Leonardi, P. M., & Barley, S. R. (2010). What's under construction here? Social action, materiality, and power in constructivist studies of technology and organizing. *Academy of Management Annals, 4*, 1–51. doi:10.1080/19416521003654160

30. Leonardi, P. M., Neeley, T. B., & Gerber, E. M. (2013). How managers use multiple media: Discrepant events, power, and timing in redundant communication. *Organization Science, 23*, 98–117. doi:10.1287/orsc.1110.0638

31. Licoppe, C. (2004). "Connected presence": The emergency of a new repertoire for managing social relationships in a changing communication technospace. *Environment and Planning D: Society and Space, 22*, 135–156. doi:10.1068/d323t

32. Ling, R. (2004). *The mobile connection: The cell phone's impact on society*. San Francisco, CA: Morgan Kaufmann.

33. Ling, R. (2012). *Taken for grantedness: The embedding of mobile communication into society*. Cambridge, MA: MIT Press.

34. Ling, R., & Donner, J. (2009). *Mobile communication: Digital media and society series*. Malden, MA: Polity Press.

35. Ling, R., & Donner, J. (2013). *Mobile phones and mobile communication*. Hoboken, NJ: Wiley.

36. Ling, R., & Yttri, B. (2002). Hyper-coordination via mobile phones in Norway. In J. E. Katz & M. Aakhus (Eds.), *Perpetual contact: Mobile communication, private talk, public performance* (pp. 139–169). Cambridge, United Kingdom: Cambridge University Press.

37. Majchrzak, A., Faraj, S., Kane, G. C., & Azad, B. (2013). The contradictory influence of social media affordances on online communal knowledge sharing. *Journal of Computer-Mediated Communication, 19*, 38–55. doi:10.1111/jcc4.12030

38. Marshall, S. (2014). IT consumerization: A case study of BYOD in a healthcare setting. *Technology Innovation Management Review, 4*, 14–18. Retrieved from https://timreview.ca/sites/default/files/article_PDF/Marshall_TIMReview_March2014.pdf

39. Mazmanian, M. (2013). Avoiding the trap of constant connectivity: When congruent frames allow for heterogeneous practices. *Academy of Management Journal, 56*, 1225–1250. doi:10.5465/amj.2010.0787

40. Mazmanian, M., Orlikowski, W. J., & Yates, J. (2005). Crackberries: The social implications of ubiquitous wireless e-mail devices. In C. Sørensen, Y. Yoo, K. Lyytinen, & J. DeGross (Eds.), *Designing ubiquitous information environments: Socio-technical issues and challenges* (pp. 337–343). New York, NY: Springer.

41. Mazmanian, M., Orlikowski, W., & Yates, J. (2013). The autonomy paradox: The implications of mobile devices for knowledge professionals. *Organization Science, 24*, 1337–1357. Retrieved from http://dx.doi.org/10.1287/orsc.1120.0806

42. Middleton, C., Scheepers, R., & Tuunainen, V. K. (2014). When mobile is the norm: Researching mobile information systems and mobility as post-adoption phenomena. *European Journal of Information Systems, 23*, 503–512. doi:10.1057/ejis.2014.21

43. Nippert-Eng, C. E. (1996). *Home and work: Negotiating boundaries through everyday life*. Chicago, IL: University of Chicago Press.

44. Orlikowski, W. J. (2007). Sociomaterial practices: Exploring technology at work. *Organizational Studies, 28*, 1435–1448. doi:10.177/0170840607081138

45. Orlikowski, W. J., & Scott, S. V. (2008). Sociomateriality: Challenging the separation of technology, work and organization. *Academy of Management Annals, 2*, 433–474. doi:10.1080/19416520802211644

46. Osterlund, C. (2007). Genre combinations: A window into dynamic communication practices. *Journal of Management Information Systems, 23*, 81–108. doi:10.2753/MIS0742-1222230405

47. Parchoma, G. (2014). The contested ontology of affordances: Implications for researching technological affordances for collaborative knowledge production. *Computers in Human Behavior, 37*, 360–368.

48. Perlow, L. A. (1998). Boundary control. The social ordering of work and family time in a high-tech corporation. *Administrative Science Quarterly, 43*, 328–357.

49. Reinsch, N. L., Turner, J. W., & Tinsley, C. H. (2008). Multicommunicating: A practice whose time has come? *Academy of Management Review, 33*, 391–403. doi:10.2307/20159404

50. Rice, R. E., Evans, S. K., Pearce, K. E., Sivunene, A., Vitak, J., & Treem, J. W. (2017). Organizational media affordances: Operationalization and associations with media use. *Journal of Communication, 67*, 106–130. doi:10.1111/jcom.12273

51. Rice, R. E., Hiltz, S. R., & Spencer, D. (2004). Media mixes and learning networks. In S. R. Hiltz & R. Goldman (Eds.), *Learning together online: Research on asynchronous learning* (pp. 215–237). Mahwah, NJ: Erlbaum.

52. Rice, R. E., & Leonardi, P. M. (2013). Information and communication technology use inorganizations. In L. L. Putnam & D. K. Mumby (Eds.), *The Sage handbook of organizational communication* (3rd ed., pp. 425–448). Thousand Oaks, CA: Sage.

53. Schrock, A. R. (2015). Communicative affordances of mobile media: Portability, availability, locatability, and multimediality. *International Journal of Communication, 9*, 1229–1246. Retrieved from http://ijoc.org/index.php/ijoc/article/view/3288/1363

54. Silverstone, R., Hirsch, E., & Morley, D. (1992). Information and communication technologies and the moral economy of the household. In R. Silverstone & E. Hirsch (Eds.), *Consuming technologies: Media and information in domestic spaces* (pp. 15–31). New York, NY: Routledge.

55. Sørensen, C. (2011). *Enterprise mobility: Tiny technology with global impact on work*. Basingstoke, United Kingdom: Palmgrave Macmillan.

56. Steelman, Z. R., Lacity, M., & Subberwal, R. (2016). Charting your organization's bring-your-own-device voyage. *MIS Quarterly Executive, 15*, 85–104.

57. Stephens, K. K. (2007). The successive use of information and communication technologies at work. *Communication Theory, 17*, 486–509. doi:10.1111/j.1468-2885.2007.00308.x

58. Stephens, K. K. (2012). Multiple conversations during organizational meetings: Development of the multicommunicating scale. *Management Communication Quarterly, 26*, 195–223. doi:10.1177/0893318911431802

59. Stephens, K. K., Cruz, I., Waters, E. D., & Zhu, Y. (2017). *Meetings as persistent conversations that use ICTs and face-to-face to build social capital.* Proceedings of the 50th Annual Hawaii International Conference on System Sciences (HICSS) (pp. 2175–2184). Washington, DC: IEEE Computer Society. Retrieved from https://scholarspace.manoa.hawaii.edu/bitstream/10125/41418/1/paper0269. pdf

60. Stephens, K. K., & Davis, J. D. (2009). The social influences on electronic multitasking in organizational meetings. *Management Communication Quarterly, 23,* 63–83. doi:10.1177/0893318909335417

61. Stephens, K. K., Mandhana, D., Kim, J., Li, X., Glowacki, E., & Cruz, I. (2017). Reconceptualizing communication overload and building a theoretical foundation. *Communication Theory, 27,* 269–289. doi:10.1111/comt.12116

62. Stephens, K. K., Sørnes, J. O., Rice, R. E., Browning, L. D., & Sætre, A. S. (2008). Discrete, sequential, and follow-up use of information and communication technology by managerial knowledge workers. *Management Communication Quarterly, 22,* 197–231. https://doi.org/10.1177/ 0893318908323149

63. Stephens, K. K., Waters, E. D., & Sinclair, C. (2014). Media management: The integration of HR, technology, and people. In M. E. Gordon & V. D. Miller (Eds.), *Meeting the challenge of human resource management: A communication perspective* (pp. 215–226). New York, NY: Routledge.

64. Stephens, K. K., Zhu, Y., Harrison, M., Iyer, M., Hairston, T., & Luk, J. (2017). *Bring your own mobile device (BYOD) to the hospital: Layered boundary barriers and divergent boundary management strategies.* Proceedings of the 50th Annual Hawaii International Conference on System Sciences (HICSS) (pp. 3517–3526). Washington, DC: IEEE Computer Society.

65. Thomas, M., & Lim, S. S. (2011). On maids and mobile phones: ICT use by female migrant workers in Singapore and its policy implications. In J. E. Katz (Ed.), *Mobile communication: Dimensions of social policy* (pp. 175–190). New Brunswick, NJ: Transaction.

66. Treem, J. W., & Leonardi, P. M. (2012). Social media use in organizations: Exploring the affordances of visability, editability, persistence, and association. *Communication Yearbook, 36,* 143–189. Retrieved from http:// citeseerx.ist.psu.edu/viewdoc/download?doi=10.1.1.726.264&rep=rep1&type= pdf

67. Turner, J. W., Grube, J. A., Tinsley, C. H., Lee, C., & O'Pell, C. (2006). Exploring the dominant media: How does media use reflect organizational norms and affect performance? *Journal of Business Communication, 43,* 220–250. doi:10.1177/0021943606288772

68. Turner, J. W., & Reinsch, N. L. (2007). The business communicator as presence allocator: Multi-communicating, equivocality, and status at work. *Journal of Business Communication, 44,* 36–58. doi:10.1177/0021943606295779.

69. Turner, J. W., & Reinsch, N. L. (2010). Successful and unsuccessful multicommunication episodes: Engaging in dialogue or juggling messages? *Information System Frontiers, 12,* 277–285. doi:10.1007/s10796-009-9185-y

70. Wajcman, J. (2010). New connections: Social studies of science and technology and studies of work. *Work, Employment and Society, 20,* 773–786.

71. Wajcman, J., Bittman, M., & Brown, J. E. (2008). Families without borders: Mobile phones, connectedness and work–home divisions. *Sociology, 42,* 635–652. doi:10.1177/0038038508091620

72. Wajcman, J., Bittman, M., & Brown, J. (2009). Intimate connections: The impact of the mobile phone. In G. Goggin & L. Hjort (Eds.), *Mobile technologies: From telecommunications to media* (pp. 9–22). New York, NY: Routledge.

73. Wellman, B., Salaff, J., Dimitrova, D., Garton, L., Gulia, M., & Haythornthwaite, C. (1996). Computer networks as social networks: Collaborative work, telework, and virtual community. *Annual Review of Sociology, 22*, 213–238. doi:10.1146/annurev.soc.22.1.213

74. Williams, M. G. (2015). Cabs, community, and control: Mobile communication among Chicago's taxi drivers, *Mobile Media & Communication, 3*, 3–19. doi:10.1177/2050157914544804

75. Yan, J., Zhang, S., Milic, N., Koch, H., & Curry, P. (2016, August). *IT consumerization and new IT practices: Discriminating, firefighting and innovating.* Paper presented at the 22nd Americas Conference on Information Systems, San Diego, CA.

76. Yang, K. (2008). A preliminary study on the use of mobile phones amongst migrant workers in Beijing. *Knowledge Technology and Policy, 21*, 65–72. doi:10.1007/s12130-008-9047-7

Chapter 1

1. Abbott, A. (1988). *The system of professions: An essay on the division of expert labor.* Chicago, IL: University of Chicago Press.

2. Alvesson, M. (2001). Knowledge work: Ambiguity, image and identify. *Human Relations, 54*, 863–886. Retrieved from http://dx.doi.org/10.1177/0018726701547004

3. Boudreau, M. C., & Robey, D. (2005). Enacting integrated information technology: A human agency perspective. *Organization Science, 16*, 3–18. doi:10.1287/orsc.1040.01

4. Browning, L. D., Sætre, A. S., Stephens, K. K., & Sørnes, J. O. (2008). *Information & communication technologies in action: Linking theory and narratives of practice.* New York, NY: Routledge.

5. Drucker, P. F. (1969). *The age of discontinuity: Guidelines to our changing society.* London, United Kingdom: William Heinemann.

6. Emirbayer, M., & Mische, A. (1998). What is agency? *American Journal of Sociology, 103*, 962–1023. doi:10.1086/231294

7. Giddens, A. (1984). *The constitution of society: Outline of the theory of structuration.* Berkeley: University of California Press.

8. Gouldner, A. W. (1960). The norm of reciprocity: A preliminary statement. *American Sociological Review, 25*, 161–178. Retrieved from http://www.jstor.org/stable/2092623

9. Ling, R. (2012). *Taken for grantedness: The embedding of mobile communication into society.* Cambridge, MA: MIT Press.

10. Ling, R., & Donner, J. (2009). *Mobile communication: Digital media and society series.* Malden, MA: Polity Press.

11. Ling, R., & Yttri, B. (2002). Hyper-coordination via mobile phones in Norway. In J. E. Katz & M. Aakhus (Eds.), *Perpetual contact: Mobile communication, private talk, public performance* (pp. 139–169). Cambridge, United Kingdom: Cambridge University Press.

12. Markus, M. L. (1987). Toward a "critical mass" theory of interactive media: Universal access, interdependence and diffusion. *Communication*

Research, 14, 491–511. Retrieved from https://doi.org/10.1177/
009365087014005003

13. Majchrzak, A., Faraj, S., Kane, G. C., & Azad, B. (2013). The contradictory influence of social media affordances on online communal knowledge sharing. *Journal of Computer-Mediated Communication, 19*, 38–55. doi:10.1111/jcc4.12030

14. Orlikowski, W. J. (2000). Using technology and constituting structures: A practice lens for studying technology in organizations. *Organization Science, 2000*, 404–428. doi:10.1287/orsc.11.4.404.14600

15. Scott, W. R. (1982). Managing professional work: Three models of control for health organizations. *Health Services Research, 17*, 213–240. Retrieved from https://www.ncbi.nlm.nih.gov/pmc/articles/PMC1068678/pdf/hsresearch00528-0008.pdf

16. Sørnes, J. O., Stephens, K. K., Sætre, A. S., & Browning, L. D. (2004). The reflexivity between ICTs and business culture: Using Hofstede's theory to compare Norway and the United States. *Informing Science, 7*, 1–30. Retrieved from http://inform.nu/Articles/Vol7/v7p001-030-211.pdf

17. Stephens, K. K. (2007). The successive use of information and communication technologies at work. *Communication Theory, 17*, 486–509. doi:10.1111/j.1468-2885.2007.00308.x

18. Stephens, K. K., Sørnes, J. O., Rice, R. E., Browning, L. D., & Sætre, A. S. (2008). Discrete, sequential, and follow-up use of information and communication technology by managerial knowledge workers. *Management Communication Quarterly, 22*, 197–231. doi:10.1111/j.1468-2885.2007.00308.x

19. Wallace, J. E. (1995). Organizational and professional commitment in professional and nonprofessional organizations. *Administrative Science Quarterly, 40*, 228–255. Retrieved from http://www.jstor.org/stable/2393637

Chapter 2

1. Bittman, M., Brown, J. E., & Wajcman, J. (2009). The mobile phone, perpetual contact, and time pressure. *Work, Employment & Society, 23*, 673–691.

2. Dunbar, R. L. M., & Statler, M. (2010). A historical perspective on organizational control. In S. B. Sitkin, L. B. Cardinal, & K. M. Bijlsma-Frankema (Eds.), *Organizational control* (pp. 16–48). Cambridge, United Kingdom: Cambridge University Press.

3. Gouldner, A. W. (1960). The norm of reciprocity: A preliminary statement. *American Sociological Review, 25*, 161–178. Retrieved from http://www.jstor.org/stable/2092623

4. Hofstede, G. (1980). *Culture's consequences: International differences in work related values.* Newbury Park, CA: Sage.

5. Jarvenpaa, S. L., & Lang, K. R. (2005). Managing the paradoxes of mobile technology. *Information Systems Management, 22*, 7–23. doi:10.1201/1078.10580530/45520.22.4.20050901/90026.2

6. Mazmanian, M. (2013). Avoiding the trap of constant connectivity: When congruent frames allow for heterogeneous practices. *Academy of Management Journal, 56*, 1225–1250. doi:10.5465/amj.2010.0787

7. Mazmanian, M., Orlikowski, W., & Yates, J. (2013). The autonomy paradox: The implications of mobile devices for knowledge professionals. *Organization Science, 24*, 1337–1357. Retrieved from http://dx.doi.org/10.1287/orsc.1120.0806

8. Mazmanian, M., Orlikowski, W. J., & Yates, J. (2005). Crackberries: The social implications of ubiquitous wireless e-mail devices. In C. Sørensen, Y. Yoo, K. Lyytinen, & J. DeGross (Eds.), *Designing ubiquitous information environments: Socio-technical issues and challenges* (pp. 337–343). New York, NY: Springer.

9. Schrock, A. R. (2015). Communicative affordances of mobile media: Portability, availability, locatability, and multimediality. *International Journal of Communication, 9*, 1229–1246. Retrieved from http://ijoc.org/index.php/ijoc/article/view/3288/1363

10. Sørnes, J. O., Stephens, K. K., Sætre, A. S., & Browning, L. D. (2004). The reflexivity between ICTs and business culture: Using Hofstede's theory to compare Norway and the United States. *Informing Science, 7*, 1–30. Retrieved from http://inform.nu/Articles/Vol7/v7p001-030-211.pdf

11. Stephens, K. K., Mandhana, D., Kim, J., Li, X., Glowacki, E., & Cruz, I. (2017). Reconceptualizing communication overload and building a theoretical foundation. *Communication Theory, 27*, 269–289. doi:10.1111/comt.12116

12. Straub, D., & Karahanna, E. (1998). Knowledge worker communications and recipient availability: Toward a task closure model of media choice. *Organization Science, 9*, 160–175. Retrieved from http://dx.doi.org/10.1287/orsc.9.2.160

13. Wajcman, J., Bittman, M., & Brown, J. E. (2008). Families without borders: Mobile phones, connectedness and work-home divisions. *Sociology, 42*, 635–652. doi:10.1177/0038038508091620

Chapter 3

1. Barker, J. R. (1993). Tightening the iron cage: Concertive control in self-managing teams. *Administrative Science Quarterly, 38*, 408–437. doi:10.2307/2393374

2. Beniger, J. (1989). *The control revolution: Technological and economic origins of the information society.* Cambridge, MA: Harvard University Press.

3. Berlo, D. K. (1960). *The process of communication.* New York, NY: Holt, Rinehart, & Winston.

4. Browning, L. D., Sætre, A. S., Stephens, K. K., & Sørnes, J. O. (2008). *Information & communication technologies in action: Linking theory and narratives of practice.* New York, NY: Routledge.

5. Cardinal, L. B., Sitkin, S. B., & Long, C. P. (2004). Balancing and rebalancing in the creation and evolution of organizational control. *Organization Science, 15*, 411–431. Retrieved from http://dx.doi.org/10.1287/orsc.1040.0084

6. Dunbar, R. L. M., & Statler, M. (2010). A historical perspective on organizational control. In S. B. Sitkin, L. B. Cardinal, & K. M. Bijlsma-Frankema (Eds.), *Organizational control* (pp. 16–48). Cambridge, United Kingdom: Cambridge University Press.

7. Emerson, R. M. (1962). Power-dependence relations. *American Sociological Review, 27*(1), 31–41.

8. Emirbayer, M., & Mische, A. (1998). What is agency? *American Journal of Sociology, 103*, 962–1023. doi:10.1086/231294

9. Etzioni, A. (1964). *Modern organizations.* Englewood Cliffs, NJ: Prentice-Hall.

10. Foucault, M. (1995). *Discipline and punish: The birth of the prison* (2nd ed., A. Sheridan, Trans.). New York, NY: Vintage Books. (Original work published 1975).

11.   French, J. P. R., Jr., & Raven, B. (1960). The bases of social power. In D. Cartwright & A. Zander (Eds.), *Group dynamics* (pp. 607–623). New York, NY: Harper & Row.

12.   Giddens, A. (1984). *The constitution of society: Outline of the theory of structuration*. Berkeley: University of California Press.

13.   Harris, J., Ives, B., & Junglas, I. (2012). IT consumerization: When gadgets turn into enterprise IT tools. *MIS Quarterly Executive, 11*, 99–112.

14.   Kaste, M. (2010, November 22). Wipeout: When your company kills your iPhone. *National Public Radio*. Retrieved from http://www.npr.org/2010/11/22/131511381/wipeout-when-your-company-kills-your-iphone

15.   Lewicki, R. J., Saunders, D. M., & Litterer, J. A. (1999). *Negotiation*. Homewood, IL: Richard D. Irwin.

16.   Lewis, L. K. (2011). *Organizational change: Creating change through strategic communication*. Chichester, United Kingdom: Wiley-Blackwell. Retrieved from http://dx.doi.org/10.1002/9781444340372

17.   Lewis, L. K., & Russ, T. L. (2012). Soliciting and using input during organizational change initiatives: What are practitioners doing? *Management Communication Quarterly, 26*, 267–294. Retrieved from http://dx.doi.org/10.1177/0893318911431804

18.   Ling, R. (2012). *Taken for grantedness: The embedding of mobile communication into society*. Cambridge, MA: MIT Press.

19.   Magee, J. C., & Galinsky, A. D. (2008). Social hierarchy: The self-reinforcing nature of power and status. *Academy of Management Annals, 2*, 351–398. Retrieved from https://doi.org/10.1080/19416520802211628

20.   Martin, J. (1990). Deconstructing organizational taboos: The suppression of gender conflict In organizations. *Organization Science, 1*, 339–359. Retrieved from http://www.jstor.org/stable/2634968

21.   Mazmanian, M. (2013). Avoiding the trap of constant connectivity: When congruent frames allow for heterogeneous practices. *Academy of Management Journal, 56*, 1225–1250. doi:10.5465/amj.2010.0787

22.   Mazmanian, M., Orlikowski, W., & Yates, J. (2013). The autonomy paradox: The implications of mobile devices for knowledge professionals. *Organization Science, 24*, 1337–1357. Retrieved from http://dx.doi.org/10.1287/orsc.1120.0806

23.   Mazmanian, M., Orlikowski, W. J., & Yates, J. (2005). Crackberries: The social implications of ubiquitous wireless e-mail devices. In C. Sørensen, Y. Yoo, K. Lyytinen, & J. DeGross (Eds.), *Designing ubiquitous information environments: Socio-technical issues and challenges* (pp. 337–343). New York, NY, Springer.

24.   Mumby, D. K. (2001). Power and politics. In F. Jablin & L. Putnam (Eds.), *New handbook of organizational communication* (pp. 585–623). Thousand Oaks, CA: Sage.

25.   Nicotera, A. M. (2009). Constitutive view of communication. In S. W. Littlejohn & K. A. Foss (Eds.), *Encyclopedia of communication theory* (pp. 175–179). Thousand Oaks, CA: Sage.

26.   Ocasio, W., & Wohlgezogen, F. (2010). Attention and control. In S. B. Sitkin, L. B. Cardinal, & K. M. Bijlsma-Frankema (Eds.), *Organizational control* (pp. 191–221). Cambridge, United Kingdom: Cambridge University Press.

27.   Pickering, A. (1993). The mangle of practice: Agency and emergence in the sociology of science. *American Journal of Sociology, 99*, 559–589. doi:10.1086/230316

28. Putnam, L. L. (2004). Dialectical tensions and rhetorical tropes in negotiations. *Organization Studies, 25,* 35–53. doi:10.1177/0170840604038170

29. Putnam, L. L. (2015). Unpacking the dialectic: Alternative views on the discourse–materiality relationship. *Journal of Management Studies, 50,* 706–716. doi:10.1111/joms.12115

30. Putnam, L. L., Fairhurst, G. T., & Banghart, S. (2016). Contradictions, dialectics, and paradoxes in organizations: A constitutive approach. *Academy of Management Annals, 10,* 65–171. doi:10.1080/19416520.2016.1162421

31. Rubin, J. Z., & Brown, B. R. (1975). *The social psychology of bargaining and negotiation.* New York, NY: Academic Press.

32. Shannon, C. E., & Weaver, W. (1949). *The mathematical theory of communication.* Urbana: University of Illinois Press.

33. Simon, H. A. (1957). *Models of man, social and rational: Mathematical essays on rational human behavior in a social setting.* New York, NY: John Wiley and Sons.

34. Sitkin, S. B., Cardinal, L. B., & Bijlsma-Frankema, K. M. (Eds.). (2010). *Organizational control.* New York, NY: Cambridge University Press.

35. Sørensen, C. (2011). *Enterprise mobility: Tiny technology with global impact on work.* New York, NY: Palgrave Macmillan.

36. Sørnes, J. O., Stephens, K. K., Sætre, A. S., & Browning, L. D. (2004). The reflexivity between ICTs and business culture: Using Hofstede's theory to compare Norway and the United States. *Informing Science, 7,* 1–30. Retrieved from http://inform.nu/Articles/Vol7/v7p001-030-211.pdf

37. Steinfatt, T. M. (2009). Definitions of communication. In S. W. Littlejohn & K. A. Foss (Eds.), *Encyclopedia of communication theory* (pp. 295–299). Thousand Oaks, CA: Sage.

38. Stephens, K. K. (2007). The successive use of information and communication technologies at work. *Communication Theory, 17,* 486–509. doi:10.1111/j.1468-2885.2007.00308.x

39. Stephens, K. K., Sørnes, J. O., Rice, R. E., Browning, L. D., & Sætre, A. S. (2008). Discrete, sequential, and follow-up use of information and communication technology by managerial knowledge workers. *Management Communication Quarterly, 22,* 197–231. Retrieved from https://doi.org/10.1177/0893318908323149

40. Tompkins, P. K., & Cheney, G. (1985). Communication and unobtrusive control in contemporary organization. In R. D. McPhee & P. K. Thompkins (Eds.), *Organizational communication: Traditional themes and new directions* (pp. 179–210). Newbury Park, CA: Sage.

41. Weber, M. (1947). *The theory of social and economic organizations.* (A. H. Henderson & T. Parson, Trans.). New York, NY: Free Press. (Original work published 1924).

42. Weber, M. (1958). *The protestant ethic and the spirit of capitalism.* New York, NY: Scribner's.

43. Weick, K. W. (1969). *The social psychology of organizing.* Reading, MA: Addison-Wesley.

Chapter 4

1. Allen, J. A., Yoerger, M. A., Lehmann-Willenbrock, N., & Jones, J. (2015). Would you please stop that!?: The relationship between counterproductive meeting behaviors, employee voice, and trust. *Journal of Management Development, 34,* 1272–1287. doi:10.1108/JMD-0202015-0032.

2.	Bandura, A. (1986). *Social foundations of thought and action*. Englewood Cliffs, NJ: Prentice Hall.

3.	Barker, J. R. (1993). Tightening the iron cage: Concertive control in self-managing teams. *Administrative Science Quarterly, 38*, 408–437. doi:10.2307/2393374

4.	Bayer, J. B., Campbell, S. W., & Ling, R. (2016). Connection cues: Activating the norms and habits of social connectedness. *Communication Theory, 26*, 128–149. doi:10.1111/comt.12090

5.	Bettenhausen, K., & Murninghan, J. K. (1985). The emergence of norms in competitive decision-making groups. *Administrative Science Quarterly, 30*, 350–372. Retrieved from http://www.jstor.org/stable/2392667

6.	Bluedorn, A. C. (2002). *The human organization of time: Temporal realities and experience*. Stanford, CA: Stanford University Press.

7.	Cameron, A., & Webster, J. (2010). Relational outcomes of multicommunicating: Integrating incivility and social exchange perspectives. *Organizational Science, 22*, 754–771. Retrieved from http://www.jstor.org/stable/20868891

8.	Cameron, A. F., & Webster, J. (2013). Multicommunicating: Juggling multiple conversations in the workplace. *Information Systems Research, 24*, 352–371. Retrieved from http://dx.doi.org/10.1287/isre.1120.0446

9.	Cardon, P. W., & Dai, Y. (2014). Mobile phone use in meetings among Chinese professionals: Perspectives on multicommunication and civility. *Global Advances in Business Communication, 3*, 1–33. Retrieved from http://commons.emich.edu/cgi/viewcontent.cgi?article=1043&context=gabc

10.	Chudoba, K. M., Watson-Manheim, M. B., Crowston, K., & Lee, C. S. (2005). Participation in ICT-enabled meetings. *Journal of Organizational and End User Computing, 23*, 15–36. doi:10.4018/joeuc.2011040102

11.	Dennis, A. R., Rennecker, J. A., & Hansen, S. (2010). Invisible whispering: Restructuring collaborative decision making with instant messaging. *Decision Sciences, 41*, 845–866. doi:10.111/j.1540-5915.2010.00290.x

12.	Drucker, P. F. (1969). *The age of discontinuity: Guidelines to our changing society*. London, United Kingdom: William Heinemann.

13.	French, J. P. R., Jr., & Raven, B. (1960). The bases of social power. In D. Cartwright & A. Zander (Eds.), *Group dynamics* (pp. 607–623). New York, NY: Harper & Row.

14.	Fulk J., & Collins-Jarvis, L. (2001). Wired meetings: Technological mediation of organizational gatherings. In F. M. Jablin & L. L. Putnam (Eds.), *The new handbook of organizational communication: Advances in theory, research, and methods* (pp. 624–663). Thousand Oaks, CA: Sage.

15.	Fulk, J., Schmitz, J., & Steinfield, C. W. (1990). A social influence model of technology use. In J. Fulk. & C. Steinfield (Eds.), *Organizations and communication technology* (pp. 117–140). Newbury Park, CA: Sage.

16.	Hall, E. T. (1983). *The dance of life: The other dimension of time*. Garden City, NY: Anchor Press/Doubleday.

17.	Jarzabkowski, P., & Seidl, D. (2008). The role of meetings in the social practice of strategy. *Organization Studies, 29*, 1391–1426. doi:10.1177/0170840608096388

18.	Leach, D. J., Rogelberg, S. G., Warr, P. B., & Burnfield, J. L. (2009). Perceived meeting effectiveness: The role of design characteristics. *Journal of Business and Psychology, 24*, 65–76. doi:10.1007/s10869-009-9092-6

19. Licoppe, C. (2004). "Connected presence": The emergency of a new repertoire for managing social relationships in a changing communication technospace. *Environment and Planning D: Society and Space, 22*, 135–156. doi:10.1068/d323t

20. Mankins, M. C. (2004, September). Stop wasting valuable time. *Harvard Business Review.* Retrieved from https://hbr.org/2004/09/ stop-wasting-valuable-time

21. Marquez, L. (2008, March 31). Going topless to office meetings. *ABC News.* Retrieved from http://abcnews.go.com/Technology/story?id=4560823

22. Mejias, R. J. (2007). The interaction of process losses, process gains, and meeting satisfaction within technology-supported environments. *Small Group Research, 38*, 156–194. doi:10.1177/1046496406297037

23. Mirivel, J. C., & Tracy, K. (2005). Premeeting talk: An organizationally crucial form of talk. *Research on Language and Social Interaction, 38*, 1–34. Retrieved from http://dx.doi.org/10.1207/s15327973rlsi3801_1

24. Reinsch, N. L., Turner, J. W., & Tinsley, C. H. (2008). Multicommunicating: A practice whose time has come? *Academy of Management Review, 33*, 391–403. doi:10.2307/20159404

25. Rennecker, J. A., Dennis, A. R., & Hansen, S. (2010). "Invisible whispering": Restructuring meeting processes with instant messaging. In D. M. Kilgour & C. Eden (Eds.), *Handbook of group decision and negotiation: Advances in group decision and negotiation, 4*, 25–45. doi:10.1007/978-90 481-9097-3_3

26. Rogelberg, S. G., Scott, C. S., & Kello, J. (2007, January 1). The science and fiction of meetings. *MIT Sloan Management Review, 48.* Retrieved from http:// sloanreview.mit.edu/article/the-science-and-fiction-of-meetings/

27. Rogelberg, S. G., Allen, J. A., Shanock, L., Scott, C., & Shuffler, M. (2010). Employee satisfaction with meetings: A contemporary facet of job satisfaction. *Human Resource Management, 49*, 149–172. doi:10.1002/hrm.20339

28. Schrock, A. R. (2015). Communicative affordances of mobile media: Portability, availability, locatability, and multimediality. *International Journal of Communication, 9*, 1229–1246. Retrieved from http://ijoc.org/index.php/ijoc/ article/view/3288/1363

29. Schwartzman, H. B. (1989). *The meeting: Gatherings in organizations and communities.* New York, NY: Plenum Press.

30. Scott, C. W., Shanock, L. R., & Rogelberg, S. G. (2012). Meetings at work: Advancing the theory and practice of meetings. *Small Group Research, 43*, 127–129. doi:10.1177/1046496411429023

31. Stephens, K. K. (2007). The successive use of information and communication technologies at work. *Communication Theory, 17*, 486–509. doi:10.1111/ j.1468-2885.2007.00308.x

32. Stephens, K. K. (2012). Multiple conversations during organizational meetings: Development of the multicommunicating scale. *Management Communication Quarterly, 26*, 195–223. doi:10.1177/0893318911431802

33. Stephens, K. K., Cho, J. K., & Ballard, D. I. (2012). Simultaneity, sequentiality, and speed: Organizational messages about multiple-task completion. *Human Communication Research, 38*, 23–47. doi:10.1111/ j.1468-2958.2011.01420.x

34. Stephens, K. K., Cruz, I., Waters, E. D., & Zhu, Y. (2017). *Meetings as persistent conversations that use ICTs and face-to-face to build social capital.* Proceedings of the 50th Annual Hawaii International Conference on System Sciences (HICSS) (pp. 2175–2184). Washington, DC: IEEE Computer Society. Retrieved from

https://scholarspace.manoa.hawaii.edu/bitstream/10125/41418/1/paper0269.pdf

35. Stephens, K. K., & Dailey, S. L. (2014). Human resources development in a technology-infused workplace. In M. Khosrow-Pour (Ed.), *Encyclopedia of information science and technology* (3rd ed., pp. 581–589). Hershey, PA: IGI Global. doi:10.4018/978-1-4666-5888-2.ch362

36. Stephens, K. K., & Davis, J. D. (2009). The social influences on electronic multitasking in organizational meetings. *Management Communication Quarterly, 23*, 63–83. doi:10.1177/0893318909335417

37. Stephens, K. K., Mandhana, D., Kim, J., Li, X., Glowacki, E., & Cruz, I. (2017). Reconceptualizing communication overload and building a theoretical foundation. *Communication Theory, 27*, 269–289. doi:10.1111/comt.12116

38. Stephens, K. K., Waters, E. D., & Sinclair, C. (2014). Media management: The integration of HR, technology, and people. In M. E. Gordon & V. D. Miller (Eds.), *Meeting the challenge of human resource management: A communication perspective* (pp. 215–226). New York, NY: Routledge.

39. Tompkins, P. K., & Cheney, G. (1985). Communication and unobtrusive control in contemporary organization. In R. D. McPhee & P. K. Thompkins (Eds.), *Organizational communication: Traditional themes and new directions* (pp. 179–210). Newbury Park, CA: Sage.

40. Tracy, K., & Dimock, A. (2004). Meetings: Discursive sites for building and fragmenting community. *Communication Yearbook, 28*, 127–165. doi:10.1207/s15567419cy2801_4

41. Turner, J. W., Grube, J. A., Tinsley, C. H., Lee, C., & O'Pell, C. (2006). Exploring the dominant media: How does media use reflect organizational norms and affect performance? *Journal of Business Communication, 43*, 220–250. doi:10.1177/0021943606288772

42. Turner, J. W., & Reinsch, N. L. (2007). The business communicator as presence allocator: Multi-communicating, equivocality, and status at work. *Journal of Business Communication, 44*, 36–58. doi:10.1177/0021943606295779

43. Turner, J. W., & Reinsch, N. L. (2010). Successful and unsuccessful multicommunication episodes: Engaging in dialogue or juggling messages? *Information System Frontiers, 12*, 277–285. doi:10.1007/s10796-009-9185-y

44. Wasson, C. (2004). Multitasking during virtual meetings. *Human Resource Planning, 27*, 47–60. Retrieved from http://search.proquest.com/openview/e06e0c345f8e52ddfc661c9076046184/1.pdf?pq-origsite=gscholar&cbl=52465

Chapter 5

1. Bureau of Labor Statistics, U.S. Department of Labor. (2014). Table 11. Employed persons by detailed occupation, sex, race, and Hispanic or Latino ethnicity. *Labor Force Statistics from the Current Population Survey*. Retrieved from https://www.bls.gov/cps/aa2014/cpsaat11.pdf

2. Campbell, D. (2001). Can the digital divide be contained? *International Labor Review, 140*, 119–141. doi:10.1111/j.1564-913x.2001.tb00217.x

3. Campbell, S. W., & Park, Y. J. (2008). Social implications of mobile telephony: The rise of personal communication society. *Sociology Compass, 2*, 321–387. doi:10.1111/j.1751-9020.2007.00080.x

4. Chapelle, C. (2003). *English language learning and technology: Lectures on applied linguistics in the age of information and communication technology* (Vol. 7). Philadelphia, PA: John Benjamins.

5. Chib, A., Malik, S., Aricat, R. G., & Kadir, S. Z. (2014). Migrant mothering and mobile phones: Negotiations of transnational identity. *Mobile Media & Communication, 2,* 73–93. doi:10.1177/2050157913506007

6. Chinnery, G. M. (2006). Emerging technologies. Going to the mall: Mobile assisted language learning. *Language Learning & Technology, 10,* 9–16. Retrieved from http://llt.msu.edu/vol10num1/pdf/emerging.pdf

7. Diefendorff, J. M., & Richard, E. M. (2003). Antecedents and consequences of emotional display rule perceptions. *Journal of Applied Psychology, 88,* 284–294. doi:10.1037/0021-9010.88.2.284

8. De Lara, P., Tacoronte, D. V., & Ding, J. T. (2006). Do current anti-cyberloafing disciplinary practices have a replica in research findings? *Internet Research, 16,* 450–467. doi:10.1108/10662240610690052

9. Donner, J. (2009). Blurring livelihoods and lives: The social uses of mobile phones and socioeconomic development. *Innovations: Technology, Governance, & Globalization, 4,* 91–101. doi:10.1162/itgg.2009.4.1.91

10. Drucker, P. F. (1969). *The age of discontinuity: Guidelines to our changing society.* London, United Kingdom: William Heinemann.

11. D'Urso, S. C. (2006). Toward a structural-perceptual model of electronic monitoring and surveillance in organizations. *Communication Theory, 16,* 281–303. doi:10.1111/j.1468-2885.2006.00271.x

12. Eisenberg, E. M. (1984). Ambiguity as strategy in organizational communication. *Communication Monographs, 51,* 227–242. doi:10.1080/03637758409390197

13. Ford, J. L., Stephens, K. K., & Ford, J. (2015). Digital restrictions at work: Exploring how selectively exclusive policies affect crisis communication. *International Journal of Information Systems for Crisis Response and Management, 7,* 19–28. doi:10.4018/IJISCRAM.2014100102

14. Gartner. (2013, April 4). Gartner says worldwide PC, tablet, and mobile phone combined shipments to reach 2.4 billion units in 2014. Retrieved from http://www.gartner.com/newsroom/id/2408515

15. Gordon, J. S. (2006). Justice or equality? *Journal for Business, Economics & Ethics, 7,* 183–201. Retrieved from https://www.ssoar.info/ssoar/bitstream/handle/document/34790/ssoar-zfwu-2006-2-gordon-Justice_or_equality.pdf?sequence=1

16. Griffiths, M. (2003). Internet abuse in the workplace: Issues and concerns for employers and employment counselors. *Journal of Employment Counseling, 40,* 87–96. doi:10.1002/j.2161-1920.2003.tb00859.x

17. Hargittai, E., & Hsieh, Y. P. (2013). Digital inequality. In W. H. Dutton (Ed.), *Oxford handbook for Internet research* (pp. 129–150). Oxford, United Kingdom: Oxford University Press.

18. Hochschild, A. R. (1983). *The managed heart: Commercialization of human feeling.* Berkeley: University of California Press.

19. Hwang, S. O., Piazza, C. L., Pierce, M. J., & Bryce, S. M. (2011). My heart want to say something: Exploring ELL vocabulary use through e-mail. *Multicultural Education & Technology Journal, 5,* 19–38. doi:10.1108/17504971111121900

20. Karasek, R. A. (1979). Job demands, job decision latitude, and mental strain: Implications for job redesign. *Administrative Science Quarterly, 24,* 285–308. doi:10.2307/2392498

21. Katz J. E., & Aakhus, M. (Eds.). (2002). *Perpetual contact: Mobile communication, private talk, public performance.* Cambridge, United Kingdom: Cambridge University Press.

22. Ling, R. (2012). *Taken for grantedness: The embedding of mobile communication into society.* Cambridge, MA: MIT Press.

23. Ling, R., & Donner, J. (2013). *Mobile phones and mobile communication.* Hoboken, NJ: Wiley.

24. Middleton, C., Scheepers, R., & Tuunainen, V. K. (2014). When mobile is the norm: Researching mobile information systems and mobility as post-adoption phenomena. *European Journal of Information Systems, 23,* 503–512. doi:10.1057/ejis.2014.21

25. National Telecommunication and Information Association, U.S. Department of Commerce. (2002). *A nation online: How Americans are expanding their use of the Internet.* Retrieved from https://www.ntia.doc.gov/files/ntia/publications/anationonline2.pdf

26. Pearce, K. E., & Rice, R. E. (2013). Digital divides from access to activities: Comparing mobile and personal computer internet users. *Journal of Communication, 63,* 721–744. doi:10.1111/jcom.12045

27. Pettigrew, T. F. (2002). Summing up: Relative deprivation as a key social psychological concept. In I. Walker & H. J. Smith (Eds.), *Relative deprivation: Specification, development, and integration* (pp. 351–373). Cambridge, United Kingdom: Cambridge University Press.

28. Pfeffer, J. (1994). *Competitive advantage through people: Unleashing the power of the work force.* Cambridge, MA: Harvard Business School Press.

29. Rodino-Colocino, M. (2006). Laboring under the digital divide. *New Media and Society, 8,* 487–511. https://doi.org/10.1177/1461444806064487

30. Siau, K., Nah, F. F., & Teng, L. (2002). Acceptable Internet use policy. *Communications of the ACM, 45,* 75–79. doi:10.1145/502269.502302

31. Sillince, J., Jarzabkowski, P., & Shaw, D. (2012). Shaping strategic action through the rhetorical construction and exploitation of ambiguity. *Organization Science, 23,* 630–650. doi:10.1287/orsc.1110.0670

32. Stephens, K. K., Barrett, A., & Mahometa, M. L. (2013). Organizational communication in emergencies: Using multiple channels and sources to combat noise and capture attention. *Human Communication Research, 39,* 230–251. doi:10.1111/hcre.12002

33. Stephens, K. K., & Davis, J. D. (2009). The social influences on electronic multitasking in organizational meetings. *Management Communication Quarterly, 23,* 63–83. doi:10.1177/0893318909335417

34. Stephens, K. K., & Ford, J. L. (2014, May). *Banning mobile devices: Workplace policies that selectively exclude can shape crisis communication.* In S. R. Hiltz, M. S. Pfaff, L. Plotnick, & A. C. Robinson (Eds.), Proceedings of the 11th International ISCRAM Conference, University Park, PA (pp. 284–288). Retrieved from http://idl.iscram.org/files/stephens/2014/975_Stephens+Ford2014.pdf

35. Stephens, K. K., & Ford, J. L. (2016). Unintended consequences of a strategically ambiguous organizational policy selectively restricting mobile device use at work. *Mobile Media & Communication, 4,* 186–204. Retrieved from https://doi.org/10.1177/2050157915619211

36. Stephens, K. K., Waters, E. D., & Sinclair, C. (2014). Media management: The integration of HR, technology, and people. In M. E. Gordon & V. D. Miller (Eds.), *Meeting the challenge of human resource management: A communication perspective* (pp. 215–226). New York, NY: Routledge.

37. Thomas, M., & Lim, S. S. (2011). On maids and mobile phones: ICT use by female migrant workers in Singapore and its policy implications. In J. E. Katz (Ed.), *Mobile communication: Dimensions of social policy* (pp. 175–190). New Brunswick, NJ: Transaction.

38. Vitak, J., Crouse, J., & LaRose, R. (2011). Personal Internet use at work: Understanding cyberslacking. *Computers in Human Behavior, 27*, 1751–1759. doi:10.1016/j.chb.2011.03.002011

39 Williams, M. G. (2015). Cabs, community, and control: Mobile communication among Chicago's taxi drivers. *Mobile Media & Communication, 3*, 3–19. doi:10.1177/2050157914544804

40. Yang, K. (2008). A preliminary study on the use of mobile phones amongst migrant workers in Beijing. *Knowledge Technology and Policy, 21*, 65–72. doi:10.1007/s12130-008-9047-7

41. Zoogah, D. B. (2010). Why should I be left behind? Employees' perceived relative deprivation and participation in development activities. *Journal of Applied Psychology, 95*, 159–173. doi:10.1037/a0018019

Chapter 6

1. Barrett, A. K., & Stephens, K. K. (2017). The pivotal role of change appropriation in the implementation of healthcare technology. *Management Communication Quarterly, 31*, 163–193. Retrieved from https://doi.org/10.1177/0893318916682872

2. Bayer, J. B., Campbell, S. W., & Ling, R. (2016). Connection cues: Activating the norms and habits of social connectedness. *Communication Theory, 26*, 128–149. doi:10.1111/comt.12090

3. Beisell, P. J. (2015). Something old and something new: Balancing "bring your own device" to work programs with the requirements of the National Labor Relations Act. *Journal of Law, Technology & Policy, 2014*, 497–530. Retrieved from http://illinoisjltp.com/journal/wp-content/uploads/2015/02/Beisell.pdf

4. Beniger, J. (1989). *The control revolution: Technological and economic origins of the information society*. Cambridge, MA: Harvard University Press.

5. Bosker, B. (2016). The binge breaker: Tristan Harris believes Silicon Valley is addicting us to our phones. He's determined to make it stop. *The Atlantic*. Retrieved from http://www.theatlantic.com/magazine/archive/2016/11/the-binge-breaker/501122/

6. Building construction agreement between Mechanical Contractors Association of Metropolitan Washington, Inc. and Steamfitters Local Union No. 602 of the United Association. (2013).

7. Center for the Protection of National Infrastructure. (2014). *BYOD guidance: Executive summary*. Retrieved from https://www.gov.uk/government/publications/byod-guidance-executive-summary/byod-guidance-executive-summary

8. Carter, M., & Petter, S. (2015, January). *Leveraging consumer technologies: Exploring determinants of smartphone use behaviors in the workplace.* Proceedings of the 48th Annual Hawaii International Conference on System Sciences (HICSS) (pp. 4619–4628). Washington, DC: IEEE Computer Society. doi:10.1109/HICSS.2015.550

9. Chen, W., & Wellman, B. (2004). The global digital divide—Within and between countries. *IT & Society, 1*, 39–45. Retrieved from https://www.

researchgate.net/publication/242208935_The_Global_Digital_Divide-Within_and_Between_Countries

10. University of Michigan Research Ethics and Compliance. (n.d.). *Data security guidelines*. Retrieved from http://research-compliance.umich.edu/data-security-guidelines

11. DeSanctis, G., & Poole, M. S. (1994). Capturing the complexity in advanced technology use: Adaptive structuration theory. *Organization Science, 5*, 121–147. Retrieved from http://dx.doi.org/10.1287/orsc.5.2.121

12. van Deursen, A. J. A. M., & van Dijk, J. A. G. M. (2014). The digital divide shifts to differences in usage. *New Media & Society, 16*, 507–526. doi:10.1177/1461444813487959

13. van Dijk, J. A. G. M. (2005). *The deepening divide: Inequality in the information society.* Thousand Oaks, CA: Sage.

14. Society for Human Resource Management. (2014). Electronic devices: Bring your own device (BYOD) policy. Retrieved from https://www.shrm.org/resourcesandtools/tools-and-samples/policies/pages/bringyourowndevicepolicy.aspx

15. National Safety Council. (2015, May). *Employer liability and the case for comprehensive cell phone policies.* Retrieved from http://www.nsc.org/DistractedDrivingDocuments/CPK/Corporate-Liability-White-Paper.pdf

16. Etzioni, A. (1964). *Modern organizations.* Englewood Cliffs, NJ: Prentice Hall.

17. Felstead, A., Jewson, N., & Walters, S. (2005). The shifting locations of work: New statistical evidence on the spaces and places of employment. *Work, Employment, and Society, 19*, 415–431. doi:10.1177/0950017005053186.

18. Foucault, M. (1977). *Discipline and punish: The birth of the prison.* London, United Kingdom: Penguin Books.

19. French workers win legal right to avoid checking work email out-of-hours. (2016, December 31). *Guardian.* Retrieved from https://www.theguardian.com/money/2016/dec/31/french-workers-win-legal-right-to-avoid-checking-work-email-out-of-hours

20. French win "right to disconnect" from out-of-hours work emails. (2016, December 31). *Telegraph.* Retrieved from http://www.telegraph.co.uk/news/2016/12/31/french-win-right-disconnect-out-of-hours-work-emails/

21. Griffiths, M. (2003). Internet abuse in the workplace: Issues and concerns for employers and employment counselors. *Journal of Employment Counseling, 40*, 87–96. doi:10.1002/j.2161-1920.2003.tb00859.x

22. European Data Protection Supervisor. (2015, December). *Guidelines on the protection of personal data in mobile devices used by European institutions.* Retrieved from https://secure.edps.europa.eu/EDPSWEB/webdav/site/mySite/shared/Documents/Supervision/Guidelines/15-12-17_Mobile_devices_EN.pdf

23. Hargittai, E., & Hsieh, Y. P. (2013). Digital inequality. In W. H. Dutton (Ed.), *Oxford handbook for Internet research* (pp. 129–150). Oxford, United Kingdom: Oxford University Press.

24. Harris, J., Ives, B., & Junglas, I. (2012). IT consumerization: When gadgets turn into enterprise IT tools. *MIS Quarterly Executive, 11*, 99–112.

25. IBM. (2015). IBM Mobile Security solutions for securing the mobile enterprise: Enable secure access to critical data and applications, while mitigating the risk of mobile malware.

26. Jarvenpaa, S. L., & Lang, K. R. (2005). Managing the paradoxes of mobile technology. *Information Systems Management, 22*, 7–23. doi:10.1201/ 1078.10580530/45520.22.4.20050901/90026.2

27. Kaneshige, T. (2013, May 14). Which workers are the best fit for a BYOD? *CIO Online*. Retrieved from http://www.cio.com/article/2385855

28. Yan, J., Zhang, S., Milic, N., Koch, H., & Curry, P. (2016, August). *IT consumerization and new IT practices: Discriminating, firefighting and innovating*. Paper presented at the 22nd Americas Conference on Information Systems, San Diego, CA.

29. Koch, H., Zhang, S., Giddens, L., Milic, N., Yan, J., & Curry, P. (2014, December). *Consumerization and IT department conflict*. Paper presented at the 35th International Conference on Information Systems, Auckland, New Zealand. Retrieved from https://pdfs.semanticscholar.org/9ffd/5c3d0511c884 1f9bbe6b38b1e542dea13da7.pdf

30. Köffer, S., Anlauf, L., Ortbach, K., & Niehaves, B. (2015). The intensified blurring of boundaries between work and private life through IT consumerisation. *ECIS Completed Research Papers*. Paper 108. doi:10.18151/ 7217396

31. Köffer, S., Ortbach, K., & Niehaves, B. (2014). Exploring the relationship between IT consumerization and job performance: A theoretical framework for future research. *Communications of the Association for Information Systems, 35*, 261–283. Retrieved from http://aisel.aisnet.org/cais/vol35/iss1/14/

32. Köffer, S., Ortbach, K., Junglas, I., Niehaves, B., & Harris, J. (2015). Innovation through BYOD? The influence of IT consumerization on individual IT innovation behavior. *Business Information System Engineering, 57*, 363–375. Retrieved from http://aisel.aisnet.org/bise/vol57/iss6/3/

33. Leclercq-Vandelannoitte, A., Isaac, H., & Kalika, M. (2014). Mobile information systems and organisational control: Beyond the panopticon metaphor. *European Journal of Information Systems, 23*, 543–557. doi:10.1057/ejis.2014.11

34. Livingston, S., & Helsper, E. J. (2007). Gradations in digital inclusion: Children, young people and the digital divide. *New Media & Society, 9*, 671–696. doi:10.1177/1461444 807080335

35. Lyon, C., & de Zwart, A. P. (2015, May 12). Developing bring-your-own-device programs for a global workforce. *Inside Counsel*, Retrieved from http://www.insidecounsel.com/2015/05/12/ developing-bring-your-own-device-programs-for-a-gl

36. Marshall, S. (2014). IT consumerization: A case study of BYOD in a healthcare setting. *Technology Innovation Management Review, 4*, 14–18. Retrieved from https://timreview.ca/sites/default/files/article_PDF/Marshall_TIMReview_ March2014.pdf

37. McConnell, J. (2016). Tracking the trends in bringing our own devices to work. *Harvard Business Review Online*. Retrieved from https://hbr.org/2016/05/ tracking-the-trends-in-bringing-our-own-devices-to-work

38. McPhee, R. D., & Poole, M. S. (2001). Organizational structures and configurations. In F. M. Jablin & L. L. Putnam (Eds.), *The new handbook of organizational communication: Advances in theory, research, and methods* (pp. 504–544). Thousand Oaks, CA: Sage.

39. Mazmanian, M. (2013). Avoiding the trap of constant connectivity: When congruent frames allow for heterogeneous practices. *Academy of Management Journal, 56*, 1225–1250. doi:10.5465/amj.2010.0787

40. Mazmanian, M., Orlikowski, W., & Yates, J. (2013). The autonomy paradox: The implications of mobile devices for knowledge professionals. *Organization Science, 24,* 1337–1357. Retrieved from http://dx.doi.org/10.1287/orsc.1120.0806

41. Mazmanian, M., Orlikowski, W. J., & Yates, J. (2005). Crackberries: The social implications of ubiquitous wireless e-mail devices. In C. Sørensen, Y. Yoo, K. Lyytinen, & J. DeGross (Eds.), *Designing ubiquitous information environments: Socio-technical issues and challenges* (pp. 337–343). New York, NY: Springer.

42. Middleton, C., Scheepers, R., & Tuunainen, V. K. (2014). When mobile is the norm: Researching mobile information systems and mobility as post-adoption phenomena. *European Journal of Information Systems, 23,* 503–512. doi:10.1057/ejis.2014.21

43. Miller, B. (2015, January 9). BYOD and employee habits—Employer concerns. *HR Daily Advisor,* Retrieved from http://hrdailyadvisor.blr.com/2015/01/09

44. Mohammadi v. Nwabuisi, 990 F. Supp. 2d 723 (Dist. Court, WD Texas, 2014). Retrieved from https://scholar.google.com/scholar_case?case=6022017784825714661&hl=en&as_sdt=6&as_vis=1&oi=scholarr

45. Mohn, T. (2012, May 29). Employees are getting the word about safer driving. *New York Times.* Retrieved from http://www.nytimes.com/2012/05/29/business/companies-move-to-ban-cellphones-while-driving.html

46. Morris, D. Z. (2017, January 1). New French law bars work email after hours. *Fortune.* Retrieved from http://fortune.com/2017/01/01/french-right-to-disconnect-law/

47. Niehaves, B., Koffer, S., & Ortbach, K. (2013, June). *IT consumerization under more difficult conditions: Insights from German local governments.* Proceedings of the 14th Annual International Conference on Digital Government Research (pp. 205–213). Quebec City, Canada. doi:10.1145/2479724.2479754

48. Office of the Privacy Commissioner. (2015). Is a bring your own device (BYOD) program the right choice for your organization? Retrieved from https://www.oipc.bc.ca/guidance-documents/1827

49. Pearce, K. E., & Rice, R. E. (2013). Digital divides from access to activities: Comparing mobile and personal computer internet users. *Journal of Communication, 63,* 721–744. doi:10.1111/jcom.12045

50. Tribune News Service. (2016, May 2). Privacy: Dump MnSCU plan to inspect employee cellphones. *Austin Daily Herald.* Retrieved from http://www.austindailyherald.com/2016/05/privacy-dump-mnscu-plan-to-inspect-employee-cellphones/

51. Schmitz, K. W., Teng, J. T. C., & Webb, K. J. (2016). Capturing the complexity of malleable IT use: Adaptive structuration theory for individuals. *MIS Quarterly, 40,* 663–686.

52. Schulze, H. (2016). *BYOD & mobile security: 2016 spotlight report.* Crowd Research Partners. Retrieved from http://crowdresearchpartners.com/wp-content/uploads/2017/07/BYOD-and-Mobile-Security-Report-2016.pdf

53. Smith, A. (2015). *Searching for work in the digital era.* Pew Research Center. Retrieved from http://www.pewinternet.org/2015/11/19/searching-for-work-in-the-digital-era/

54. Sørensen, C. (2011). *Enterprise mobility: Tiny technology with global impact on work.* Basingstoke, United Kingdom: Palmgrave Macmillan.

55. Steelman, Z. R., Lacity, M., & Subberwal, R. (2016). Charting your organization's bring-your-own-device voyage. *MIS Quarterly Executive, 15*, 85–104.

56. Stephens, K. K., & Dailey, S. L. (2014). Human resources development in a technology-infused workplace. In M. Khosrow-Pour (Ed.), *Encyclopedia of information science and technology* (3rd ed., pp. 581–589). Hershey, PA: IGI Global. doi:10.4018/978-1-4666-5888-2.ch362

57. Stephens, K. K., & Davis, J. D. (2009). The social influences on electronic multitasking in organizational meetings. *Management Communication Quarterly, 23*, 63–83. doi:10.1177/0893318909335417

58. Stephens, K. K., Waters, E. D., & Sinclair, C. (2014). Media management: The integration of HR, technology, and people. In M. E. Gordon, & V. D. Miller (Eds.), *Meeting the challenge of human resource management: A communication perspective* (pp. 215–226). New York, NY: Routledge.

59. Stephens, K. K., Zhu, Y., Harrison, M., Iyer, M., Hairston, T., & Luk, J. (2017). *Bring your own mobile device (BYOD) to the hospital: Layered boundary barriers and divergent boundary management strategies.* Proceedings of the 50th Annual Hawaii International Conference on System Sciences (HICSS) (pp. 2175–2184). Washington, DC: IEEE Computer Society.

60. Temple University Computer Services. (2014). *Storage and cloud computing approved usage.* Retrieved from https://computerservices.temple.edu/ storage-and-cloud-computing-approved-usage

61. Tompkins, P. K., & Cheney, G. (1985). Communication and unobtrusive control in contemporary organization. In R. D. McPhee & P. K. Thompkins (Eds.), *Organizational communication: Traditional themes and new directions* (pp. 179–210). Newbury Park, CA: Sage.

62. Torode, C. (2011). Securing and supporting a bring-your-own-device program at Ford. *TechTarget.* Retrieved from http://searchcio.techtarget.com/news/2240074385/ Securing-and-supporting-a-bring-your-own-device-program-at-Ford

63. Venkatesh, V., Morris, M. G., Davis, G. B., & Davis, F. D. (2003). User acceptance of information technology: Toward a unified view. *MIS Quarterly, 27*, 425–478. Retrieved from http://www.jstor.org/stable/ 30036540

64. Venkatesh, V., Thong, J. Y. L., & Xu, X. (2012). Consumer acceptance and use of information technology: Extending the unified theory of acceptance and use of technology. *MIS Quarterly, 36*, 157–178. from https://papers.ssrn.com/sol3/ papers.cfm?abstract_id=2002388

65. Vitak, J., Crouse, J., & LaRose, R. (2011). Personal Internet use at work: Understanding cyberslacking. *Computers in Human Behavior, 27*, 1751–1759. doi:10.1016/j.chb.2011.03.002

66. Volvo. (2012). Gestion du BYOD. L'exemple de Volvo IT. (Reprinted in Leclercq-Vandelannoitte, A., Isaac, H., & Kalika, M. (2014). Mobile information systems and organisational control: Beyond the panopticon metaphor. *European Journal of Information Systems, 23*, 543–557. doi:10.1057/ejis.2014.11)

67. Wajcman, J. (2010). New connections: Social studies of science and technology and studies of work. *Work, Employment and Society, 20*, 773–786.

68. Wajcman, J., Bittman, M., & Brown, J. E. (2008). Families without borders: Mobile phones, connectedness and work–home divisions. *Sociology, 42,* 635–652. doi:10.1177/0038038508091620

69. Wajcman, J., Bittman, M., & Brown, J. (2009). Intimate connections: The impact of the mobile phone. In G. Goggin & L. Hjort (Eds.), *Mobile technologies: From telecommunications to media* (pp. 9–22). New York, NY: Routledge.

70. Walt, V. (2017, January 4). France's "right to disconnect" law isn't all it's cracked up to be. *Time.* Retrieved from http://time.com/4622095/france-right-to-disconnect-email-work/

71. Willis, D. A. (2013). Bring your own device: The facts and the future. *Gartner.* Retrieved from https://www.gartner.com/doc/2422315/bring-device-facts-future

72. Zillien, N., & Hargittai, E. (2009). Digital distinction: Status-specific types of internet usage. *Social Science Quarterly, 90,* 274–291. doi:10.1111/j.1540-6237.2009.00617.x

Chapter 7

1. Baron, N. (2008). Adjusting the volume: Technology and multitasking in discourse control. In J. E. Katz (Ed.), *Mobile communication and social change in a global context* (pp. 117–194). Cambridge, MA: MIT Press.

2. Harris, J., Ives, B., & Junglas, I. (2012). IT consumerization: When gadgets turn into enterprise IT tools. *MIS Quarterly Executive, 11,* 99–112.

3. Köffer, S., Ortbach, K., & Niehaves, B. (2014). Exploring the relationship between IT consumerization and job performance: A theoretical framework for future research. *Communications of the Association for Information Systems, 35,* 261–283. Retrieved from http://aisel.aisnet.org/cais/vol35/iss1/14/

4. Köffer, S., Ortbach, K., Junglas, I., Niehaves, B., & Harris, J. (2015). Innovation through BYOD? The influence of IT consumerization on individual IT innovation behavior. *Business Information System Engineering, 57,* 363–375. Retrieved from http://aisel.aisnet.org/bise/vol57/iss6/3/

5. Lyon, C., & de Zwan, A. P. (2015, May 12). Developing bring-your-own-device programs for a global workforce. *Inside Council.* Retrieved from http://www.insidecounsel.com/2015/05/12/developing-bring-your-own-device-programs-for-a-gl

6. Marshall, S. (2014). IT consumerization: A case study of BYOD in a healthcare setting. *Technology Innovation Management Review, 4,* 14–18. Retrieved from https://timreview.ca/sites/default/files/article_PDF/Marshall_TIMReview_March2014.pdf

7. McConnell, J. (2016). Tracking the trends in bringing our own devices to work. *Harvard Business Review Online.* Retrieved from https://hbr.org/2016/05/tracking-the-trends-in-bringing-our-own-devices-to-work

8. Pearce, K. E., & Rice, R. E. (2013). Digital divides from access to activities: Comparing mobile and personal computer internet users. *Journal of Communication, 63,* 721–744. doi:10.1111/jcom.12045

9. Schmitz, K. W., Teng, J. T. C., & Webb, K. J. (2016). Capturing the complexity of malleable IT use: Adaptive structuration theory for individuals. *MIS Quarterly, 40,* 663–686.

10. Sørensen, C. (2011). *Enterprise mobility: Tiny technology with global impact on work*. Basingstoke, United Kingdom: Palmgrave Macmillan.
11. Stephens, K. K., Houser, M. L., & Cowan, R. L. (2009). R U able to meat me: The impact of students' overly casual email messages to instructors. *Communication Education, 58*, 303–326. doi:http://dx.doi.org/10.1080/03634520802582598

Chapter 8

1. Aarts, J., Ash, J., & Berg, M. (2007). Extending the understanding of computerized physician order entry: Implications for professional collaboration, workflow and quality of care. *International Journal of Medical Informatics, 76*, 4–13. doi:10.1016/j.ijmedinf.2006.05.009
2. American Association of Critical-Care Nurses. (n.d.). Retrieved from www.aacn.org
3. Baldwin, L. P., Low, P. H., Picton, C., & Young, T. (2006). The use of mobile devices for information sharing in a technology-supported model of care in A & E. *International Journal of Electronic Healthcare, 3*, 90–106. doi:10.1016/j.ijmedinf.2016.09.002
4. Bautista, J. R., & Lin, T. T. C. (2016). Sociotechnical analysis of nurses' use of personal mobile phones at work. *International Journal of Medical Informatics, 95*, 71–80. doi:10.1016/j.ijmedinf.2016.09.002
5. Berenson, R. A., Ginsburg, P. B., & May, J. H. (2006). Hospital–physicians relations: Cooperation, competition, or separation. *Health Affairs, 26*, w31–w43. doi:10.1377/hlthaff.26.1.w31
6. Bleakley, A. (2013). Working in "teams" in an era of "liquid" healthcare: What is the use of theory? *Journal of Interprofessional Care, 27*, 18–26. doi:10.3109/13561820.2012.699479
7. Cameron, A. F., & Webster, J. (2005). Unintended consequences of emerging communication technologies: Instant messaging in the workplace. *Computers in Human Behavior, 21*, 85–103. doi:10.1016/j.chb.2003.12.001
8. Chrisholm-Burns, M. A., Kim Lee, J., Spivey, C. A., Slack, M., Herrier, R. N., Hall-Lipsy, E., . . . Wunz, E. (2010). US Pharmacists' effect as team members on patient care: Systematic review and meta-analyses. *Medical Care, 48*, 923–933. doi:10.1097/MLR.0b013e3181e57962
9. Dala-Ali, B. M., Lioyd, M. A., & Al-Abed, Y. (2011). The uses of the iPhone for surgeons. *Surgeon, 9*, 44–48. doi:10.1016/j.surge.2010.07.014
10. Dean, M., Gill, R., & Barbour, J. B. (2016). "Let's sit forward": Investigating interprofessional communication, professional roles, and physical space in emergency departments. *Health Communication, 31*, 1506–1516. doi:10.1080/10410236.2015.1089457
11. Elias, B. L., Fogger, S. A., McGuinness, T. M., & D'Alessandro, K. R. (2014). Mobile apps for psychiatric nurses. *Journal of Psychosocial Nursing and Mental Health Services, 52*, 42–47. doi:10.3928/02793695-20131126-07
12. Epstein, R. M., & Street, R. L. (2011). The values and value of patient-centered care. *Annals of Family Medicine, 9*, 100–103. doi:10.1370/afm.1239
13. Erskine, J., Hunter, D. J., Small, A., Hicks, C., McGovern, T., Lugsden, E., . . . Eccles, M. P. (2013). Leadership and transformational change in healthcare organizations: A qualitative analysis of the North East Transformation system. *Health Services Management Research, 26*, 29–37. doi:10.1177/0951484813481589

14. Essen, A., & Lindblad, S. (2013). Innovation as emergence in healthcare: Unpacking change from within. *Social Science & Medicine, 93*, 203–211. doi:10.1016/j.socscimed.2012.08.035

15. Hall, P. (2005). Interprofessional teamwork: Professional cultures as barriers. *Journal of Interprofessional Care, 19*, 188–196. doi:10.1080/13561820500081745

16. Jarvenpaa, S. L., & Leidner, D. E. (1998). Communication and trust in global virtual teams. *Journal of Computer-Mediated Communication, 3*. doi:10.1111/j.1083-6101.1998.tb00080.x

17. Katz-Sidlow, R. J., Ludwig, A., Miller, S., & Sidlow, R. (2012). Smartphone use during inpatient attending rounds: Prevalence, patterns, and potential for distraction. *Journal of Hospital Medicine, 8*, 595–599. doi:10.1002/jhm.1950

18. Kuokkanen, L., & Leino-Kilpi, H. (2000). Power and empowerment in nursing: Three theoretical approaches. *Journal of Advanced Nursing, 31*, 235–241.

19. Lewis, L. K., & Seibold, D. R. (1993). Innovation modification during intra-organizational adoption. *Academy of Management Review, 18*, 322–354. doi:10.5465/AMR.1993.3997518

20. Lewis, L. K. (2011). *Organizational change: Creating change through strategic communication.* Chichester, United Kingdom: Wiley-Blackwell.

21. Ling, R. (2012). *Taken for grantedness: The embedding of mobile communication into society.* Cambridge, MA: MIT Press.

22. Ling, R., & Donner, J. (2009). *Mobile communication.* London, United Kingdom: Polity.

23. Ling, R., & Yttri, B. (2002). Hyper-coordination via mobile phones in Norway. In J. E. Katz & M. Aakhus (Eds.), *Perpetual contact: Mobile communication, private talk, public performance* (pp. 139–169). Cambridge: United Kingdom: Cambridge University Press.

24. Lo, V., Wu, R. C., Morra, D., Lee, L., & Reeves, S. (2012). The use of smartphones in general and internal medicine units: A boon or bane to the promotion of interprofessional collaboration? *Journal of Interprofessional Care, 26*, 276–282. doi:10.3109/13561820.2012.663013

25. Luxton, D. D., McCann, R. A., Bush, N. E., Mishkind, M. C., & Reger, G. M. (2011). mHealth for mental health: Integrating smartphone technology in behavioral healthcare. *Professional Psychology: Research and Practice, 42*, 505–512. doi:10.1037/a0024485

26. Malone, T. W., & Crowston, K. (1990, October). What is coordination theory and how can it help design cooperative work systems? In *Proceedings of the 1990 ACM conference on computer-supported cooperative work* (pp. 357–370). New York, NY: ACM. doi:10.1145/99332.99367

27. Marcus, L. (1987). Toward a "critical mass" theory of interactive media: Universal access, interdependence, and diffusion. *Communication Research, 14*, 491–511. doi:10.1177/009365087014005003

28. Massey, A. P., Montoya-Weiss, M. M., & Hung, Y. (2003). Because time matters: Temporal coordination in global virtual project teams. *Journal of Management Information Systems, 19*, 129–155. Retrieved from http://dx.doi.org/10.1080/07421222.2003.11045742

29. McBride, D., LeVasseur, S. A., & Li, D. (2015). Nursing performance and mobile phone use. Are nurses aware of their performance decrements? *JMIR Human Factors, 2*, e6. doi:10.2196/humanfactors.4070

30. McCallin, A. (2001). Interdisciplinary practice—a matter of teamwork: An integrated literature review. *Journal of Clinical Nursing, 10*, 419–428. doi:10.1046/j.1365-2702.2001.00495.x

31. McElroy, L. M., Ladner, D. P., & Holl, J. L. (2013). The role of technology in clinician-to-clinician communication. *BMJ Quality Safety, 22*, 981–983. doi:10.1136/bmjqs-2013-002191

32. Nguyen, C., McElroy, L. M., Abecassis M. M., Holl, J. L., & Ladner, D. (2015). The use of technology for urgent clinician to clinician communications: A systematic review of the literature. *International Journal of Medical Informatics, 84*, 101–110. doi:10.1016/j.ijmedinf.2014.11.003

33. Ozdalga, E., Ozdalga, A., & Ahuja, N. (2012). The smartphone in medicine: A review of current and potential use among physicians and students. *Journal of Medical Internet Research, 14*, e128. doi:10.2196/jmir.1994

34. Parkin, P. (2009). *Managing change in healthcare: Using action research.* London, United Kingdom: Sage Publications.

35. Putnam, R. D. (2000). *Bowling alone: The collapse and revival of American community.* New York, NY: Simon & Schuster.

36. Quan, S. D., Wu, R. C., Rossos, P. G., Arany, T., Groe, S., Morra, D., . . . Lau, F. Y. (2013). It's not about pager replacement: An in-depth look at the interprofessional nature of communication in healthcare. *Journal of Hospital Medicine, 8*, 137–143. doi:10.1002/jhm.2008

37. Reddy, M. C., McDonald, D. W., Pratt, W., & Shabot, M. M. (2005). Technology, work, and information flows: Lessons from the implementation of a wireless alert pager system. *Journal of Biomedical Informatics, 38*, 229–238. doi:10.1016/j.jbi.2004.11.010

38. Reeves, S., McMillan, S. E., Kachan, N., Paradis, E., Leslie, M., & Kitto, S. (2015). Interprofessional collaboration and family member involvement in intensive care units: Emerging themes from a multi-sited ethnography. *Journal of Interprofessional Care, 29*, 230–237. doi:10.3109/13561820.2014.955914

39. Rogers, E. M. (2003). *Diffusion of innovations* (5th ed.). New York, NY: Free Press.

40. Rose, L. (2011). Interprofessional collaboration in the ICU: How to define? *Nursing in Critical Care, 16*, 5–10. doi:10.1111/j.1478-5153.2010.00398.x

41. Smith, T., Darling, E., & Searles, B. (2010). Survey on cell phone use while performing cardiopulmonary bypass. *Perfusion, 5*, 375–380. doi:10.1177/0267659111409969

42. Solvoll, T., Scholl, J., & Hartvigsen, G. (2013). Physicians interrupted by mobile devices in hospitals: Understanding the interaction between devices, roles, and duties. *Journal of Medical Internet Research, 15*, e56. doi:10.2196/jmir.2473

43. Stephens, K. K., Sørnes, J. O., Rice, R. E., Browning, L. D., & Sætre, A. S. (2008). Discrete, sequential, and follow-up use of information and communication technology by managerial knowledge workers. *Management Communication Quarterly, 22*, 197–231. https://doi.org/10.1177/0893318908323149

44. Stephens, K. K., Zhu, Y., Harrison, M., Iyer, M., Hairston, T., & Luk, J. (2017). *Bring your own mobile device (BYOD) to the hospital: Layered boundary barriers and divergent Boundary management strategies.* Proceedings of the 50th Annual Hawaii International Conference on System Sciences (HICSS) (pp. 2175–2184). Washington, DC: IEEE Computer Society.

45. Vitak, J., Crouse, J., & LaRose, R. (2011). Personal Internet use at work: Understanding cyberslacking. *Computers in Human Behavior, 27*, 1751–1759. doi:10.1016/j.chb.2011.03.002

46. Walther, J. B. (1992). Interpersonal effects in computer-mediated communication: A relational perspective. *Communication Research, 19*, 52–90. doi:10.1177/009365092019001003

47. Whitlow, M. L., Drake, E., Tullmann, D., Hoke, G., & Barth, D. (2014). Bringing technology to the bedside: Using smartphones to improve interprofessional communication. *Computers, Informatics, Nursing, 32*, 305–311. doi:10.1097/CIN.0000000000000063

48. World Health Organization. (2010). Framework for action on interprofessional education and collaborative practice. Retrieved from http://apps.who.int/iris/bitstream/10665/70185/1/WHO_HRH_HPN_10.3_eng.pdf?ua=1

49. World Health Organization. (2008). Integrating mental health into primary care: A global perspective. Retrieved from http://apps.who.int/iris/bitstream/10665/43935/1/9789241563680_eng.pdf

50. Wu, R., Rossos, P., Quan, S., Reeves, S., Lo, V., Wong, B., . . . Morra, D. (2011). An evaluation of the use of smartphones to communicate between clinicians: A mixed-methods study. *Journal of Medical Internet Research, 13*, e59. doi:10.2196/jmir.1655

51. Wu, R. C., Tran, K., Lo, V., O'Leary, K. J., Morra, D., Quan, S. D., & Perrier, L. (2012). Effects of clinical communication interventions in hospitals: A systematic review of information and communication technology adoptions for improved communication between clinicians. *International Journal of Medical Informatics, 81*, 723–732.

52. Zerubavel, E. (1979). *The patterns of time in hospital life: A sociological perspective.* Chicago, IL: University of Chicago Press.

53. Zwarenstein, M., Rice, K., Gotlib-Conn, L., Kenaszchuk, C., & Reeves, S. (2013). Disengaged: A qualitative study of communication and collaboration between physicians and other professions on general internal medicine wards. *BMC Health Services Research, 13*, e494. doi:10.1186/1472-6963-13-494

Chapter 9

1. Atchley, P., & Warden, A. C. (2012). The need of young adults to text now: Using delay discounting to assess informational choice. *Journal of Applied Research in Memory and Cognition, 1*, 229–234. doi:10.1016/j.jarmac.2012.09.001

2. Bayer, J. B., Campbell, S. W., & Ling, R. (2016). Connection cues: Activating the norms and habits of social connectedness. *Communication Theory, 26*, 128–149. doi:10.1111/comt.12090

3. Bayer, J. B., Dal Cin, S., Campbell, S. W., & Panek, E. (2016). Consciousness and self-regulation in mobile communication. *Human Communication Research, 42*, 71–97. doi:10.1111/hcre.12067

4. Billieux, J., Philippot, P., Schmid, C., Maurage, P., De Mol, J., & Van der Linden, M. (2014). Is dysfunctional use of the mobile phone a behavioural addiction? Confronting symptom-based versus process-based approaches. *Clinical Psychology, & Psychotherapy, 22*, 460–468. doi:10.1002/cpp1910

5. Bayer, J. B., Campbell, S. W., & Ling, R. (2016). Connection cues: Activating the norms and habits of social connectedness. *Communication Theory, 26*, 128–149. doi:10.1111/comt.12090

6. Chau, S. L., Dahling, J. J., Levy, P. E., & Diefendorff, J. M. (2009). A predictive study of emotion labor and turnover. *Journal of Organizational Behavior, 30*, 1151–1163. doi:10.1002/job.617

7. Cheever, N. A., Rosen, L. D., Carrier, L. M., & Chavez, A. (2014). Out of sight is not out of mind: The impact of restricting wireless mobile device use on anxiety levels among low, moderate and high users. *Computers in Human Behavior, 37*, 290–297. doi:10.1016/j.chb.2014.05.002

8. Chib, A., Malik, S., Aricat, R. G., & Kadir, S. Z. (2014). Migrant mothering and mobile phones: Negotiations of transnational identity. *Mobile Media & Communication, 2*, 73–93. doi:10.1177/2050157913506007

9. Cumiskey, K. M., & Ling, R. (2015). The social psychology of mobile communication. In S. Sundar (Ed.), *The handbook of the psychology of communication technology* (pp. 228–246). Oxford, United Kingdom: John Wiley & Sons.

10. Diefendorff, J. M., & Richard, E. M. (2003). Antecedents and consequences of emotional display rule perceptions. *Journal of Applied Psychology, 88*, 284–294. doi:10.1037/0021-9010.88.2.284

11. Donner, J. (2009). Blurring livelihoods and lives: The social uses of mobile phones and socioeconomic development. *Innovations: Technology, Governance, & Globalization, 4*, 91–101. doi:10.1162/itgg.2009.4.1.91

12. Gallo, C. (2012). *The Apple experience: Secrets to building insanely great customer loyalty.* New York, NY: McGraw-Hill.

13. Golden, A. G. (2012). The structuration of information and communication technologies and work–life interrelationships: Shared organizational and family rules and resources and implications for work in a high-technology organization. *Communication Monographs, 80*, 101–123. doi:10.1080/03637751.2012.739702

14. Golden, A. G., & Geisler, C. (2007). Work–life boundary management and the personal digital assistant. *Human Relations, 60*, 519–551. doi:10.1177/0018726707076698

15. Hall, J., & Baym, N. K. (2012). Calling and texting (too much): Mobile maintenance expectations, (over)dependence, entrapment, and friendship satisfaction. *New Media & Society, 14*, 316–331. doi:10.1177/1461444811415047

16. Hochschild, A. R. (1983). *The managed heart: Commercialization of human feeling.* Berkeley: University of California Press.

17. Ishii, K., & Markman, K. M. (2016). Online customer service and emotional labor: An exploratory study. *Computers in Human Behavior, 62*, 658–665. doi:10.1016/j.chb.2016.04.037

18. Kirby, E. L. (2006). "Helping you make room in your life for your needs": When organizations appropriate family roles. *Communication Monographs, 73*, 474–480. doi:10.1080/03637750601061208

19. Kirby, E. L., Golden, A. G., Medved, C. E., Jorgenson, J., & Buzzanell, P. M. (2003). An organizational communication challenge to the discourse of work and family research: From problematics to empowerment. In P. J. Kalbfleisch (Ed.), *Communication yearbook, 27* (pp. 1–43). Thousand Oaks, CA: Sage.

20. LaRose, R. (2010). The problem of media habits. *Communication Theory, 20*, 194–222. doi:10.1111/j.1468-2885.2010.01360.x

21. LaRose, R., Kim, J., & Peng, W. (2011). Social networking: Addictive, compulsive, problematic, or just another media habit? In Z. Papacharissi (Ed.), *A networked self* (pp. 59–81). New York, NY: Routledge.

22.   LaRose, R., Lin, C. A., & Eastin, M. S. (2003). Unregulated Internet usage: Addiction, habit, or deficient self-regulation? *Media Psychology, 5*, 225–253. Retrieved from http://dx.doi.org/10.1207/S1532785XMEP0503_01

23.   Licoppe, C. (2004). "Connected presence": The emergence of a new repertoire for managing social relationships in a changing communication technospace. *Environment and Planning D: Society and Space, 22*, 135–156. doi:10.1068/d323t

24.   Ling, R. (2004). *The mobile connection: The cell phone's impact on society.* San Francisco, CA: Morgan Kaufmann.

25.   Ling, R. (2012). *Taken for grantedness: The embedding of mobile communication into society.* Cambridge, MA: MIT Press.

26.   Ling, R., & Horst, H. A. (2011). Mobile communication in the global south. *New Media & Society, 13*, 363–374. doi:10.10.1177/1461444810393899

27.   Ling, R., & Yttri, B. (2002). Hyper-coordination via mobile phones in Norway. In J. E. Katz & M. Aakhus (Eds.), *Perpetual contact: Mobile communication, private talk, public performance* (pp. 139–169). Cambridge, United Kingdom: Cambridge University Press.

28.   Ling, R., & Yttri, B. (2006). Control, emancipation, and status: The mobile telephone in the teens' parental and peer relationships. In R. Kraut, M. Brynin, & S. Kiesler (Eds.), *Computer, phones, and the Internet: Domesticating information technology* (pp. 219–234). New York, NY: Oxford University Press.

29.   Maslach, C. (1982). *Burnout: The cost of caring.* Englewood Cliffs, NJ: Prentice Hall.

30.   Maslach, C., Schaufeli, W., & Leiter, M. (2001). Job burnout. *Annual Review of Psychology, 52*, 397–422. doi:10.1146/annurev.psych.52.1.397

31.   Miller, K. I., Birkholt, M., Scott, C., & Stage, C. (1995). Empathy and burnout in human service work: An extension of a communication model. *Communication Research, 22*, 123–147. doi:10.1177/009365095022002001

32.   Miller, K. I., Ellis, B. H., Zook, E. G., & Lyles, J. S. (1990). An integrated model of communication, stress, and burnout in the workplace. *Communication Research, 17*, 300–326. https://doi.org/10.1177/009365090017003002

33.   Miller, K. I., Stiff, J. B., & Ellis, B. H. (1988). Communication and empathy as precursors to burnout among human service workers. *Communication Monographs, 55*, 250–265. doi:10.1080/03637758809376171

34.   Miller, K. I., Zook, E. G., & Ellis, B. H. (1989). Occupational differences in the influence of communication on stress and burnout in the workplace. *Management Communication Quarterly, 3*, 166–190. Retrieved from https://doi.org/10.1177/0893318989003002002

35.   Nippert-Eng, C. E. (1996). *Home and work: Negotiating boundaries through everyday life.* Chicago, IL: University of Chicago Press.

36.   Perlow, L. A. (1998). Boundary control. The social ordering of work and family time in a high-tech corporation. *Administrative Science Quarterly, 43*, 328–357. Retrieved from http://dx.doi.org/10.2307/2393855

37.   Schrock, A. R. (2015). Communicative affordances of mobile media: Portability, availability, locatability, and multimediality. *International Journal of Communication, 9*, 1229–1246. Retrieved from http://ijoc.org/index.php/ijoc/article/view/3288/1363

38.   Starnaman, S. M., & Miller, K. I. (1992). A test of a causal model of communication and burnout in the teaching profession. *Communication Education, 41*, 40–53. doi:10.1080/03634529209378869

39. Stephens, K. K., Mandhana, D., Kim, J., Li, X., Glowacki, E., & Cruz, I. (2017). Reconceptualizing communication overload and building a theoretical foundation. *Communication Theory, 27*, 269–289. doi:10.1111/comt.12116

40. Ter Hoeven, C. L., van Zoonen, W., & Fonner, K. L. (2016). The practical paradox of technology: The influence of communication technology use on employee burnout and engagement. *Communication Monographs, 83*, 239–263. Retrieved from http://dx.doi.org/10.1080/03637751.2015.1133920

41. Van Dijck, J. (2013). *The culture of connectivity: A critical history of social media.* New York, NY: Oxford University Press.

42. Vitak, J., Crouse, J., & LaRose, R. (2011). Personal Internet use at work: Understanding cyberslacking. *Computers in Human Behavior, 27*, 1751–1759. doi:10.1016/j.chb.2011.03.002011

43. Williams, M. G. (2015). Cabs, community, and control: Mobile communication among Chicago's taxi drivers. *Mobile Media & Communication, 3*, 3–19. doi:10.1177/2050157914544804

Chapter 10

1. Alvesson, M. (2001). Knowledge work: Ambiguity, image and identity. *Human Relations, 54*, 863–886. Retrieved from https://doi.org/10.1177/0018726701547004

2. Bardram, J. E., & Bossen, C., (2003, September). Moving to get ahead: Local mobility and collaborative work. In K. Kuutti, E. H. Karsten, G. Fitzpatrick, P. Dourish, & K. Schmidt (Eds.), *Proceedings of the Eighth European Conference on Computer-Supported Cooperative Work* (pp. 355–374). Norwell, MA: Kluwer Academic. Retrieved from https://pdfs.semanticscholar.org/09af/a78b426848e923b58db6c6327e240f956093.pdf

3. Castells, M. (2013). *Communication power.* Oxford, United Kingdom: Oxford University Press.

4. Cowan, R., & Hoffman, M. F. (2007). The flexible organization: How contemporary employees construct the work/life border. *Qualitative Research Reports in Communication, 8*, 37–44. Retrieved from http://dx.doi.org/10.1080/17459430701617895

5. Frenkel, S., Korczynski, M., Donoghue, L., & Shire, K. (1995). Re-constituting work: Trends towards knowledge work and info-normative control. *Work, Employment & Society, 9*, 773–796. Retrieved from https://doi.org/10.1177/095001709594008

6. Glaser, B. G. (1965). The constant comparative method of qualitative analysis. *Social Problems, 12*, 436–445. doi:10.2307/798843

7. Glaser, B., & Strauss, A. (1967). *The discovery of grounded theory.* Chicago, IL: Transaction.

8. Golden, A. G., & Geisler, C. (2007). Work–life boundary management and the personal digital assistant. *Human Relations, 60*, 519–551. doi:10.1177/0018726707076698

9. Hill, E. J., Grzywacz, J. G., Allen, S., Blanchard, V. L., Matz-Costa, C., Shulkin, S., & Pitt-Catsouphes, M. (2008). Defining and conceptualizing workplace flexibility. *Community, Work, & Family, 11*, 149–163. Retrieved from http://dx.doi.org/10.1080/13668800802024678

10. Hofstede, G. (1998). Identifying organizational subcultures: An empirical approach. *Journal of Management Studies, 35*, 1–12.

11. Jarvenpaa, S. L., & Lang, K. R. (2005). Managing the paradoxes of mobile technology. *Information Systems Management, 22*, 7–23. doi:10.1201/1078.10580530/45520.22.4.20050901/90026.2

12. Kelley, R. (1990). *The gold collar worker—harnessing the brainpower of the new workforce.* Reading, MA: Addison-Wesley.

13. Ling, R., & Horst, H. A. (2011). Mobile communication in the global south. *New Media & Society, 13*, 363–374. doi:10.10.1177/1461444810393899

14. Ling, R. & Yttri, B. (2006). Control, emancipation, and status: The mobile telephone in the teens' parental and peer relationships. In R. Kraut, M. Brynin, & S. Kiesler (Eds.), *Computer, phones, and the Internet: Domesticating information technology* (pp. 219–234). New York, NY: Oxford.

15. Mazmanian, M., Orlikowski, W., & Yates, J. (2013). The autonomy paradox: The implications of mobile devices for knowledge professionals. *Organization Science, 24*, 1337–1357. Retrieved from http://dx.doi.org/10.1287/orsc.1120.0806

16. Putnam, L. L., Myers, K. K., & Gailliard, B. M. (2014). Examining the tensions in workplace flexibility and exploring options for new directions. *Human Relations, 67*, 413–440. doi:10.1177/0018726713495704

17. Robertson, M., & Swan, J. (2003). "Control—what control?" Culture and ambiguity within a knowledge intensive firm. *Journal of Management Studies, 40*, 831–858. doi:10.1111/1467-6486.00362

18. Susskind, R. E., & Susskind, D. (2015). *The future of the professions: How technology will transform the work of human experts.* Oxford, United Kingdom: Oxford University Press.

19. Susskind, R. E. (2017). *Tomorrow's lawyers: An introduction to your future* (2nd ed.). Oxford, United Kingdom: Oxford University Press.

20. Wallace, J. E. (1995). Organizational and professional commitment in professional and nonprofessional organizations. *Administrative Science Quarterly, 40*, 228–255. Retrieved from http://www.jstor.org/stable/2393637

21. Yang, K. (2008). A preliminary study on the use of mobile phones amongst migrant workers in Beijing. *Knowledge Technology and Policy, 21*, 65–72. doi:10.1007/s12130-008-9047-7

Chapter 11

1. Arnold, M. (2003). On the phenomenology of technology: The "Janus-faces" of mobile phones. *Information and Organization, 13*, 231–256.

2. Barker, J. R. (1993). Tightening the iron cage: Concertive control in self-managing teams. *Administrative Science Quarterly, 38*, 408–437.

3. Baron, N. S. (2008). *Always on: Language in an online and mobile world.* New York, NY: Oxford University Press.

4. Bayer, J. B., Campbell, S. W., & Ling, R. (2016). Connection cues: Activating the norms and habits of social connectedness. *Communication Theory, 26*, 128–149. doi:10.1111/comt.12090

5. Beniger, J. (1989). *The control revolution: Technological and economic origins of the information society.* Cambridge, MA: Harvard University Press.

6. Birnholtz, J., Hancock, J., Smith, M., & Reynolds, L. (2012). Understanding unavailability in a world of constant connection. *Interactions, 19*(5), 32–35. doi:10.1145/2334184.2334193

7. Birnholtz, J., Reynolds, L., Smith, M. E., & Hancock, J. (2013). "Everyone has to do it": A joint action approach to managing social inattention. *Computers in Human Behavior, 29*, 2230–2238. doi:10.1016/j.chb.2013.05.004

8. Canary, H. E. (2010). Structurating activity theory: An integrated approach to policy knowledge. *Communication Theory, 20*, 21–49. doi:10.1111/j.1468-2885.2009.01354.x

9. Cheney, G., Christensen, L. T., Zorn, T. E., & Ganesh, S. (2011). *Organizational communication in an age of globalization: Issues, reflections, practices* (2nd ed.). Long Grove, IL: Waveland.

10. Deetz, S. (1992). *Democracy in the age of corporate colonization.* Albany: State University of New York.

11. DeSanctis, G., & Poole, M. S. (1994). Capturing the complexity in advanced technology use: Adaptive structuration theory. *Organization Science, 5*(2), 121–147.

12. Etzioni, A. (1964). *Modern organizations.* Englewood Cliffs, NJ: Prentice Hall.

13. Evans, S. K., Pearce, K. E., Vitak, J., & Treem, J. W. (2017). Explicating affordances: A conceptual framework for understanding affordances in communication research. *Journal of Computer-Mediated Communication, 22*, 35-52. doi: 10.1111/jcc4.12180

14. Fairhurst, G., & Putnam, L. (2004). Organizations as discursive constructions. *Communication Theory, 14*, 5–26.

15. Gibbs, J. L., Rozaidi, N. A., & Eisenberg, J. (2013). Overcoming the "ideology of openness": Probing the affordances of social media for organizational knowledge sharing. *Journal of Computer-Mediated Communication, 19*, 102–120. doi: 10.1111/jcc4.12034

16. Gibson, J. J. (1986). *The ecological approach to visual perception.* Mahwah, NJ: Erlbaum.

17. Giddens, A. (1979). *Central problems in social theory: Action, structure and contradiction in social analysis.* Berkeley: University of California Press.

18. Giddens, A. (1982). Power, the dialectic of control, and class structuration. In A. Giddens & G. Mackenzie (Eds.), *Social class and the division of labor* (pp. 29–45). New York, NY: Cambridge University Press.

19. Giddens, A. (1984). *The constitution of society: Outline of the theory of structuration.* Berkeley: University of California Press.

20. Glaser, B. G. (1965). The constant comparative method of qualitative analysis. *Social Problems, 12*, 436–445. doi:10.2307/798843

21. Glaser, B., & Strauss, A. (1967). *The discovery of grounded theory.* Chicago, IL: Transaction.

22. Golden, A. G. (2012). The structuration of information and communication technologies and work–life interrelationships: Shared organizational and family rules and resources and implications for work in a high-technology organization. *Communication Monographs, 80*, 101–123. doi:10.1080/03637751.2012.739702

23. Golden, A. G., & Geisler, C. (2007). Work–life boundary management and the personal digital assistant. *Human Relations, 60*, 519–551. doi:10.1177/0018726707076698

24. Hagel, J., Brown, J. S., & Jelinek, M. (2013). Relational networks, strategic advantage: Collaborative control is fundamental. In S. B. Sitkin, L. B. Cardinal, & K. M. Bijlsma-Frankema (Eds.), *Organizational control* (pp. 251–300). Cambridge, United Kingdom: Cambridge University Press.

25. Harris, J., Ives, B., & Junglas, I. (2012). IT consumerization: When gadgets turn into enterprise IT tools. *MIS Quarterly Executive, 11*, 99–112.

26. Helles, R. (2013). Mobile communication and intermediality. *Mobile Media & Communication, 1*, 14–19.

27. Hill, E. J., Grzywacz, J. G., Allen, S., Blanchard, V. L., Matz-Costa, C., Shulkin, S., & Pitt-Catsouphes, M. (2008). Defining and conceptualizing workplace flexibility. *Community, Work, & Family, 11*, 149–163.

28. Jarvenpaa, S. L., & Lang, K. R. (2005). Managing the paradoxes of mobile technology. *Information Systems Management, 22*, 7–23.

29. Kärreman, D., & Alvesson, M. (2004). Cages in tandem: Management control, social identity, and identification in a knowledge-intensive firm. *Organization, 11*, 149–175.

30. Katz, J. E. (2007). Mobile media and communication: Some important questions. *Communication Monographs, 74*(3), 389–394.

31. Katz, J. E., & Aakhus, M. (2002). *Perpetual contact: Mobile communication, private talk, public performance.* Cambridge, United Kingdom: Cambridge University Press.

32. Kirby, E., & Krone, K. (2011). "The policy exists but you can't really use it": Communication and the structuration of work–family policies. *Journal of Applied Communication Research, 30*, 50–77. doi:10.1080/00909880216577

33. Köffer, S., Ortbach, K., & Niehaves, B. (2014). Exploring the relationship between IT consumerization and job performance: A theoretical framework for future research. *Communications of the Association for Information Systems, 35*(1), 261–283.

34. Köffer, S., Ortbach, K., Junglas, I., Niehaves, B., & Harris, J. (2015). Innovation through BYOD? The influence of IT consumerization on individual IT innovation behavior. *Business Information System Engineering, 57*, 363–375.

35. Leclercq-Vandelannoitte, A., Isaac, H., & Kalika, M. (2014). Mobile information systems and organisational control: Beyond the panopticon metaphor. *European Journal of Information Systems, 23*, 543–557. doi:10.1057/ejis.2014.11

36. Leonardi, P. M. (2011). When flexible routines meeting flexible technologies: Affordance, constraint, and the imbrication of human and material agencies. *MIS Quarterly, 35*, 147–167.

37. Leonardi, P. M. (2013). When does technology use enable network change in organizations? A comparative study of feature use and shared affordances. *MIS Quarterly, 37*, 749–775.

38. Leonardi, P. M. (2014). Social media, knowledge sharing, and innovation. Toward a theory of communication visibility. *Information Systems Research, 25*, 796–816.

39. Lewis, L. K. (2000). "Blindsided by that one" and "I saw that one coming": The relative anticipation and occurrence of communication problems and other problems in implementers' hindsight. *Journal of Applied Communication Research, 28*, 44–67. Retrieved from http://dx.doi.org/10.1080/00909880009365553

40. Lewis, L. K. (2007). An organization stakeholder model of change implementation communication. *Communication Theory, 17*, 176–204. Retrieved from http://dx.doi.org/10.1111/j.1468-2885.2007.00291.x

41. Lewis, L. K. (2011). *Organizational change: Creating change through strategic communication.* Chichester, United Kingdom: Wiley-Blackwell. Retrieved from http://dx.doi.org/10.1002/9781444340372

42. Lewis, L. K., & Russ, T. L. (2012). Soliciting and using input during organizational change initiatives: What are practitioners doing? *Management Communication Quarterly, 26,* 267–294. Retrieved from http://dx.doi.org/10.1177/0893318911431804

43. Lewis, L. K., Schmisseur, A., Stephens, K. K., & Weir, K. E. (2006) Advice on communicating during organizational change: The content of popular press books. *Journal of Business Communication, 43,* 113–137.

44. Licoppe, C. (2004). "Connected presence": The emergency of a new repertoire for managing social relationships in a changing communication technospace. *Environment and Planning D: Society and Space, 22,* 135–156. doi:10.1068/d323t

45. Ling, R. (2004). *The mobile connection: The cell phone's impact on society.* San Francisco, CA: Morgan Kaufmann.

46. Ling, R. (2012). *Taken for grantedness: The embedding of mobile communication into society.* Cambridge, MA: MIT Press.

47. Majchrzak, A., Faraj, S., Kane, G. C., & Azad, B. (2013). The contradictory influence of social media affordances on online communal knowledge sharing. *Journal of Computer-Mediated Communication, 19,* 38–55.

48. Mazmanian, M., Orlikowski, W., & Yates, J. (2013). The autonomy paradox: The implications of mobile devices for knowledge workers. *Organization Science, 24,* 1337–1357.

49. McPhee, R. D., & Poole, M. S. (2001). Organizational structures and configurations. In F. M. Jablin & L. L. Putnam (Eds.), *The new handbook of organizational communication: Advances in theory, research, and methods* (pp. 504–544). Thousand Oaks, CA: Sage.

50. Menezes, B., Taylor, B., & Dulaney, K. (2015). 2015 strategic roadmap for BYOD/CYOD split-billing solutions. Retrieved from http://www.gartner.com/search/site/premiumresearch/simple?tabChg=true&keywords=BYOD

51. Meyerson, D. E. (2001). *Tempered radicals: How people use difference to inspire change at work.* Boston, MA: Harvard Business School.

52. Mumby, D. K. (2001). Power and politics. In F. Jablin & L. Putnam (Eds.), *New handbook of organizational communication* (pp. 585–623). Thousand Oaks, CA: Sage.

53. Mumby, D. K. (2005). Theorizing resistance in organizational studies: A dialectical approach. *Management Communication Quarterly, 19,* 1–26.

54. Nippert-Eng, C. E. (1996). *Home and work: Negotiating boundaries through everyday life.* Chicago, IL: University of Chicago Press.

55. Oliver, C. (1990). Determinants of interorganizational relationships: Integration and future directions. *Academy of Management Review, 15,* 241–265. doi:10.5465/AMR.1990.4308156

56. O'Mahoney, S., & Barley, S. R. (1999). Do telecommunications technologies affect work and organizations? The state of our knowledge. In B. Staw & R. Sutton (Eds.), *Research in organizational behavior* (Vol. 21, pp. 125–161). Greenwich, CT: JAI Press.

57. Parchoma, G. (2014). The contested ontology of affordances: Implications for researching technological affordances for collaborative knowledge production. *Computers in Human Behavior, 37,* 360–368.

58. Perlow, L. A. (1998). Boundary control. The social ordering of work and family time in a high-tech corporation. *Administrative Science Quarterly, 43,* 328–357.

59. Poole, M. S., Van de Ven, A. H., Dooley, K., & Holmes, M. E. (2000). *Organizational change and innovation processes: Theory and methods for research.* New York, NY: Oxford University Press.

60. Poole, M. S., Seibold, D. R., & McPhee, R. D. (1985). Group decision-making as a structurational process. *Quarterly Journal of Speech, 71,* 74–102. doi:10.1080/00335638509383719

61. Putnam, L. L. (2004). Dialectical tensions and rhetorical tropes in negotiations. *Organization Studies, 25,* 35–53. doi:10.1177/0170840604038170

62. Putnam, L. L. (2015). Unpacking the dialectic: Alternative views on the discourse–materiality relationship. *Journal of Management Studies, 52,* 706–716. doi:10.1111/joms.12115

63. Putnam, L. L., Fairhurst, G. T., & Banghart, S. (2016). Contradictions, dialectics, and paradoxes in organizations: A constitutive approach. *Academy of Management Annals, 10,* 65–171. doi:10.1080/19416520.2016.1162421

64. Putnam, L. L., Myers, K. K., & Gailliard, B. M. (2014). Examining the tensions in workplace flexibility and exploring options for new directions. *Human Relations, 67,* 413–440. doi:10.1177/0018726713495704

65. Rice, R. E., Evans, S. K., Pearce, K. E., Sivunene, A., Vitak, J., & Treem, J. W. (2017). Organizational media affordances: Operationalization and associations with media use. *Journal of Communication, 67,* 106–130. doi:10.1111/jcom.12273

66. Reinsch, N. L., Turner, J. W., & Tinsley, C. H. (2008). Multicommunicating: A practice whose time has come? *Academy of Management Review, 33,* 391–403. doi:10.2307/20159404

67. Rogers, E. M. (1995). *Diffusion of innovations* (4th ed.). New York, NY: Free Press.

68. Rogers, E. M. (2003). *Diffusion of innovations* (5th ed.). New York, NY: Free Press.

69. Samuel, A. (2014, February 6). Limit the time you spend on email. *Harvard Business Review.* Retrieved from https://hbr.org/2014/02/limit-the-time-you-spend-on-email

70. Schrock, A. R. (2015). Communicative affordances of mobile media: Portability, availability, locatability, and multimediality. *International Journal of Communication, 9,* 1229–1246.

71. Scott, W. R., & Davis, G. F. (2007). *Organizations and organizing: Rational, natural, and open system perspectives.* New York, NY: Pearson Education.

72. Scott, C., & Myers, K. (2010). Toward an integrative theoretical perspective on organizational membership negotiation: Socialization, assimilation, and the duality of structure. *Communication Theory, 20,* 79–105.

73. Sheer, V. C., & Rice, R. E. (2017). Mobile instant messaging use and social capital: Direct and indirect associations with employee outcomes. *Information & Management, 54,* 90–102. doi:10.1016/j.im.2016.04.001

74. Sitkin, S. B., Cardinal, L. B., & Bijlsma-Frankema, K. M. (Eds.). *Organizational control.* Cambridge, United Kingdom: Cambridge University Press.

75. Sørensen, C. (2011). *Enterprise mobility: Tiny technology with global impact on work.* Basingstoke, United Kingdom: Palmgrave Macmillan.

76. Stephens, K. K. (2012). Multiple conversations during organizational meetings: Development of the multicommunicating scale. *Management Communication Quarterly, 26,* 195–223. doi:10.1177/0893318911431802

77.	Stephens, K. K., Mandhana, D., Kim, J., Li, X., Glowacki, E., & Cruz, I. (2017). Reconceptualizing communication overload and building a theoretical foundation. *Communication Theory, 27*, 269–289. doi:10.1111/comt.12116

78.	Stephens, K. K., Waters, E. D., & Sinclair, C. (2014). Media management: The integration of HR, technology, and people. In M. E. Gordon, & V. D. Miller (Eds.), *Meeting the challenge of human resource management: A communication perspective* (pp. 215–226). New York: Routledge.

79.	Treem, J. W., & Leonardi, P. M. (2012). Social media use in organizations: Exploring the affordances of visability, editability, persistence, and association. *Communication Yearbook, 36*, 143–189.

80.	Wellman, B., Salaff, J., Dimitrova, D., Garton, L., Gulia, M., & Haythornthwaite, C. (1996). Computer networks as social networks: Collaborative work, telework, and virtual community. *Annual Review of Sociology, 22*, 213–238. doi:10.1146/annurev.soc.22.1.213

81.	Whittington, R. (1992). Putting Giddens into action: Social systems and managerial agency. *Journal of Management Studies, 29*(6), 693–712.

82.	Willis, D. A. (2012). Bring your own device: New opportunities, new challenges. *Gartner,* https://www.gartner.com/doc/2422315/bring-device-facts-future

Chapter 12

1.	Bayer, J. B., Campbell, S. W., & Ling, R. (2016). Connection cues: Activating the norms and habits of social connectedness. *Communication Theory, 26*, 128–149. doi:10.1111/comt.12090

2.	Beniger, J. (1989). *The control revolution: Technological and economic origins of the information society*. Cambridge, MA: Harvard University Press.

3.	Bureau of Labor Statistics. (2017). Building and grounds cleaning: Janitors and building cleaners. Retrieved from https://www.bls.gov/ooh/building-and-grounds-cleaning/janitors-and-building-cleaners.htm

4.	Canary, H. E. (2010). Structurating activity theory: An integrated approach to policy knowledge. *Communication Theory, 20*, 21–49. doi:10.1111/j.1468-2885.2009.01354.x

5.	Canary, H. E., Riforgiate, S. E., & Montoya, Y. (2013). The policy communication index: A theoretically based measure of organizational policy communication practices. *Management Communication Quarterly, 27*, 471–502. doi:10.1177/0893318913494116

6.	Covey, S. R. (1994). *First things first*. New York, NY: Simon & Schuster.

7.	Donner, J. (2009). Blurring livelihoods and lives: The social uses of mobile phones and socioeconomic development. *Innovations, Technology, Governance, Globalization, 4*, 91–101. doi:10.1162/itgg.2009.4.1.91

8.	Donovan, E., Crook, B., Brown, L. E., Pastorek, A. E., Hall, C. A., Mackert, M. S., & Stephens, K. K. (2014). An experimental test of medical disclosure and consent documentation: Assessing patient comprehension, self-efficacy, and uncertainty. *Communication Monographs, 81*, 239–260. Retrieved from http://dx.doi.org/10.1080/03637751.2013.876059

9.	Hagel, J., Brown, J. S., & Davison, L. (2010, April 5). Are all employees knowledge workers? *Harvard Business Review*. Retrieved from https://hbr.org/2010/04/are-all-employees-knowledge-wo.html

10.	Hartley, S. (2015, June, 30). The future of digital jobs is blue collar. *Forbes*. Retrieved from http://www.forbes.com/sites/scotthartley/2015/06/30/future-digital-jobs-blue-collar/#7cfb01f0775c

11. Kaneshige, T. (2013, May 14). Which workers are the best fit for BYOD? *CIO Online*. Retrieved from http://www.cio.com/article/2385855

12. Kirby, E., & Krone, K. (2011). "The policy exists but you can't really use it": Communication and the structuration of work–family policies. *Journal of Applied Communication Research, 30*, 50–77. doi:10.1080/00909880216577

13. Kirby, E. L., Golden, A. G., Medved, C. E., Jorgenson, J., & Buzzanell, P. M. (2003). An organizational communication challenge to the discourse of work and family research: From problematics to empowerment. In P. J. Kalbfleisch (Ed.), *Communication yearbook, 27* (pp. 1–43). Thousand Oaks, CA: Sage.

14. Ling, R. (2012). *Taken for grantedness: The embedding of mobile communication into society*. Cambridge, MA: MIT Press.

15. Pink, S., Morgan, J., & Dainty, A. (2014). Safety in movement: Mobile workers, mobile media. *Mobile Media & Communication, 2*, 335–351. doi:10.1177/2050157914537486

16. Torlina, J. (2011). *Working class: Challenging myths about blue collar labor*. Boulder, CO: Lynne Riernner.

17. Tracy, B. (2013). *Time management*. New York, NY: AMACOM.

18. Van Dijck, J. (2013). *The culture of connectivity: A critical history of social media*. New York, NY: Oxford University Press.

Appendix A

1. Charmaz, K. (2006). *Constructing grounded theory: A practical guide through qualitative analysis*. Thousand Oaks, CA: Sage.

2. Corbin, J. M., & Strauss, A. (1990). Grounded theory research: Procedures, canons, and evaluative criteria. *Qualitative Sociology, 13*, 3–21. doi:10.1007/BF00988593

3. Corbin, J., & Strauss, A. (2008). *Basics of qualitative research: Techniques and procedures for developing grounded theory*. Thousand Oaks, CA: Sage.

4. Glaser, B. G. (1965). The constant comparative method of qualitative analysis. *Social Problems, 12*, 436–445. doi:10.2307/798843

5. Glaser, B., & Strauss, A. (1967). *The discovery of grounded theory*. Chicago, IL: Transaction.

6. Miles, M. B., Huberman, A. M., & Saldaña, J. (2013). *Qualitative data analysis: A methods sourcebook*. Thousand Oaks, CA: Sage.

7. Tracy, S. J. (2013). *Qualitative research methods: Collecting evidence, crafting analysis, communicating impact*. Chichester, United Kingdom: Wiley.

8. Weiss, R. S. (1994). *Learning from strangers: The art and method of qualitative interview studies*. New York, NY: Simon & Schuster.

INDEX